TRUE NORTH

TRUE
NORTH

A LIFE IN THE MUSIC BUSINESS

BERNIE FINKELSTEIN

Foreword by Murray McLauchlan

McCLELLAND & STEWART

LIBRARY AND ARCHIVES CANADA CATALOGUING IN PUBLICATION

Finkelstein, Bernie
True North : a life inside the music business / Bernie Finkelstein.

ISBN 978-0-7710-4793-0

1. Finkelstein, Bernie. 2. Concert agents – Canada – Biography. 3. Sound recording
executives and producers – Canada – Biography. 4. True North Records – History.
5. Record labels – Canada – History. I. Title.

ML429.F499A3 2012   781.64092   C2011-904432-3

We acknowledge the financial support of the Government of Canada through the Canada Book
Fund and that of the Government of Ontario through the Ontario Media Development
Corporation's Ontario Book Initiative. We further acknowledge the support of the Canada
Council for the Arts and the Ontario Arts Council for our publishing program.

Published simultaneously in the United States of America by McClelland & Stewart Ltd.,
P.O. Box 1030, Plattsburgh, New York 12901

Library of Congress Control Number: 2011931121

Typeset in Van Dijck

Printed and bound in Canada

 ANCIENT FOREST
FRIENDLY

This book is printed on acid-free paper that is 100% recycled,
ancient-forest friendly (100% post-consumer waste).

McClelland & Stewart Ltd.
75 Sherbourne Street
Toronto, Ontario
M5A 2P9
www.mcclelland.com

1 2 3 4 5   16 15 14 13 12

To my Mom and Dad

FOREWORD

by Murray McLauchlan

As I write this, I am sixty-three years old. I am still making records. I am still performing, both as a solo act and with a band called Lunch at Allen's. Mostly it is in nice theatres or good festivals. It is considered miraculous in this country to be making the music you want under your own terms and to have been doing it as long as I have and to be able to make a living at it while remaining in your own country. It has something to do with being good at it. It has a lot to do with the guy who wrote this book.

This is a self-penned biography and so it is up to Bernie to tell his own story in his own way. But in spite of his fearsome reputation for planting himself in people's offices and hectoring them until he gets what he wants, he has always been better at blowing other people's horns than his own. Compliments leave him speechless. So this is in some ways a book that alludes to things and that in its judgments of people and situations tends towards a kindly diplomacy. Of course, many of the people in it are still alive and kicking, as well as still working in the music industry (how we all used to hate that term), so some reticence about shooting first and asking questions later is understandable.

If this was the United States, Bernie would be revered in the same way as Ahmet Ertegun or Sam Phillips are. He should be! But this is Canada, after all, and we don't do that. Generally you have to succeed somewhere else in order to earn your star on the walk of fame in this funny little country.

Curiously enough, Bernie has succeeded elsewhere, but he is still underappreciated as one of the founders and driving forces of a cultural movement that became an industry. Go figure. Perhaps it was something he said. He does point out rather eloquently that elements in the music industry can be somewhat small and more than a little vindictive.

What is important is this: In a world of bean counters, Bernie has always shone brightly as a pure music man. That's why I would put him in the same league as those other guys I mentioned. He is the most passionate appreciator of what Keith Richards calls "the real shit" that I have ever met. I think that is why he has been able to do what he has done in the face of indifference and opposition. When he was starting out, he had no idea what he was doing and was thrown back on that passion. It gave him a drive to doggedly outgun anyone who got in his way and to make them believe that whatever he was representing was the single most important thing to ever be created in human history.

What was it like to be an artist and work with Bernie? In the early days we were like a merry band of outlaws making up the rules as we went along. Bernie had a tremendous respect for the freedom that people needed to create the work that was in them. He had a very open mind about social matters and a revolutionary's disposition. That was what allowed him to embrace the political leanings of Cockburn, the outrageousness of Rough Trade, and my bullheadedness, all at the same time. He went at the world on our behalf with everything he had. We also had a hell of a lot of fun.

On a more serious note, we all came up at a time of great change, during a wave of cultural nationalism that coincided with the advent of a new medium (FM radio). Bernie read the tea leaves and understood better than anyone else the changes that were taking place. I still remember us talking to Pierre Juneau at L'Hibou coffee house in Ottawa in those days. Bernie expressed great frustration that the art being produced, no matter its quality, was destined for the trash, just because it was homegrown. That was the climate then, but you could tell he categorically refused to accept it.

It's hard to imagine the mountains Bernie moved to get True North Records up and running and built into one of the most progressive independent labels in the world, but move them he did!

For me? Bernie was a champion; a guy who stuck up for you. In the cocoon of True North and the management company I was happily shielded from negative opinion and lived in a climate of optimism that allowed me to take chances with my art, which I might not have been able to do under different circumstances. Do I regret coming back from New York to join up with him? Not for one second!

Bernie convinced people that what I had to offer was important, and to this day there seem to be a lot of people who remain so convinced.

I read this book in a single night at the cottage. I thought that was a good sign.

Yes, there are references to sex, drugs, and rock 'n' roll, but Bernie also takes a good hard look at how we view our artists, as well as at the institutions we've created that control our culture.

Bernie and I remain close friends. We get together for a dinner or a lunch a couple of times a month. I always joke that ceasing to work with him probably saved our friendship, and I suppose many a true word has been said in jest. Bernie was always drawn to the idea of getting hits. In his view, the most important thing was plugging a song into that classic marriage of radio and the record business, and then motivating the promotions people to drive the project home, internationally, but especially in the U.S.A. That's why Bernie got on so well with guys like Walter Yetnikoff, Bill Graham, and Donnie and Jimmy Ienner. In his heart, he really was one of them, and they accepted him as such. If he couldn't make the record happen, he took it hard and he took it personally.

So Bernie duked it out with the big guys and in the process helped to put Canada's music industry on the map. Bruce Cockburn, Dan Hill, and the world at large were the beneficiaries. Bernie got his hits!

As for me? Well, suffice it to say I had other fish to fry. It all worked out. I'm still out there, making music, doing what I want. Yay, Canada!

AUTHOR'S NOTE

Before we get started, just a couple of things.

This is not a history of the Canadian music business. Why do I even bother to mention this? Well, to put it simply, just about everyone I happen to tell that I'm writing a book says, "Great, we need a history of the Canadian music business."

That may be true, although I happen to think there are a few good ones out there, but this book isn't a history. It's my story, and although I've attempted to be as honest and accurate as possible, it remains the world of music as seen through my eyes and experience. If your favourite band is not in here, it's because I didn't work with them. I'm sure they're great and there's a book coming soon.

Also, in the music game nothing ever happens on its own. There is always a team of people involved. Agents, publicists, road crews, promoters, producers, assistants, salespeople, lawyers, accountants – the list is endless.

I'm sure they have lots of stories to tell but this isn't their book either.

I owe them all big-time and have no real way to properly thank them beyond what I've expressed in the past, but, once again, "Thanks."

Now get out there and write your own books.

PROLOGUE

On December 17, 2007, I sold True North Records, a company I started in 1969. I didn't quite get out of the music business that day. I kept my management company and some of my music publishing interests. Nonetheless, the sale represented the end of my direct involvement in the record business. It's a day I'm not going to forget for many reasons, not the least of which is that there was a snowstorm in Toronto, bad and big enough that my accountant couldn't get downtown for the sale's closing, which was being held in my lawyer's office high up in one of the bank towers smack in the middle of Toronto's financial district.

I had built a company that had become so complicated that at the closing I had to sign fifty-two separate contracts. Besides the complexity of the paperwork, I had mixed feelings. True North had been my baby for almost forty years and I cared about it deeply. However, I was also overjoyed to be selling. I had begun to lose my deep-rooted love for the record business. I could see the great promise of the digital age but I just didn't seem to care. I was burned out. At sixty-three, the time had come to make a change if I was to have any kind of a second act. But I wasn't too old to be involved in great music. In fact, on the day I sold, I was still putting out terrific new records, and many considered True North to be the leading independent music company in Canada.

At the end of the signing I received the payment. It was in the seven figures, not a fortune, but more than I ever thought I would see the day I got into the business. Money had never been the issue for me. I hadn't given it too much thought, apart from its usefulness to keep things going. If money had concerned me, I would have put out much different music over the years.

A series of underground walkways knits together much of Toronto's downtown into a subterranean labyrinth. As the snowstorm swirled around the tower outside, I was going to walk from my lawyer's office through this indoor web of tunnels to another building, surface in the nearest Royal Bank, and make a very large deposit. It all felt somewhat surreal. The strange fact was that this was going to be the first time I had personally gone to a bank to make a deposit in over twenty years. I had always had a bookkeeper or, later on, a financial director who made all my deposits and withdrawals, both for business and personal banking. No doubt about it, this was going to be a special occasion. Bernie Finkelstein goes to the bank. I thought for sure bells would go off and the teller would turn a spotlight on both me and my deposit. Surely the teller would demand more identification than I usually carried or at least ask me a few skill-testing questions before accepting my deposit.

But none of that happened. The teller barely blinked, took the deposit, stamped it a few times, and told me to have a nice day. I said I would give it a try, and that was that. I headed out into the snowstorm.

Here's how I got to the bank.

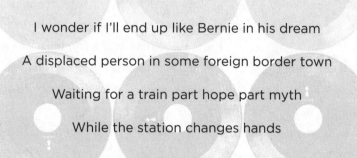

I wonder if I'll end up like Bernie in his dream

A displaced person in some foreign border town

Waiting for a train part hope part myth

While the station changes hands

"How I Spent My Fall Vacation"
Bruce Cockburn

CHAPTER ONE

It was early March 2009 when the ring of the phone shook me from my daydream. I'd been staring out the window of our little library at the farm my wife and I had bought in Prince Edward County a few hours east of Toronto, deep in Ontario's newest wine district.

I'd been watching the birds hopping around on the ground and eating at the feeders I'd put up. Grosbeaks, blue jays, and the occasional brilliant red cardinal. They were strikingly beautiful against the snow. It was easy to get lost in watching them, and why not? I'd sold True North about eighteen months earlier and had gone from being involved in twenty-one acts to only working hands-on with one, Bruce Cockburn.

Luckily for me, Bruce had decided to take off some time just around the period I had made the sale. So I had time on my hands, and I was spending a whole lot of it looking out this window, and a few others in the County, and I was loving it. I knew it was just a matter of time till things started to happen again, but I also knew it would never be the same.

When I picked up the phone, it was Michael Cohl on the line. Michael Cohl. If I could be considered successful at all then Michael was Croesus himself.

Was it really forty years ago that we had casually smoked a joint together in Yorkville? Things were different then. We both were getting started in Toronto's Yorkville district. While I had already been managing two bands, the Paupers and Kensington Market, there was no question that Michael was going to become someone special. And he certainly did. In 1989, he bought the rights to, and produced, the Rolling Stones' *Silver Wheels* tour, which went on to become the world's most successful tour to that date.

Receiving Michael's call startled me. As much as I'd liked him, we hadn't stayed in touch. He told me he was going to produce a show at New York's Madison Square Garden to celebrate Pete Seeger's ninetieth birthday on May 3 and wanted to know if Bruce would like to participate. The only other act he'd booked at the time of the call was the other Bruce – Springsteen – but he was now working on the lineup and it promised to be a good one. After a quick call to Cockburn, who was more than happy to do the show, I called Michael back and confirmed.

Of course we would do the show. It was a no-brainer. What a great way to start things rolling again, and the concert was a natural fit. This would not be the first show we had done to celebrate the great Peter Seeger. Bruce had done a concert in Philadelphia on May 15, 2005, to acknowledge Pete's fifty years of writing the "Appleseeds" column in the venerable folk magazine *Sing Out!* That concert, at the 1,400-seat Keswick Theatre, included Judy Collins, Natalie Merchant, Janis Ian, and Pete himself. But now that Michael had become involved, the event had moved to the 18,000-seat Madison Square Garden. When I mentioned this to Michael his modest response was, "That's what happens when you have Bruce Springsteen involved."

The show ended up with more than fifty artists on the bill, including Dave Matthews, John Mellencamp, Joan Baez, Emmylou Harris, Kris Kristofferson, and Ani DiFranco, just to name a few. PBS signed on to broadcast the concert across the United States and then to release it on DVD. Because of the number of acts on the show, various artist pairings and ensemble numbers were going to be set up.

Everyone was to do one or two Pete Seeger numbers, or at least songs associated with Pete over the years. We had requested that Bruce do "Turn, Turn, Turn," a song he had recorded on a Pete Seeger tribute album, *Where Have All the Flowers Gone*, in 1998. But when Roger McGuinn from the Byrds was added to the show, naturally he was given the song that the group had taken all the way to number 1 in 1965.

Bruce Cockburn, Pete Seeger, Billy Bragg, and Cara Tivey at the Riverside Church, New York, 1991 (Phil Jacobs)

But all's well that ends well. Bruce was paired up with his friend Ani DiFranco to do the old union working song "Which Side Are You On?" His other number would be done with the only other Canadians on the show, Kate & Anna McGarrigle, and Kate's children, Rufus and Martha Wainwright. They chose to perform "Dink's Song," which is also known as "Fare Thee Well." In fact, Fred Neil's version of "Fare Thee Well" is one of my all-time favourite records. Check it out if you can. Sadly, the performance at Madison Square Garden would be one of Kate's last public performances before she passed away from a rare form of cancer.

It was an amazing evening. Both of Bruce's "duets" were remarkable and extremely well received. The tickets had sold out in a matter of minutes and the love and respect for Pete Seeger throughout the backstage area and the entire audience was palpable. At ninety years of age, his performance and energy were enough to give you hope for the aging process.

Every inch of the backstage area was crawling with people I'd met and worked with over the past forty-five years, from Steve Earle to Taj Mahal to Billy Bragg to Joan Baez. The music director for the evening was Torontonian Bob Ezrin, whose production credits included Pink Floyd, Alice Cooper, and Peter Gabriel. I had worked with Bob back in the eighties on a Murray McLauchlan album. I spent some time talking to Danny Goldberg, former president of Warner Records and currently Steve Earle's manager. I had first met Danny when he owned Gold Castle Records, the American record company that had released Cockburn's *Stealing Fire* with the hits "If I Had a Rocket Launcher" and "Lovers in a Dangerous Time."

It was a bit like an old-fashioned school reunion. The neat thing was that just about every conversation had something to do with music and songs, which was a refreshing change from the current ongoing dialogue that seems to always revolve around bandwidth, piracy, or some other tech issue. Important stuff no doubt, but in my life there was nothing more important than a good song, and it was good to be somewhere where that was the main topic. Everywhere I turned there was an artist whom I had either toured with or presented in concert at one time or another. And with them came their managers, agents, and others, many who'd become my friends over the years. Lots of great – and occasionally not so great – memories.

The show was a signal to me that although I had left the record business, I hadn't left the music business, and it represented a fine re-entry into the hustle and frenzied world of management, something I had seemed to have a knack for and hadn't yet lost.

Goodbye Momma goodbye to you too Pa

Little sister you'll have to wait a while to come along

Goodbye to this house and all its memories

We just got too old to say we're wrong

Got to make one last trip to my bedroom

Guess I'll have to leave some stuff behind

"Child's Song"
Murray McLauchlan

CHAPTER TWO

I was born August 12, 1944, in the old Mount Sinai Hospital on Yorkville Avenue in the middle of Toronto. Strangely enough, it was within a few yards of that hospital that I would begin to make my mark in the world some eighteen years later, at a time when Yorkville was emerging as the epicentre of Canada's burgeoning music industry.

I think of it as a strange coincidence because I could have been born anywhere in the world where there was a Canadian air force base. My father was in the Royal Canadian Air Force and he was constantly being posted to new places. Many years later, it was Toronto where my father would choose to retire with me, my sister, Rozanne, and my mother, Eve.

What I mostly remember from my childhood is the constant moving. Some of it was great fun, like going to England on an ocean liner or crossing Canada on old steam trains. But some of it was pretty unnerving. Imagine being the only Finkelstein in small towns in the 1950s and early '60s and you'll know what I mean. I learned how to make friends and to be alone at the same time. I learned how to fight and how to negotiate my way out of fights; how to survive and move on. But before I leave you with the wrong impression, let me say that I had a happy childhood that prepared me well for the life I was to live in the music busi-ness. My mother always told the story about one of those train voyages across the country during which I returned to our com-partment in the sleeper car with my pockets full of change. Apparently I had gone through the dining car and picked up all the tips, not understanding why the money had been left on the tables. She made me take it all back to the chief dining car stew-ard, who had a good laugh at my expense and then gave me a tip for being honest. They don't teach you that in school.

Over the years, we lived in Edmonton, Winnipeg, Trenton, Toronto, and Nottingham, England. I attended about thirteen schools and, in the end, never finished grade eleven. Clearly, I was a terrible student.

In 1955, the RCAF transferred my father to England. To me, at eleven years old, it seemed like it was going to be the worst thing that could happen. I'd be going so far away, I thought, that they wouldn't have Coke in cans or grilled cheese sandwiches. We were to be stationed to RCAF Langar, an airbase outside of Nottinghamshire. Langar was the supply base for the five fighter wings that Canada had stationed in Germany and France. The Second World War had ended only ten years earlier and Canada was doing its part for NATO, which included maintaining a mission in West Germany. RCAF Langar was adjacent to the tiny village of Radcliffe-on-Trent and about fifteen miles from the city of Nottingham. We sailed to England on the SS *Homeric*, a grand transatlantic ship flying the Italian flag. It left from Quebec City, where my grandfather had arrived when he immigrated to Canada from Russia. It was the first time I had ever been on a ship that size. Spending six days at sea, some of them very rough, was the kind of adventure I loved. The ship was a floating palace with a swimming pool, a library, a shuffleboard, and several decks where I was able to spend loads of time just staring out to sea.

The SS *Homeric* crossed the Atlantic to the French port of Le Havre, and then moved on to Liverpool, where we disembarked. The first thing I remember discovering about England was that, my God, I was right, there was no cola, just something called mineral water. We made our way from Liverpool to Nottingham, where we occupied a flat on the second floor of an old house right in the centre of the city. (The Canadian airbase didn't have its married quarters finished yet but eventually we moved onto the base.)

Of course I knew Nottingham as the home of Robin Hood and it didn't take me long to get caught up in the romance of those legendary tales. The city was dominated by Nottingham Castle, and everywhere you went there were statues of one kind or another dedicated to Robin and his Merry Men. I was particularly taken by an old pub from the thirteenth century now called "Ye Old Trip to Jerusalem." Local lore had it that this had been a place where knights would go to have a pint. After someone, perhaps the bartender, had spiked their drinks, the knights would pass out and be dropped down a tunnel hidden under a trap door located just behind the bar. At the bottom of the tunnel there was a small stream that led directly to the ocean, where the knights would be heaved into a small rowboat that then carried them downstream to a larger ocean-going ship. By the time the knights had regained consciousness, they were halfway to Jerusalem, where they'd be forced into battle against the Saracens during the Crusades.

Our house was near a park called Sherwood Forest, although the real Sherwood Forest was just outside the city. Rob from the rich and give to the poor — I think that idea stayed with me as I made my way through the world.

But I wasn't the only one to arrive in the U.K. in 1955. So did Elvis, with a force that hit the Island like a tsunami. I was already being seduced by the music of Bill Haley, who with his band the Comets recorded "Rock Around the Clock" and "See You Later, Alligator." Everyone was talking about the birth of something new called rock 'n' roll. I remember, in particular, Elvis's cover of Roy Brown's "Good Rockin' Tonight," his second release on Sun Records. It contained the memorable lines, "I heard the news there's good rocking tonight." I think that song set me on a road that I'm still travelling today.

For my birthday that summer, my parents bought me a small record player, the kind that opened like a brief case. You lifted up the top and there it was in all its splendour: a turntable, an arm with a needle, and a speaker. Along with it were three 78s: Guy Mitchell's "Singing the Blues," Frankie Vaughan's "The Green Door" (Jim Lowe had the hit version of this in North America), and also Elvis's unforgettable version of Big Mama Thornton's "Hound Dog," with "Heartbreak Hotel" on the B-side. God bless my parents.

For me and rock 'n' roll it was instant love. Not that this was the first time I'd had records. When I was five and living just outside of Edmonton in Jasper Place, I had loads of kids' records that came complete with picture books. You'd put the record on, read along with the story, and when there was a beep or a bell you would turn the page. I was in grade one at Jasper Place Public School at the time. Many years later, in 2005, my long career in the music business brought me an improbable honour: the Order of Canada. One of the many nice and unexpected consequences of that event was a phone call I received shortly after the ceremony. An elderly woman's voice asked, "Is that Bernie Finkelstein? Is it the Bernie Finkelstein that once went to school at Jasper Place Public School?"

"Yes, it is," I said.

"Well," the lady said, "it's Miss Brower, your teacher from grade one."

Unbelievable! On the phone was my favourite teacher of all time. She'd been retired for years, living on a farm just outside of Red Deer. Miss Brower had read about my award in the local paper. She told me that she always knew I would do something of note, that she could tell from my bright shiny eyes in school that I was going somewhere, somehow. I think I fell in love with her at that moment, for the second time.

England turned out to be one of the greatest experiences of my life. At first I attended Cambridge House, a public school, which in Canada we would call a private school. Going to Cambridge

I receive the Order of Canada from Michaëlle Jean

House meant wearing a uniform – a school cap, tie, and jacket, a blue blazer with a crest – the whole works. I adjusted, but not as well as I could have, I guess. I kept getting into trouble with the teachers, usually for not doing my schoolwork. (The only subject I liked was English Literature.) The normal punishment was to be caned, usually on the palms, but occasionally you had to bend over with your hands on your knees and take it on the rear end. That was the English way, at least at that school.

I was the only Canadian in the school. With the great interest in all things American, brought on by the success of Elvis and rock 'n' roll – and with the kids assuming that being Canadian really meant I was American – I became a popular student. I was also the *only* kid with a brush cut, which was considered quintessentially American. Naturally, I became the expert on all things North American. To be honest, I knew very little, but since Canada and the U.S. shared so many cultural trends, I talked knowledgeably about yo-yos, Bolo bats, baseball, hockey, chewing gum with cards, and all the usual kid stuff we had in Canada.

When Elvis's first movie, *Love Me Tender*, opened, my parents took me to see it. I cried, not because it was so moving, but because it only had one song in it. At twelve, I had already become a hard-core music fan. They also took me to see Buddy Holly & the Crickets when that great band played a concert in a movie theatre in Nottingham. That was one of the greatest thrills of my young life. Over on the left-hand side of the stage, a mike had been set up on a stand only two or three feet off the stage floor. Every once in awhile, Buddy would go over and lean into that mike, singing and strumming his guitar for theatrical effect. I was amazed and delighted. I count myself lucky to have seen Buddy Holly & the Crickets in person. Buddy truly was one of the great musical innovators of all time.

Later on, after we had moved from Nottingham to Radcliffe-on-Trent to be nearer to the airbase in Langar, my week's big activity was the Saturday morning trip on the double-decker bus into Nottingham to hear the latest records that were coming into the shops. I would stand in line in front of a sound booth that had a turntable and a headset. Finally I'd get my chance to listen to the new releases. If luck was smiling my way I'd have a few shillings to buy a record or two.

Usually we were the only Jewish family stationed on base, either in England or back in Canada. My bar mitzvah at a local synagogue in Nottingham turned out to be quite the public event. The Canadian air force was big news in the Nottingham area and when it turned out the commanding officer was coming to the synagogue for the ceremony, I made the front page of the daily

My dad and I at my bar mitzvah in Nottingham, England

paper in a picture with my dad and the commanding officer. It wasn't often that a member of a Canadian Forces family had a bar mitzvah in England, so it became a bit of a public relations event for both the air force and the synagogue.

My father, Harold, was a non-commissioned officer in the air force. By the time he retired his rank was warrant officer class 2. I used to joke that he was the Phil Silvers of the Canadian air force. Phil Silvers played Master Sergeant Bilko, a wisecracking wheeler-dealer on the wildly popular '50s TV show *The Phil Silvers Show*. To be fair to my father, he really wasn't much like Ernie Bilko. Still, I could see the similarities, and in many ways enjoyed the comparison.

Shortly after my bar mitzvah we moved from Nottingham right onto the Canadian base at Langar and I enrolled in what was called a secondary school in the small town of Radcliffe-on-Trent. This was entirely a different kind of school from Cambridge House. Here I was surrounded by kids who weren't going to go on to colleges or universities. It was a working-class school and I enjoyed it as much as I did Cambridge House, even though I was only there for about half a year before I started going to another new school on the airbase itself.

Around this time a new kind of music, called skiffle, was sweeping England. Skiffle was usually played by a trio with a washboard, a guitar, and a tea-chest bass. It was a strange amalgamation of old-time jug band music, country music, and blues. Lonnie Donegan was its leading progenitor. Donegan would have many hits including his cover of "Rock Island Line," "Cumberland Gap," and "Don't You Rock Me Daddy-O." About ten years later the Lovin' Spoonful would ride the same influence of jug band music to enormous success. It wasn't long before I found myself in a skiffle group playing the tea-chest bass. I wasn't too good at it, but, boy, did I have fun.

In October of 2008 I had the occasion to talk about my introduction to skiffle. It was during my acceptance speech for the Estelle Klein Award for Lifetime Achievement, from the Ontario Council of Folk Festivals.

I told the gathering about hearing this song "Diggin' My Potatoes" on BBC radio by Lonnie Donegan. Soon after, I decided to call the station to request the song, but when I finally got through I was told the record had been banned. Banned . . . wow! When I figured out what that meant, I ran right out and bought the record, and my skiffle group made that song a regular part of our repertoire.

So, as a teenager, I had already learned the value of having something banned. I wish it had happened more often to my artists during my career! The few times it did always led to something good, even if the banning itself was an uncomfortable experience. When U.S. stations began to ban Bruce Cockburn's "Call It Democracy," I found myself in several knock-down, drag-'em-out fights with our record company. Yet, in the end, the song found its audience, and it remains one of Bruce's most popular songs, even these many years later. I have always said that when a song is banned in the U.S. it gets noticed, but when it's banned in Canada it stays unknown. Another way to put this is to say that Canadians are very good at sweeping things under the carpet, while Americans are very good at selling the carpets.

Part of being in a skiffle group meant going to public contests where the various bands would compete for fame and glory. By the late '50s there were an estimated 30,000 to 50,000 skiffle groups in Britain. It turns out that John Lennon was listening to exactly the same songs on the radio as me, at the same time that I was. He had formed a skiffle group called the Quarrymen, which became the foundation for the Beatles. I've often wondered if our little group and the Quarrymen might have played at some of the same contests. What I do know for sure is that we never won a contest. But, hey, I was playing in the band, even if it was the first and last time I ever played music in public.

Curiously, for a guy who has made a career out of representing performers, being a performer myself was never a big obsession of mine. I was too busy listening and enjoying the music to learn how to play it, even though I can think of no talent that I admire more than the ability to write and play a great song.

While in England I also got my first tape recorder, an old Studer reel-to-reel, and started using it to record songs from the radio, usually late at night. There was no commercial radio in England during this period. The BBC had a government-sanctioned monopoly on the airwaves and didn't really embrace rock 'n' roll.

However, a reaction against the dominance of the BBC developed around this time: pirate radio. The most famous station, Radio Luxembourg, broadcast at night from the Grand Duchy of Luxembourg, a tiny country bordered by France, Germany, and Belgium. During the '50s, Luxembourg's stations targeted the growing teenage market by emphasizing pop music, similar to top-forty radio stations in North America. (By the early '60s, pop music stations like Radio Caroline and Radio London began providing the same service by broadcasting pop music from ships anchored in international waters.) I used to stay up late into the night taping the various shows on Radio Luxembourg so I could listen to the music whenever I wanted to.

Sometimes the disc jockeys would only play part of the records, like maybe a minute and a half, but still, what great stuff I was listening to: the Everly Brothers, Mickey & Sylvia, the Coasters, the Del-Vikings, Johnnie & Joe. Such terrific music and just about all of it holds up today. Strange to think about taping the music way back then, in light of today's controversy over digital downloading and copyright infringement. I guess there really isn't anything new under the sun.

My parents encouraged me to join the boy scouts, and I agreed to give it a try. By chance, a World Jamboree was to be held in England during 1957 and my troop was selected to go. It was held for a week in a place called Sutton Park, outside of Birmingham, and would end on August 12, my birthday. Well, it turned out to be a week of incredible heat coupled with torrential rains that seemed, to me, of biblical proportions. I soon had enough of waking up to a soaking tent and wet food. Without warning either my scout master or my parents back home, I took off from the campsite.

Around the time my scout troop, and no doubt the Jamboree's organizers, were sounding the alarm that a boy had gone missing, I had stopped at an outdoor pavilion with a long lineup in front of a jukebox. (The English would queue up for anything and everything.) I got in the line, and when my turn came, I deposited my sixpence and played "Young Blood" by the Coasters. Later that day, I was picked up by the local police and my parents arrived at the camp to take me home. I don't recall celebrating my birthday that summer but I remember playing that Coasters record like it was only yesterday, and it's a record I still like a lot.

So the die was cast. The sound and message of rock 'n' roll were a stronger lure to me than anything else. No boy scout badges or even my parents' most fervent wishes for me could hope to compete with the powerful attraction of that jukebox and its treasures in that park.

Soon after my ill-fated episode with the boy scouts, we were transferred back to Canada, this time to Eighth Wing in Trenton,

Ontario. Again we sailed on a grand ship, a Canadian Pacific liner called *Empress of England*. After the six-day ocean crossing we stopped to visit relatives in Ottawa on our way to the base in Trenton. There I was at fifteen, in Canada again after a three-year absence, excited to be back in the world of baseball and hockey, and within striking distance of the home of rock 'n' roll. We spent a few days at my grandmother's cottage in Britannia, now an Ottawa neighbourhood but at that time a small town to the west of the city. The cottage was really small – just a couple of rooms and a tiny, always crowded kitchen – but very magical to me. The family of Lorne Greene, the CBC news anchorman – who that year began a new job playing Pa Cartwright on a U.S. TV show called *Bonanza*, which would make him a star – lived next door, but I don't remember meeting Lorne Greene while I was there. I spent most of my time reading *Comics Illustrated* and drinking loads of Pure Spring pop. It was summer, and life was good.

When the talk with my Ottawa cousins turned to music, some interesting things became apparent. When I enthused about the song "Tutti Frutti," surely one of the greatest records ever made by Little Richard, they didn't know what I was talking about. They'd been listening to Pat Boone's version of "Tutti Frutti" on local radio. And the same thing was true for many other songs, including Pat Boone's cover version of the great Fats Domino's "Ain't That a Shame." There was no comparison in the quality of the recordings or performances. The originals were, well, primal, and the covers were like white bread. Something was wrong here, but what was it?

Several years later I understood it to be race discrimination on radio playlists. A fact of life in the U.S., but a sad commentary on Canadian radio's willingness to play follow the leader. All of this would have a big impact on me later in my career but, at fifteen, I didn't really know anything about radio, other than that I enjoyed listening to it.

While my father worked at the military base in Trenton, I furthered my education. I learned to drive, shoot pool, smoke cigarettes, and find a bootlegger. By then I didn't just like music, the way other teenagers did; I couldn't get enough of it. Everything from Elvis and Buddy Holly to Chuck Berry and Little Richard. But there was more, not just rock 'n' roll but the records that my parents liked: Sinatra, the show tunes from Broadway, Judy Garland. You name it, I liked it. The big event of my day was turning on Dick Clark's *American Bandstand* after I got home from school and watching the dancers move to the hit records.

About the only time I wasn't listening to music was when I was in the pool hall in downtown Trenton. Shortly after we'd arrived in town I found my way there. It was on the main drag and there was something about it that instantly attracted me. The dark room, lit by shaded lamps hanging over the tables, the air filled with smoke and a slight scent of danger, gave me the the feeling I was a character in a noir movie. The sound of the balls bouncing off each other on the green felt was as clear and crisp as the sound of twigs snapping on a cold winter day. Everything seemed urgent in a pool hall – the constant state of suspense at each table put everything else into sharp relief. My kind of place for sure.

I got pretty good at the game, too. Good enough to play for money. One of the unwritten rules of pool is that what counts "isn't what you make, but what you leave." There's no sense trying to make an impressive shot if it could leave an easy set-up on the table for your opponent.

I had a bit of natural skill in me, and more than a little of the natural-born hustler. Sure, I loved shooting pool – but I really loved it when I was playing for money. The game I most liked was called golf, played on the largest table in the room, usually with five or six players. The object was to use the shared white cue ball to shoot your assigned coloured ball into all six pockets clockwise around the table. When it was your turn, you had to shoot the cue ball from wherever the player before you had left it. It was truly a game of skill and strategy. Sometimes we'd also put little mini skittles around the table to make the game even tougher. Points were added to your score any time you scratched, or knocked over, a skittle. Once you got your colour ball into the pocket, every stroke after that counted against you. The player with the most points against him would pay everyone above him, right through to the top player, who would be collecting from all the people below him. As you can imagine, it was a cutthroat game, but loads of fun. Depending how much you were playing for per stroke, you could win – or lose – a lot of money. I started spending more time in the pool hall than at school, but I was getting an education anyway.

My father taught me to drive around the base in his 1956 blue and white Chevy Bel Air. It was just a six-cylinder, but what a great car it was. There was nothing like having several square miles of almost deserted roads on which to practice. I just had to make sure I steered clear of big planes taxiing by. It didn't take me long to get my license, and shortly after that I had my first night out, alone with the car.

One of the other things I learned at the pool hall was where and how to buy a mickey or two from a bootlegger. Off I went with a couple of friends to visit the town's friendly dealer of illicit alcohol. Sadly for me, it happened to be the night the cops were staking him out, and when they saw three teenagers driving away with a couple of bottles of rum, they just couldn't resist making the arrest. A few minutes later, I was in the local jail. It wouldn't be the last time I would spend a bit of time behind bars, but it was the scariest. My father and mother were not pleased, and it took me a few months to get the car again.

Do you want to know the definition of paradise for a sixteen-year-old? Driving and music. There just wasn't anything better in the world. Rolling the window down and cranking the radio up as loud as you could. And it was paradise, four years later, hearing one of the first records I was involved with playing on the car radio. It's still a big thrill when I'm lucky enough to hear them today.

Still, when I was sixteen, I didn't have a single thought about being involved in music. I knew as much about the music business as I knew about physics, which was nothing at all, judging by my report cards. I just loved the songs. I thought these records magically appeared like some sort of manna from heaven. Records like "Cathy's Clown" by the Everly Brothers, "Stay" by Maurice Williams, "Stagger Lee" by Lloyd Price, and "Running Bear" by Johnny Preston, to name but a few that were all over the radio at the time. It never occurred to me that there was a business involving music. This subject wasn't on my school's curriculum, or anywhere near the air base, or at my primary hangout, the pool hall. If I had any ambition at all back then, it might have been to become a professional pool hustler.

At school dances, I mostly leaned against the back wall or stood outside smoking, but I loved hearing the music. Usually there'd be a DJ playing records but occasionally we'd have a live band. The sound of a record from the back of a gym is pretty impressive. This hit home years later, when we were doing Murray McLauchlan's one-off single "Little Dreamer." (I always really liked this song even though it wasn't one of Murray's biggest records.) While we were doing the final mix, I asked the recording engineer to make it sound like we were listening from the back of a high-school gym. He knew exactly what I meant and I think we got the sound right.

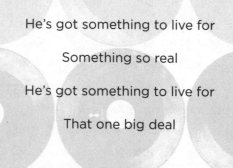

He's got something to live for

Something so real

He's got something to live for

That one big deal

"Something to Live For"
(Barney Bentall and Gary Fraser)
Barney Bentall & the Legendary Hearts

CHAPTER THREE

At fifteen I began working two jobs, both part-time. One was as a rink rat at the air base's local arena. It didn't pay much but, boy, did I love that job. I cleaned the ice between periods at hockey games and then, after the crowd had gone home, I could play on the ice in the evening. The rink's manager was a kind old guy named Charlie, who had a little office at the back of the rink with a small wood-burning stove in it. Charlie and I'd sit around that stove, keeping warm and talking, and drinking the best hot chocolate I've ever had in my life. The highlight during that time was when future NHL stars Bobby and Dennis Hull came to Trenton to play junior hockey. We all knew they were destined for greatness.

My other job was working for Allied Van Lines. I would show up early in the morning at the office and wait to see if they'd call me to help out on the big moving trucks. The company's owners always started the day with a prayer session, sitting around in a circle, praying to Jesus to help us with our work. It never bothered me, since I really didn't have any clear idea of what I thought about religion. But when my mother found out about these sessions, she spoke to the owners to request that I be excused from them.

Although I'd always been a reader, it was about this age that I developed a real passion for it. In school it was Thomas Hardy's *The Mayor of Casterbridge*, Emily Brontë's *Wuthering Heights*, and Shakespeare. All great, but it was the stuff I was reading after school that was leaving the biggest impression on me. Books like *A Stone for Danny Fisher* and *The Carpetbaggers*, both by Harold Robbins; *Atlas Shrugged* by Ayn Rand; Jack Kerouac's *On the Road*; Walter Tevis's pool-hall novel, *The Hustler*; and loads of science fiction by authors like Isaac Asimov and the Canadian writer A. E. van Vogt.

By 1961, I had failed grade nine and was having a second try at it. In those days, my head was spinning with ideas as I tried to learn more about this fascinating world and figure out my place in it. Then my father announced he was being transferred from Trenton to Toronto. We'd be moving halfway through the school year, so I'd be completing my second kick at the grade-nine can in Toronto.

Well, to be exact, he was posted to RCAF Station Downsview, an air base located at Keele Street and Sheppard Avenue, in what was then the far northwestern corner of Toronto. It really felt like it was a long way from the city. Off the southern end of the base was Downsview Collegiate, my new school.

The married quarters on the base were full so we temporarily moved into what the military euphemistically called LDH, or Low Dividend Housing – dirty, rundown, four-storey apartment buildings. They were so bad that the small Nottingham flat we'd briefly lived in now seemed like a palace. But this new situation did have one advantage: the buildings were located just behind a small plaza at Keele and Sheppard where there was a good pool hall: lots of tables and lots of action. I was right at home.

Many things happened all at once around the time of our move to Downsview. My mother helped me get a part-time job working at Honest Ed's, the landmark discount department store at Bloor and Bathurst Streets in downtown Toronto. She had been a lifelong friend of Honest Ed Mirvish's sister, Lakey, and when we moved back to Toronto they picked up their friendship where it had left off. Next thing you know, I found myself working in the hardware department of the world's craziest store. I loved that job and the people I worked with, but I hated packing my lunch in a brown paper bag and waiting in line to catch the bus downtown. I promised myself that I would find a way to avoid this kind of life in the future.

I became an expert on floor tiles, toilet seats, and light switches. I saved enough money to buy a sports car – a little red Sunbeam Alpine – and I began driving Honest Ed's mother home at the end of the workday. (She lived with Lakey and their house wasn't too far away from the air base.) Honest Ed used to love seeing his mother with her kerchief tied around her head sitting in my Alpine with the roof down.

It was at Honest Ed's that I met Randy Markowitz who later – known as Randy Dandy – would become the producer of *The Hilarious House of Frightenstein*, an early Canadian children's program syndicated across Canada and the United States. Starring Billy Van and Vincent Price, the show used off-beat humour and up-to-the-minute cultural references that made it ahead of its time. (It's still being shown on television today.) But when I first knew him, Randy was the in-store announcer at Honest Ed's. A huckster and joker of the first order, he told customers about the specials throughout the store, from the red-hot deals in the hardware section to the deeply discounted hourly sales in women's clothing and home furnishings. He always managed to inject some humour into the proceedings.

We had no way of knowing that just a few months after meeting, Randy and I would find ourselves in a friendly, but none-theless serious, competition in Yorkville. We each managed one of the two hottest new bands in Toronto, both of them about to get international record contracts.

At the same time as I was getting to know Randy at Ed's, I was becoming fast friends with two people who were to have a great influence on my life: Peter Simpson and Al Fisher. Peter and Al were pals before they ran into me. Al's brother, Stan, had been a member of the Diamonds but had left that band just before they recorded the seminal hit "Little Darlin'." Some fifty-odd years after its release in 1957 and its rocketing to number 2 on the inter-national singles charts, "Little Darlin'" is still one of the best records ever recorded by Canadians.

I met Peter at Bill's, our local pool hall in that little plaza in Downsview. He fancied himself a good pool player, and he was. Peter went on to have a great career in both advertising and the film business. His most successful movie was *Prom Night* but probably his biggest accomplishment was starting Media Buying Services, a company that revolutionized the advertising world and made him rich. However, when I first met Peter, he, like Al and I, was just beginning to dream and scheme about show business.

Despite these vague notions of some kind of show business future, I still didn't really know what I wanted to do with my life, except that it didn't involve staying in school. If I wasn't going to be kicked out of class, I would quit on my own. Not because I was a hooligan or falling into a criminal underworld, but because the school didn't know what to do with someone who was getting 9 per cent in French and 11 per cent in Algebra. Even though I knew I could do better, I was bored out of my mind. All I wanted to do was spend time in the pool hall, work part-time, and dream.

I saw being in school as being institutionalized and that wasn't my idea of how to spend my time productively.

One day in 1962, a friend took me downtown to Yorkville for the first time. Yorkville was a mixed area, a jumble of upscale antique shops, boarding houses, greasy-spoon diners, and poets standing on street corners reciting their work. Small coffee houses were decorated with posters on the walls and showcased folk and jazz music as well as poetry readings. Often the entertainment featured flamenco guitarists or European folk-style duos like Malka and Joso.

You could go into any of the coffee houses, order an espresso, play some chess, and hear some pretty interesting music. And there were loads of girls around. I was confident that if I hung around Yorkville long enough, I'd meet Jack Kerouac or someone like him and end up on the road. Keep in mind that even though this is still a year or two before Bob Dylan and the Beatles changed the world, I sensed endless possibilities in Yorkville, and decided it was a possible destination in the not-too-distant future.

While Peter and I were figuring things out, Al suddenly made the first move. He signed up for one of those radio courses you could take by correspondence, the ones that used to be advertised on the back of match books. I think he even got a free tape recorder when he signed up to take the course. One day, shortly after he started the lessons, he had an opportunity to be the turntable operator for the all-night radio show on CFGM in Richmond Hill. (This was back in the days when radio still played vinyl records and the better DJs could demand that the station hire them a turntable operator.) During this period, CFGM was the leading country music station in the Toronto area, and when the all-night disc jockey quit his job, Al was hired to replace him. After he'd been on the air for a while we started to think of him as the only kosher ham in Richmond Hill.

Sometimes I would go to the station and stay all night, watching Al work and helping him answer the phones. In the morning, I'd either drag myself to school, dead tired, or just as often take the day off and not get to school at all. Every once in a while Al would have to go down to the Horseshoe Tavern on Queen Street West and host a live show. When he did, he'd often invite me to go along with him as his guest. I remember seeing Ferlin Husky singing "Wings of a Dove" one evening. That remains even today an unforgettable experience. But for me the real excitement at the Horseshoe during those days was all those country music–loving women in their bouffants. Who knew what mysteries lurked under those wild hairdos?

Meanwhile, Peter and I came up with the idea that we should start providing entertainment at Downsview Collegiate. Of course, our first event would be to book Al as the DJ for a sock hop. This turned out to be a success. It was time to start a business.

First we needed a name. We decided on the Specter Agency. It was a play on two of the things that were then current in our imaginations. First, Spectre was the name of the criminal organization that Ian Fleming's character, James Bond, was always fighting in those spy novels. (The name stood for *SP*ecial *E*xecutive for *C*ounter-intelligence, *T*errorism, *R*evenge and *E*xtortion and was led by the evil genius Ernst Stavro Blofeld.) Hard to imagine naming your company after something like that today.

The second inspiration for our company name came from Phil Spector, the great record producer responsible for the "wall of sound" heard on hit songs like "To Know Him Is to Love Him" by the Teddy Bears, the Crystals' "He's a Rebel," and the Ronettes' "Be My Baby." Spector produced "You've Lost That Lovin' Feelin'" by the Righteous Brothers, worked with the Beatles, and produced solo records by John Lennon, George Harrison, and Leonard Cohen.

He was so successful that journalist Tom Wolfe named him "the First Tycoon of Teen."

I quit school and Peter and I opened a small office on the second floor of an old house on Davenport Road, not far from Yorkville. Our company was doomed to be short-lived but it was fun while it lasted. One of my fondest memories was meeting with Peter each morning at the little greasy spoon across the road from the office, where we would split a toasted Danish for breakfast. Every morning we would toss a coin to see who would get the side with the icing on it. It would be a great understatement to say we were broke.

But things were changing quickly. Around the time I moved to Yorkville, I was still working part-time at Honest Ed's. Then an opportunity came up. The Mirvishes were renting the Poor Alex Theatre on Brunswick Avenue, just a few blocks from Yorkville – a kind of second cousin to Ed Mirvish's more prestigious Royal Alex Theatre – to outside groups, and they needed a representative in the house. My job had two distinctive parts. During the

THE SPECTER AGENCY

S

PROMOTERS

OFFICE - 1893 DAVENPORT RD.

B. L. FINKELSTEIN
ME. 6-3993

P. R. SIMPSON
ME. 3-1169

My first business card – the Specter Agency
(Photo courtesy of Quinn Simpson)

day, I would clean it up. In other words, I was the janitor. And in the evening I'd put on a suit and be the Mirvishes' representative in the theatre. Yale Simpson, who was in charge of both the Royal Alex and the Poor Alex, called my mother one day to tell her that a good Jewish boy shouldn't be a janitor, and my mother broke the news to me that I should move on.

I was living on the second floor of a house located on the west side of Avenue Road, across from Yorkville Avenue. I shared a one-room flat with an old friend of mine from Downsview. Just down the hall was the common toilet we shared with the other boarders in the house. This arrangement only worked because my friend had a day job and I was working at night. I would appear at

Working at the Poor Alex

around 7 a.m. just as he was getting up for work. After sleeping, I'd be sure to be gone by around 6 p.m., when he returned.

It was at this time that I smoked my first joint. I was already a big smoker of regular cigarettes but this was something different. It put a different spin, both literally and figuratively, on everything. Dylan and the Beatles had arrived. I'll never forget the first time I heard Dylan on the radio, on the weekly Toronto show hosted by Randy Farris. When Randy played Dylan's "Song for Woody," a tribute to the great folksinger Woody Guthrie, I thought I was hearing the voice of all ages, or even the voice of God. I thought it was directed right at me.

Little did I know that within four years I would be in New York, forming a partnership with Dylan's manager, Albert Grossman. And then there were the Beatles. Like everyone else, I got caught up in their ethos and never once did I feel let down. The times were electric and the possibilities seemed endless. The sixties had begun.

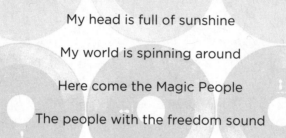

My head is full of sunshine

My world is spinning around

Here come the Magic People

The people with the freedom sound

"Magic People"
(Adam Mitchell and Skip Prokop),
The Paupers

CHAPTER FOUR

One day Peter Simpson told me that he was going to elope with his high-school sweetheart, Gordine, and asked if I would help him out with his wedding. There was just one little problem. His high-school sweetheart was still in grade twelve. Peter wanted me to be his best man, which I was delighted to do, so we cooked up a plan. With Gordine still attending high school the trick was going to be to get her out of Downsview Collegiate for the day without her parents or anyone else knowing what was going on. Peter forged a note to the school principal, saying that Gordine would have to leave school at 11 a.m. for an appointment with her dermatologist, which he signed as her father. I made arrangements to get a limo with a driver for the day. Then Peter, Gordine's maid of honour, Marianne, and I parked around the corner from the school. At eleven, Gordine showed up, and we took off to Toronto's City Hall for the wedding. There were only the four of us in attendance, but it was the finest of all weddings. After the ceremony we went to the Ports of Call, a restaurant considered to be one of the very best in Toronto at the time. The

Ports had several sections, each one dedicated to some exotic part of the world. I had booked a private booth in the Polynesian section. That same night, right after the dinner, Gordine went back to her parents' place to do her homework, and Peter returned to his family's house in Downsview. It would be several months before Peter and Gordine told their parents they were married and moved in together.

That year, I was living in a mostly abandoned University of Toronto frat house, not far from Yorkville Village and empty for

My first business partner, Peter Simpson. We're still at Downsview Collegiate here (Photo courtesy of Quinn Simpson)

the summer. Sometimes I put my emerging entrepreneurial instincts to work making a few bucks by illegally parking cars in the unused lots behind the frat houses, charging whatever I could.

I was also working two jobs in Yorkville. One was at a basement club right in the heart of the Village, Café El Patio. At that time, the street was teeming with young people of all types: hippies, greasers, bikers, and just plain tourists looking for what everyone was looking for in the sixties: music, drugs, sex, and – don't laugh – freedom. Freedom from what? Well, maybe that wasn't certain, but change was in the air and everyone wanted to be part of it.

I had several duties at Café El Patio. Mostly I worked in the kitchen washing dishes and running the espresso machine, but I also set up for the evening's shows and would occasionally act as the club's bouncer, making sure that the kids – many of them not much younger than me – were orderly while waiting in line. I'm glad I never had to deal with any serious trouble. I wasn't much of a tough guy and, given the freewheeling culture of the mid-sixties, I was stoned a good deal of the time.

One night, Tony, the Spaniard with whom I worked in the kitchen, showed up wearing high rubber boots. Tony didn't speak much English but I got the message: I clumsily slopped too much soapy dishwater on the floor. Thankfully, I had other things on my mind, and didn't see dishwashing in my future.

I was also working with a rock group called the Dimensions, from Downsview, who later changed their name to A Passing Fancy and had a few minor hits on Columbia Records, including "I'm Losing Tonight" and "I Believe in Sunshine." I was helping them to get gigs around town. The leader of the Dimensions was Jay Telfer, also from Downsview Collegiate, whom I originally met back when he had a folk group called the Voyageurs. For the brief time that the Specter Agency was a going concern, one of the best things we did was to book the Voyageurs at the Village Corner, one of the leading folk clubs in Toronto. We booked them as an opening act, which meant they were expected to perform three twenty-minute sets, but as luck would have it the headliner didn't show up, and the Voyageurs became the evening's headliner. They'd have to do three forty-minute sets. They ended up repeating material and faking it a lot that evening, but it was a memorable night for me. Just being in this legendary Toronto club with my sudden headliner felt like a real accomplishment.

The Village Corner was a Toronto institution. It was there that Ian & Sylvia had made their mark and still occasionally played. I was in complete awe of both Ian & Sylvia and Gordon Lightfoot; to be anywhere in the vicinity of where they worked was a thrill. Not only were their songs and records incredible, but knowing they lived right here in Toronto was inspiring and extremely encouraging. There's no doubt that they opened my eyes to what was possible. I was always hoping to run into them in Yorkville and find out how they did it. Eventually I did meet them, quite some time later, but it was worth the wait. Needless to say, I also got the Dimensions a few bookings at the El Patio.

Around the same time I was booking the Dimensions into the Café El Patio, I also had a job at the Kiki Rouge, a disco around the corner in Old York Lane. I would be at the El Patio until around midnight and then would report to the Kiki Rouge for work until 3 or 4 a.m. I worked in the kitchen making coffee and washing dishes, but soon I became involved in a bit of a scheme there. The two main waitresses were named Solveigh and Jutta, simply the most beautiful women I'd ever seen and for whom I would pretty much do anything they asked. They knew how to look after their customers and how to get tips – I knew, because they kept the tips in a big glass jar in the kitchen, which they would divide at the end of the night. To increase the size of those tips they needed two things from me. First, I had to be fast, so their customers could get their orders in a hurry. Second . . . well, the Kiki Rouge, like most Yorkville clubs during that period, didn't have an alcohol licence. Instead, regular customers knew to bring in their own booze. The waitresses would take their bottles to the kitchen, ask me to hide them, and then surreptitiously spike their coffee orders.

Of course I cooperated, and I started to notice that the harder the girls pushed me, the larger the tips got. Finally I got wise to my importance in the set-up and asked them to split their tips with me. This seemed reasonable, given my contribution to their ever-increasing earning power. They agreed, although I can't say I ever paid too much attention to how much they were giving me. It just felt good to be part of the operation. Later both Butta and Solvie married members of the band Steppenwolf, which at that time was called the Sparrow, and before that, Jack London and the Sparrow.

The floor of the Kiki Rouge was littered with used amyl nitrite poppers and those, along with alcohol, were the drugs of choice there. Notwithstanding the seductiveness of the Kiki Rouge and my fondness for its waitresses, I always liked my job at the El Patio much more. Maybe it was because that club was full of teens and they were there to have a good time listening to the local bands.

Although most of the clubs were on Yorkville Avenue, there were also several rooms strung along Avenue Road north of Yorkville to Davenport. There were even a few south of Yorkville on Cumberland. Each was unique: the Devil's Den, Boris's, the Red Gas Room, the Purple Onion, the Mynah Bird, the Inn on the

Parking Lot, the Riverboat, the Night Owl, the Penny Farthing, the Mousehole, the Village Corner Club, and many more. They all had one thing in common: great music. Rock, folk, and rhythm and blues and it was all good, real good.

So how good was it? Well, listen to this. On any night you could hear David Clayton-Thomas (later to become an international sensation as the lead singer with Blood, Sweat & Tears), with or without his band, the Shays; the Sparrow, soon to score several hit records under a new name, Steppenwolf; and the Mynah Birds, whose members included future funk star Rick James, Neil Young, and Bruce Palmer (who played with Neil in the seminal California folk-rock group, Buffalo Springfield). There were bands like the Paupers, Luke & the Apostles, Jon & Lee & the Checkmates, and the great Mandala, not to mention acoustic artists like Joni Mitchell, Gordon Lightfoot, Ian & Sylvia, and Bonnie Dobson. All of this great music was concentrated in this small area called the Village.

Yorkville was jammed with people from all over the city and right across the country, everyone from political activists like David DePoe, June Callwood, and the Diggers (a group of community activists and improv actors), to bikers, dealers, writers, and musicians. There were artists hanging out just down the road at the Pilot Tavern, poets selling their work on the street, and lots and lots of marijuana. I don't want to over-romanticize grass or drugs of any kind but you can't – at least, I can't, given my experience – tell the story of the sixties without talking about drugs. Drugs, mostly soft, permeated the world we all lived in throughout this period and they were deeply infused in much of the music.

For a while, after Yorkville was well slammed shut and turned into Rodeo Drive North, it became fashionable to deny that anything special really happened in the sixties or in Yorkville, to say that those remembering it that way were just members of another generation feeling nostalgic about its youth. But now, as even more time has gone by, it seems clear that something extraordinary did, indeed, take place there. I really don't have an axe to grind one way or the other, but it's hard to deny its quality and the magic, when all you have to do is turn on the radio to hear the music that was innocently being made during this period still being played, over and over again. And I was lucky enough to be in the middle of it, living and breathing it, and, soon enough, involved in getting some of it out to the street.

By this time I had moved to a flat on the second floor of a house on Walmer Road. I stored a large bowl of pot in the oven of my stove, just about the only thing I ever opened the oven for. I'd wake up, roll a few joints, light one up, and walk down to the El Patio getting high.

Occasionally the El Patio's owner allowed bands to rehearse during the afternoon. One of them was a group called the Paupers, made up of drummer Skip Prokop, guitarists Chuck Beal and Bill Marion, and bassist Denny Gerrard. The Paupers had already made a couple of singles for a small label called Roman Records and owned by Duff Roman, then a DJ at CHUM and one of the pioneers in the Canadian music business. Duff made a handful of some of the greatest Canadian records ever, not only by the Paupers, but also by David Clayton-Thomas when he was with the Shays, and later when he had joined the Bossmen. If you can get hold of it, check out "Brainwashed" by David. Awesome. At that same time Stan Klees had a label called Red Leaf Records. He was turning out some pretty strong stuff as well, including Little Caesar and the Consuls' hit version of "My Girl Sloopy."

But things weren't going well for the Paupers. Remember, this is five years before Canadian-content regulations were introduced and decades before the concept of financial support for the Canadian music business came into being. There were no schools that taught anything about the music business and very few people you could go to for advice. No one really knew the way home, which was good news for someone like me. I may not have known a lot but it was as much as, or even more than, anyone else.

During those afternoons at the Café El Patio, as I was preparing the club for the evening, I would spend my time listening to the Paupers rehearsing. I thought they were great, but it was apparent they didn't know which steps to take next, and even more apparent that they were flat broke. Although I was under strict orders from the owner not to feed the musicians in the afternoon, when the deliveries of baguettes and cold cuts came into the club I'd open up the fridge and do what anyone would do – make the band sandwiches. We'd sit around and talk about everything under the sun while getting high,

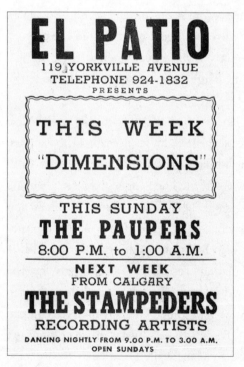

My first two acts, the Dimensions and the Paupers, at Yorkville's El Patio

but then we'd get to talking about the state of their band. Most of the stuff was pretty mundane, I suppose, but it seemed important at the time. Should they wear suits? Should they have long or short hair? Should they play more or less original material? Should they play twelve-string guitars, and if so, where would they get the money to buy them? I had answers for everything and I wasn't just fooling around; I really thought I did know the answers. I also didn't have self-serving motives at the time, as I still didn't have a clear idea, let alone an ambition, about getting into the business of music. I can't really tell you what was on my mind as far as long-term thinking went, but I'm pretty sure it had more to do with meeting girls, reading books, getting high, and maybe somehow making some money. But making money from Canadian music in the mid-sixties? That didn't really occur to me.

The one thing I did know for sure was that this was one great band. They had several terrific songs, a good look, and they could really play. I don't know whether it was the sandwiches or my advice but one night, Skip, who was the leader of the band, met me on the back patio of the club and asked if I'd like to manage them. I jumped at the opportunity. I'd been watching my old friend from my Honest Ed's days, Randy Markowitz, working with the Mandala (earlier known as the Rouges), a soul and R&B band who were playing lots of shows just around the corner at the Devil's Den. And I'd been thinking, If Randy can do it, so can I.

During this period, the Yorkville scene had two main camps of music. There was the "blue-eyed soul" sound of bands like the Mandala and Jon & Lee & the Checkmates, whose main fans were known as greasers, and the rock bands like the Ugly Ducklings and the Paupers, whose main followers were more or less hippies. Skip and the rest of the Paupers were giving me the opportunity to get something going with what I thought for sure was the best band on the street. I said yes to Skip that day, even though I wasn't exactly sure what a manager's responsibilities were. I found out soon enough.

We met that same evening after the band's last set at the El Patio and got down to work. The first thing I found out was just how broke they were. To make things worse they had some of their equipment in hock with Long & McQuade, the big music equipment dealer in town. They were going to need that equipment for a show coming up at a high school on the weekend. Turned out they needed one hundred dollars, which was a small fortune to all of us. I told them not to worry about it. I'd get it figured out, even though I didn't have two nickels to rub together.

The next day I went home to visit my parents, who were living in an apartment at Bathurst and Steeles in Toronto's north end. By now my father had retired from the air force and, after twenty-six years in the military, had taken another job in the area working for a potato chip company. Our relationship had become stormy and from time to time things would really blow up. Let's face it, I wasn't exactly the dutiful son they might have expected, yet they always supported me to the best of their abilities and never let me down. The air force had provided a good life but certainly there was never any extra money to speak of. I told them that I had just been handed a great opportunity but I needed one hundred dollars to get things started. My father opened his wallet and pulled out seventy-four bucks. He told me he was glad to give it to me but I shouldn't come back and ask again as there wasn't more money to be had.

I was grateful, and said so, but I guess something prompted my dad to tell me that I shouldn't get too full of myself. Even though I may have been thinking I was going places, as far as he could see I hadn't yet gone a hundred yards from where I started. And that's when it finally dawned on me that I had been born in the old Mount Sinai Hospital just a few doors away from the Café El Patio.

I took the money and headed back down to the Village on the subway and walked over to Long & McQuade, where I made my first deal for the band. I convinced the company that it was better to take seventy dollars and give the band their equipment than to hold out for the hundred. I was off to a good start.

We decided that the best way forward was for the band to be as original as it could be, so they began replacing the cover tunes with as many of their own songs as possible. Sounds like a simple enough thing to do, but this still was an era when local bands weren't expected to play a lot of original material. I couldn't see the point of being the best at imitating someone else. It didn't make sense to me then and it still doesn't today, although many musicians get away with copying other people while cleverly disguising it as original work. Skip Prokop, whose background included being a champion marching-drum-band member, came up with the idea of having two of the Paupers playing marching drums (essentially snare drums) during some numbers. This would mean that now there would be sections of some songs where the band would have three drummers. Chuck Beal had also come up with the idea of using an electronic loop machine that he had rigged up on his own with his guitar. With the three drummers, the electronic guitar loops, and the original material, the band was starting to sound like nothing else anywhere on the planet.

But as always in the music business, disaster was lurking just around the corner. For one reason or another Bill Marion, the main vocalist and rhythm guitar player, decided he had had enough of the Paupers, and with little notice he got up and quit on us. It seemed like a major setback for a moment, but I had the answer in a blink of the eye.

From time to time I had been going across the road from the El Patio to a little club called the Mousehole that primarily featured up-and-coming folk musicians. Despite being involved with a psychedelic rock 'n' roll band, I had a deep love of folk music going back to my time in England. The Mousehole was owned by Bernie and Patti Fiedler, who also owned the more famous Riverboat located a little further down Yorkville. I would later become partners with Bernie and we would have a very successful run together.

I had been watching a talented young singer-songwriter named Adam Mitchell. Adam's folk background and vocal sound seemed like a great fit for the Paupers, merging in well with the more psychedelic and rock leanings of the band. I imagined the sounds to be both compatible and different at the same time, further distinguishing the Paupers from the pack. The band liked the idea, Adam loved the idea, and the modern Paupers were born.

Between the drums, the electronic enhanced guitar, and the addition of Adam, we really had something going. Adam brought another kind of songwriting to the group. The songs written by Skip and Adam created a dynamic and dynamite repertoire. After the Paupers broke up both Adam and Skip went on to bigger things. Skip was a founding member of Lighthouse, a band that had several international hits, and Adam's songs were covered by artists like Merle Haggard, Kiss, and Olivia Newton-John.

The band worked and worked, especially when it came to rehearsing. We rented a rehearsal space on Yonge Street not too far from the famous Le Coq d'Or. There, on any given night, you could hear Ronnie Hawkins and his backup group, which eventually became known as the Band. Ronnie was something else and the music he was making was different again from what was being heard on Yorkville. But it was cool. Ronnie, who had come to Toronto via

Arkansas, scored big in 1959, with the top-forty hits "Forty Days" and "Mary Lou." Rompin' Ronnie, as he was affectionately called, was the king of Yonge Street, and I'm glad that I got to know him. Larger than life – just like the rock 'n' roll he sang.

The Paupers had a terrific work ethic. I tried to attend every rehearsal and was always quick to make suggestions on how to improve things, some of them good, and some of them . . . well, just suggestions. They would rehearse all night long and soon the sound began to shape up as something special, as did the whole show. Bass player Denny Gerrard started doing a solo to end each night's set that was truly amazing. Sometimes he would play so ferociously that his fingers bled. His performances were truly show-stopping. The band's reputation, as well as its audience, was growing. It didn't take long before there were lineups for their Toronto shows. It was time to make a move. There had to be more than Yorkville.

Gradually I was learning about the music business, such as it was, in Toronto. The biggest booking agency in the city was called Bigland and located in a small building on Yonge Street near Merton. I heard that there would often be last-minute cancellations on a Wednesday or Thursday for that coming weekend's one-nighters, so if you happened to be close by the right agent when the cancellations were called in, you could clinch last-minute shows for your band. I had given up both of my club jobs by now and was only working with the Paupers, so with the time to spare I started hanging out in the Bigland lobby.

Right upstairs from the agency was a small magazine run by Walt Grealis and Stan Klees called *RPM* known as the voice of the nascent "Canadian music business" – three words I had never heard strung together before and really wouldn't much hear together again until somewhat later in the seventies, but nonetheless ones that signalled a business busy being born. Between my time hanging out in the lobby of Bigland and talking to the guys at *RPM*, I was learning more and more about the music game. So I decided that it was time to make a demo and try to get the Paupers a record deal.

Everything was about to move into overdrive. We made the demo in a matter of a few days with the assistance of the great and masterful music arranger Ben McPeek and the tremendously talented organist, pianist, songwriter, and session musician Doug Riley, known as Doctor Music. Then I decided to take it to New York. It wasn't like I was passing up too many opportunities in Toronto. There really weren't any record companies in 1966 that were signing acts in Toronto. The only band I knew that had a

Walt Grealis and me

record deal of any consequence was the Mandala, with Decca Records in New York. When the Mandala went into the studio to record their first single, "Opportunity," it was so exciting that we would receive hourly reports on how the recording was going. Things like, "Hey, they are now recording Domenic Troiano's guitar solo," or "They are now editing together, bit by bit, piece by piece, the lead vocal by George Oliver." The information buzzed around the Toronto music scene like it was front-page news coming off the wire services. Truly magic.

Talking about Domenic Troiano, he and I became great friends even though our respective audiences were the "greasers" and the "hippies." We would often meet after our shows at an all-night restaurant in the newly opened Colonnade on Bloor Street, along with musicians from various bands, including our own. Although the edgy psychedelic rock of the Paupers and the blue-eyed soul of the Mandala couldn't have been further apart, Donny and I agreed that the egg-salad sandwiches at the Colonnade were the best.

It was an exciting time and I wanted the Paupers to be part of the same action. One of the very few places that the band had been able to play outside of Toronto was at a terrific Ottawa club called Le Hibou, owned by Harvey Glatt. I met Harvey at the club when I was travelling with the band and he became a lifelong friend. (In fact, Harvey, along with Geoff Kulawick and Mike Pilon, was one of the buyers of True North Records.) He was quite familiar with the music scene in New York, and at the beginning of our friendship he helped me set up a meeting with the president of MGM Records, Jerry Schoenbaum.

Not only had I never been to New York before, I had never even flown on an airplane, despite the fact that my father had been in the air force and I'd grown up on air bases. Whenever we had travelled as a family, it had always been by car, train, or boat. Let me paint you a picture of how I looked, airline ticket in hand, in August 1966. I looked like the prototypical hippie. My hair was down to my shoulders, and my wardrobe consisted of an old army jacket, a black tee-shirt, a pair of jeans, and an old pair of boots. Like René Lévesque, I was covered in ashes, although in my case more of it was from grass than cigarettes. In my pocket I had what I considered to be the greatest demo anyone had ever heard and here I was, taking it to New York. At twenty-two, I didn't really have a care in the world, including the outcome of this meeting. It never occurred to me that things wouldn't work out. When the plane had reached its cruising altitude, I looked out the window and saw a wonderful spread of thick white clouds looking like giant pillows. And I thought to myself, *Well, this can't be too bad. In a worst-case scenario, if something goes wrong with the plane, it can just make a soft landing on those clouds.* Hard to say if I was just naive or completely stoned, but in any case the plane arrived at La Guardia just fine and I was off to MGM.

New York City, what can you say? I can tell you this, I felt at home right from the beginning. I loved the hustle and the speed of the city, and I loved the people. I thought they were friendly and bold with great humour, three qualities I liked. I hailed a cab and headed for my meeting in one of those large sky-scrapers on Sixth Avenue at 56th Street. It was one in a row of looming skyscrapers that housed most of the large media and record companies, such as CBS, RCA, ABC, and MGM.

I walked into the MGM building and met with Jerry. I'd love to tell you that I did something amazing, but all that happened was that I pulled out the tape, Jerry put it on, and said, "Okay, I'll give you a deal. First we'll make a single and then, if it works out, we'll do an album."

"How about two guaranteed singles and then an album?" I asked, thinking two chances were better than one. He agreed, we shook hands on it, and then started talking about what would happen next. He asked me if I was staying in New York that evening and when I said yes, he told me it would make sense to have the band play in New York as soon as possible. He sent me down to Greenwich Village to meet with Howard Solomon, the owner of the legendary Café Au Go Go on Bleecker Street. I thanked Jerry and walked out the door with a record contract in my pocket, although the actual papers didn't get signed for a while.

It's strange to say this but, honestly, I wasn't that excited about the deal. I had truly expected it, and like any good manager, I believed there was nobody better than my act and it was just a question of getting people to listen. When I look back on it with the knowledge I have today, I can see that I should have been dancing and clicking my heels, but I was actually more excited about my trip downtown to the Village – I had dreamed of visiting the Village since I was in high school. Somewhere in the back of my mind I still thought I might find Jack Kerouac and the bohemian life, and certainly Greenwich was at its centre. And it was also the current home of one of my newer heroes, Bob Dylan.

I'd heard a lot about the Café Au Go Go. I knew it was Howard who, just a year or so earlier, had presented the wonderful but controversial comedian Lenny Bruce and ended up getting arrested with him on obscenity charges. I'd always found it easy to talk to club owners because of my time spent at the Kiki Rouge, the Café El Patio, and the Poor Alex. I understood the issues involved in running a club and could speak their language.

Greenwich Village amazed me. First off, how large it was compared to the Yorkville district and how old it felt. And just how cool it was. There were all the famous names, one after another – the Bitter End, Café Wha?, the Tin Angel, the Village Vanguard – right there in front of me, and I was going in to meet the owner of one of the greatest of them all.

So in I go. Howard turned out to be a great guy. He tells me he'll book the band and opens up his booking ledger, which was one of those big month-to-month books with a square for each day of the month and lots of scribbling in it. He looks it over and says, Hey, I've got the perfect show for you, with Ian & Sylvia. He tells me they are going to fill the place and, given that they are from Canada, it should be a good fit.

Now there are times in your life when you have to take a shot. Think about it. I'm twenty-two; I'm in the Café Au Go Go, one of the most important clubs in the music world. I've got the president of my new record company waiting to hear about what show we are going to have in New York and how soon it'll be, and I'm being offered a gig with one of the greatest Canadian acts of all time, the duo who had written and recorded a handful of the finest songs ever, including Ian's "Four Strong Winds" and Sylvia's "You Were On My Mind."

And what did I say? "No thanks." And then I asked him if I could look at the upcoming schedule.

Now, anything could have happened at that moment. Howard could have said, "Get outta here kid, maybe I'll call you later." But instead he said, "Sure, take a look."

And there it was – the Jefferson Airplane were coming in for their first-ever New York appearance. I explained that as much as I loved Ian & Sylvia, I just didn't think it would be the best match.

"Could we have the Jefferson Airplane instead?"

Howard says, "Yes, you can have that show," marks it in his book, and off I go.

Let me tell you what I knew about the Jefferson Airplane at the time. Just about nothing. But I knew enough to place the Airplane as one of the leading lights in San Francisco's burgeoning music scene. There was a kind of informal information exchange between the different underground scenes around North America in the sixties. News travelled quickly, especially between Yorkville, Haight-Ashbury, and Greenwich Village. I'd been hearing a lot about the music coming out of Haight-Ashbury but I had yet to hear the Airplane. This was just before their first hits, "Somebody to Love" and "White Rabbit," broke and charted in the top-ten around the world.

On my way to the airport, I stopped at a record store and picked up the Airplane's album *Jefferson Airplane Takes Off*. When I arrived back in Toronto the first thing I did was to get together with the Paupers to listen to the record. To be truthful we didn't think too much of it. It just didn't seem to be that good, and with that in mind we couldn't wait to play that gig. I immediately called Howard at the Café Au Go Go to reconfirm the show, and the band continued their hectic rehearsal schedule, playing as many shows as possible.

As fall turned to winter we started hearing the Airplane all over the place with songs from their new album *Surrealistic Pillow*. As it turns out, the album I had bought was the first Jefferson Airplane record, made before Grace Slick joined the band. This newer version of the Airplane was something else again. Not only were they riding a terrific album to the top of the charts but they were also among the leaders of the psychedelic San Francisco movement that was beginning to rival the long-running British invasion. This was good news and bad. Bad only because the opportunity to get noticed at the Café Au Go Go was going to be possibly diminished by the onslaught of publicity and curiosity of this phenomenon out of the West Coast. More than just any music show, a new social and music movement was going to be making its New York debut at the Paupers' gig. We were up for it. We had our own movement and our own ideas, and by the time the band got to New York in early '67 we were ready for anything. As expected, the hottest ticket in town was the Airplane, with all of the shows sold out well in advance and almost no chance of getting in last-minute, no matter who you were.

Happening almost simultaneously with my trip to New York and my return with the MGM record contract was a large promotional show at Maple Leaf Gardens called the Toronto Sound Show. By this time, people in Toronto were waking up to the tremendous amount of local talent and were becoming more and more interested in it. This show was supposed to help put that music on the map. I was somewhat dubious of this kind of promotion as it felt pretty mainstream – what those of us from Yorkville would have called "manufactured." However, I believed in the cause, so I agreed to the organizer's request for the Paupers to appear. After all, it was Maple Leaf Gardens, and it was rumoured that a lot of foreign-record-company people would be attending the show. Who knew what might happen? So we put aside our worries and started getting ready for the concert.

As luck would have it, between the time I accepted the booking and the date of the show I had made the deal with MGM. Well, the show was truly a great success, especially for the Paupers who were one of the hits of the night. I had purposely held off announcing our MGM deal until after the show and now I was able to use the show's positive impact to claim that the Paupers had been such a success that it had triggered a recording contract in the States. Not strictly true but close enough, and the story got big play in the media. The Paupers were becoming big news not only in Toronto but right across the country. This wouldn't be the last time I would slightly fudge the truth to make a good story, but I figured none of it would have happened anyway if the band's music and live performances weren't so powerful. And as the expression goes, "It was good enough for folk music."

The big night of the Paupers' first show in New York finally arrived. The club was jammed with just about every significant player in the music business, from the Beatles' manager Brian Epstein to Dylan's manager Albert Grossman, not to mention Paul Simon; the rock world's leading concert promoter, Bill Graham; bluesman Johnny Winter; and countless more, many arriving from San Francisco with the Airplane. It was like a circus that night; New York's first look at West Coast flower power in full bloom, hippiedom at its best and most powerful. It was February 1967 and an early beginning to the summer of love.

And love it was for the Paupers. By then the Airplane had little to teach us about psychedelics and little to teach us about music, although let me clearly tell you how much I liked their show and their attitude that night. Their music had a certain majesty and they couldn't have been cooler, which I mean in the best possible way. Still, the Paupers blew the audience away that night. It's all well documented by the press, including a stunning review that ran in the *Village Voice* from the dean of all rock writers at that time, Richard Goldstein. Richard had many fine things to say, including: "They have a power and discipline I've never seen before in a performance."

In some ways music, especially live music, is like sports. Sometimes the artists have to reach deep and just be better than they ever have been, no matter what the circumstances. In other words you have to be, to use a sports term, a big-money player and learn to win. That's what the Paupers did that night.

Now I know that won't make me popular among the music purists out there, and I never put that theory forward to pressure any of my acts, but nonetheless, over the years, I've learned that it's true. I've seen plenty of nights when artists were able to take things over the top and, unfortunately, many nights where they couldn't. To the unschooled eye and ear the differences between a good night and a bad night can be very subtle, but to me they were always clear. Many acts fold under the pressure and never quite get it together on the big nights. And who can blame them. Professional music, like all professional activities, can sometimes be one big pressure-cooker.

That doesn't mean good things can't come out of an ordinary show. That's where music differs from sports – musicians aren't playing in a fixed season. Still, there are nights where you have a chance to win big and, for the Paupers, that first show at the Café Au Go Go was one of those nights when they magnificently rose to the occasion. I swear you could feel the whole club rising a few feet into the air while the band played. Nobody had ever heard anything like this before. Three drummers, electronically enhanced lead guitar, and a stunning bass solo had the crowd on its feet during the last number. They didn't sit down until the band came back out and took a bow. After the set, there was pandemonium backstage. Everyone wanted to talk to the band and to me, especially the executives from our record company who were all suddenly talking about doing a full album right away, never mind just another single.

We had arrived and it felt good. Of course it was just a beginning, but at that time, in that moment, I didn't know that, and I was riding high, literally and figuratively. It was a four-day gig for us and we were staying at the Gorham Hotel on 55th Street, which became my home away from home for several years.

But during those few days of 1967 a few more notable things happened.

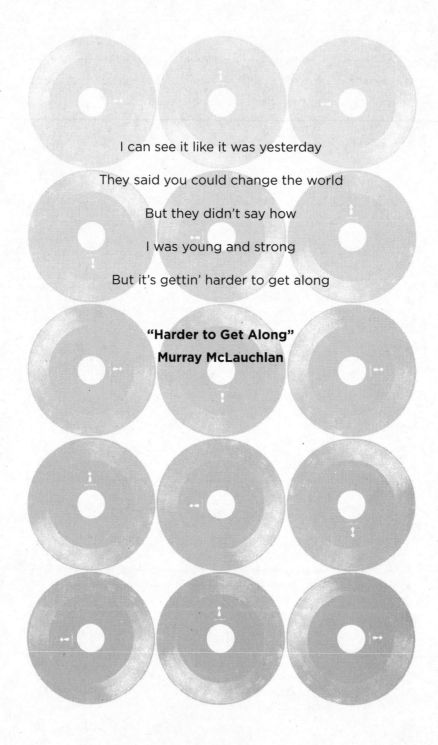

I can see it like it was yesterday

They said you could change the world

But they didn't say how

I was young and strong

But it's gettin' harder to get along

"Harder to Get Along"
Murray McLauchlan

CHAPTER FIVE

One afternoon I heard a knock at my hotel door. Opening it, I saw a pretty blonde woman with two joints in her hand. She introduced herself as Linda Eastman. We lit a joint and she told me she'd been at the opening night show and thought the Paupers were great. As it turned out, she was a photographer and a good one at that. She had brought a portfolio of her work and I was impressed. She wanted to shoot the band. What could I say to a pretty, talented, and very nice photographer who arrived with joints and was willing to shoot the band for nothing? So I spoke to Skip and we scheduled a shoot in Central Park for the next day. We used her shots as promo pictures for a while. As time passed I lost track of Linda, but certainly noticed when she later married Paul McCartney.

Among the many other people who contacted me that week was Albert Grossman, Bob Dylan's manager. Grossman's impressive roster included Peter, Paul & Mary, as well as my fellow Canadians Gordon Lightfoot and Ian & Sylvia. Albert asked if I could meet him after one of the shows at his townhouse in fashionable Gramercy Park. That was an invitation I certainly wasn't going to refuse. So after that night's show I made my way to Gramercy, riding a high, as I would after each of the band's hugely successful shows during this gig. I was just twenty-two and the world seemed to be unfolding in wonderful ways that I couldn't have predicted just a year earlier. But I was taking it in stride, or so I thought.

When the door opened to Albert's place I was greeted by the very beautiful Sally Grossman, although at that exact moment I didn't know who she was. What I did know was that she was on the cover of my absolutely favourite Bob Dylan album at that time, *Bringing It All Home*. I must have played that record a hundred times in a row and while playing it I'd stare at the cover and read the liner notes over and over again. That's the power those records had on me, and on so many other people. And standing

Linda Eastman shoots The Paupers (Photo by Linda Eastman)

right there in front of me was the woman with Dylan on the album jacket, asking me to come in. *Alice's Adventures in Wonderland* comes to mind.

Although I got to know Sally better in the future, that evening she just kind of disappeared and I don't recall seeing her again on that occasion. I sat down with Albert in his living room and we started talking. Albert was an interesting-looking guy. I thought he looked like Benjamin Franklin with his granny glasses and white hair tied back in a ponytail.

Albert was impressed with the band. He'd seen the future of rock – represented by bands like mine, and others from the West Coast – and was very interested in getting involved with me and the Paupers. At the time Albert wasn't managing rock of any kind. It was all folk or blues music, although Bob Dylan had already gone electric and "Just Like a Rolling Stone" had been a major hit, but I suppose for Albert it was still folk music. He had yet to start working with Janis Joplin, and the Band was still Dylan's backup group; the group's amazing *Big Pink* was a year away. I was flattered and not just a little excited. Here I was, in the home of the manager of some of the artists I liked the most in the world – Gordon Lightfoot, Ian & Sylvia, and the great Dylan himself. We started smoking a joint, and I don't know exactly why but I got higher that night on grass than I had ever been before. As we talked I was looking around the room, and at first I thought the two large paintings of Elvis pointing a gun, each slightly different from the other, were hallucinations. I liked Elvis of course, but I couldn't figure out why you would want two large paintings of him pointing a gun in your living room. What I didn't realize was that they were original Andy Warhol prints, the silkscreens Warhol had made from publicity stills from Elvis's 1960 western *Flaming Star*. At that moment I knew absolutely nothing about Andy Warhol. As time moved on, I got it, and a few years later I had the opportunity to meet Andy at his famous Factory.

That night, however, I kept getting higher and higher, and found myself wondering if Bob Dylan was going to walk into the room. (Although if he had, I'm not sure I could even have managed to get off the couch to say hello.) Finally, I left Albert's, agreeing that I'd come to his office to discuss a possible partnership in the management of the Paupers.

The next day I headed out to Albert's office in midtown Manhattan. In these days, back in Toronto, I didn't have an office of any kind. I had a phone in my flat on Walmer Avenue but no files, desks, nothing like that. My whole business was being run out of my two back pockets. I had started hanging out across the road from the El Patio at an outdoor café called the Upper Crust, and if anyone needed me, they could find me there. I conducted all my meetings in the corner on the outside patio or at a window table inside the café. I used the pay phone at the corner outside the Upper Crust for business calls both in and out, although sometimes the owner of the café, the great Werner Graeber, would let me use the kitchen phone if I could convince him something important was going on. Werner, who was one of the longest-running inhabitants and club owners on the Yorkville coffee house scene, once told me, "Sell them junk, Bernie, it's what they like." Maybe I should have listened to him.

The café world was wonderful. The street was growing more interesting and crowded with each passing day. The times were changing again and now it was becoming the full-on age of the hippie. I've never liked labels of any kind and hippie's one I also never liked at all, although I've got to admit it, I most likely looked like one and thought like one. I suppose I was somewhere between a hippie and a reject from a biker gang. Still, I thought the hippie thing was cool. Peace and love. I couldn't find anything wrong with that. I enjoyed my afternoons at the Upper Crust, sitting outside taking in the street, drinking cup after cup of coffee, and smoking the odd joint throughout the day. Evenings were devoted to the Paupers. Life could have been worse.

Albert's office in Manhattan was a world away from the Upper Crust. He had a full floor with a central hallway and several offices on either side of the hall in a building on 45th near Lexington. There was lots of activity and you could feel the buzz the moment you walked through the front door. Sometimes I felt like I was in the back room of a small bank; the decor was simple but there was a real feeling of success about the place. After talking about the management situation I decided that it would make sense to enter into a partnership with Albert for the Paupers. Albert talked enthusiastically about me getting further involved in his company and working with him on other artists in one capacity or another. We started to work out a plan that included getting the MGM/Verve contract changed so the band could immediately start an album. Albert called Jerry Schoenbaum and we agreed to meet at MGM the next day. There was also talk about a pending offer for the band to play this brand-new show called the Monterey Pop Festival that was just being put together and not yet announced. When it was announced, the Paupers would be part of the show. Nobody really knew too much about rock festivals, because there had never been one before, but this looked like it was going to be something big.

Well, of course, the Monterey Pop Festival did happen in June 1967, with a star-studded lineup that included Jimi Hendrix, the Who, Otis Redding, Eric Burdon & the Animals, Jefferson Airplane, and a future Albert Grossman client, Janis Joplin. It set the template for all the festivals – including Woodstock – that followed. The Paupers did appear at it, but I wasn't there myself. In fact, by the time of the Monterey festival I was no longer working with the Paupers or Albert. By my own choice.

On the way out of Albert's office that day I finally met Bob Dylan. I'm not sure why he was there, maybe waiting to meet with Albert, but we were introduced. I shook his hand, and that was that. A thrill, of course, but now I had business of my own to get on with.

Our meeting with Jerry went well. He was happy about, or more likely really motivated by, the fact that Albert had become involved with the Paupers. He agreed on the spot to change the contract to include the immediate recording of a full-length album that would appear on the new MGM imprint, Verve Forecast, which Jerry had founded that year. Meant to be an extension of the iconic label Verve Folkways, the new label would be home to not only the Paupers but a whole new generation of talent that included Tim Hardin, Al Kooper's Blues Project, Laura Nyro, and Richie Havens. Our album would be recorded in New York but first we had to go back to Toronto and start fine-tuning the material.

When we left Jerry's office it was getting dark and beginning to rain. There was just one last show left at the Café Au Go Go, on that evening. As we waited to hail a cab to take us down to the Village, I stared into the window of a Mercedes-Benz dealership. Albert assumed I was thinking about owning one but, in fact, I was really just thinking about how unusual it was to see a car dealership on the ground floor of a skyscraper in the middle of a city. Not something you saw in Toronto. I'll never forget, though, Albert saying to me, "You know, Bernie, you'll have a Mercedes whenever you want one. You know why? Because you know more about rock 'n' roll than any of the people in the business here in New York and you've only just begun."

That was pretty much the nicest thing Albert ever said to me. It may seem as if I had fallen under Albert's spell – his relationship with Bob Dylan, alone, was enough to do that to anyone – so, yes, there's probably some truth to that. But it wasn't quite that simple. I felt ready to go down the road with Albert and learn what I could, and I was certainly able to take a compliment without letting it cloud my judgment. Yet the scene in Toronto was beginning to feel like a movement or a revolution of some kind. Canadian music was beginning to matter both at home and abroad. I was somewhere in the middle of it and wasn't too anxious to leave it just when we were having fun. I wasn't too sure where all of this was going but it felt like a ride in the right direction and I figured I would know where to get off when I got to the right station. But the next day, I headed back to Toronto; the beginning of what would become a series of frequent trips between Toronto and New York.

One of the first things I did when I got home was move from my apartment on Walmer Road to the area around Avenue Road and Davenport, closer to the Yorkville area. I rented a loft that had once been the old changing rooms at the Aura Lee sports grounds, just off Pears Avenue running right on to Ramsden Park. It's where a former Toronto Maple Leaf from the 1930s, the great Charlie "The Big Bomber" Conacher, used to play hockey. The rink was now abandoned. However, they had left up the changing rooms building, and I moved in. One of the rooms was about fifty feet long. For some reason, which now escapes me, I bought a bow and arrow and set up a target at one end of the room. I used to sit at the other end and practise shooting.

The success of the Paupers in New York, and especially the MGM record deal, had become big news in Toronto, and spread right across the country among those who were involved in the fledgling Canadian music business. Their success was seen as a real breakthrough, not only for the Paupers but possibly for all Canadian bands. I even made it to the cover of Canada's most prestigious monthly magazine, *Saturday Night*.

There were, of course, other Canadians starting to do well internationally. The Paupers, however, represented the new music that had been emerging from the streets of major cities like London, New York, San Francisco, and, yes, Toronto. The band had a sound that was identifiably Canadian. And, even more importantly, the band hadn't needed to move south to be recognized. It was an affirmation that Canadian bands had something valid and creative to say to the world. So even though the Paupers weren't riding high on the charts – they hadn't even released an album yet – they had nonetheless taken New York by storm, landed a U.S. record deal, and attracted the interest of the most powerful manager in the business.

Along with the band and Albert, I started piecing together the Paupers' recording schedule. We had already decided to call the first album *Magic People*, one of the most popular songs in the band's live repertoire and also the song that spoke most clearly to the band's image and sound. After much discussion among Jerry Schoenbaum, Albert, the band, and myself, we decided to get Rick Shorter (the brother of the great jazz trumpeter Wayne Shorter, who was playing in Miles Davis's band at that time), to produce the first album. Rick would be coming to Toronto for a few days of rehearsal and then the band would be off to New York to start the record.

We decided to rehearse at the same place we had always used on Yonge Street, near Le Coq d'Or. Rick arrived in Toronto and began working with the band. I wasn't really all that excited by the rehearsals. It seemed like the energy of the band was being toned down by the changes being made to the arrangements, but I didn't have much experience with the process of making records at that time, so even though I discussed my concerns with the band I didn't feel I was in a position to make too much of a scene. I know now that we should have had Rick spend much more time with the group at live performances so he could better capture the full dynamics of the band. However, I was really looking forward to seeing what would happen when we hit the studio in New York.

Yorkville was reaching a zenith during this same time period. It was getting intensely crowded with teens and university students, but also with musicians and other artists of every stripe and, yes, with heaps of grass and acid and just a hint of everything else. The interesting thing was that with the drinking age being twenty-one in those days, almost none of the clubs had liquor licences, so alcohol wasn't a big part of the equation. I think this made a difference to the music. Because the clubs didn't sell booze, there was no age restriction on who could come in. The rooms were full of kids being entertained by bands whose members were the same age as them, and everyone was there to listen to, and enjoy, the music. There was a real feeling of community in the air. I always thought that the day the beer companies began to sell their products in the music clubs – quickly followed by sponsorship deals for both bands and venues – something got lost. I'm not unrealistic; I can see how selling beer in clubs may have been a financial necessity, and I can think of a lot worse things to sell. But in the end, a certain direct connection between the music and the audience was lost somewhere along the way, and along with it a kind of honesty. When it's about money first, in my opinion, the music begins to suffer. But those days had yet to come. The energy, the sweat, and those sweet sounds were pouring out of the clubs, into the street, and people were paying attention.

Unfortunately, there was no real music business in Canada that I was aware of, and that seemed especially true in Toronto. As a consequence there was no foundation to build on. Yes, there were a few notable pioneers out there trying to make things happen, but with there being no real industry to work in, we started to lose such great artists as Neil Young, Joni Mitchell, and Steppenwolf to the States, and you couldn't blame them for leaving. Despite the burgeoning scene in Yorkville, in the end there just weren't the opportunities here to make a career, never mind a record, so they left. One day you would see a band like the Sparrow pack their car and leave for Los Angeles, and just a few months later they would be back with a new name, in this case Steppenwolf, and a hit record riding high on the charts.

However, I have to admit that building an industry wasn't really at the top of my mind during this time. We had a record to make. An exciting experience for sure, and the first full-length album I was ever involved with. What a thrill. We were booked into New York's Columbia recording studios and were back staying at the Gorham Hotel. But for me two things were going wrong. I just didn't think the record was turning out right, and I was missing Toronto, in particular, being in Yorkville.

From time to time I would make suggestions as to how the record might be improved but it seemed that my advice was falling on unreceptive ears. I can't really blame the band. Here we were, in one of the best studios in the world with a great producer, getting loads of positive feedback from our record company and Albert Grossman, and here I was, voicing my concerns. I was a lone voice in the wilderness and a pretty inexperienced one at that. Night after night we would go to the studio, and gradually the record was nearing completion. On many of those nights Albert would show up and we'd spend time talking about the business and his early days in Chicago running the Gate of Horn, one of the most famous folk clubs in America. We'd get visits from various people every night, including Linda Eastman and Jerry Schoenbaum, as well as various members of the staff from Verve, along with the occasional press person who had been assigned to do a story on the band.

One night a deliveryman approached Albert with a package. After handing him it, he asked Albert "if he was Jewish." Albert said no and the deliveryman smiled and said, "I thought so." Then Albert told him, "Don't be so happy, my parents are." Albert was always quick-witted and very droll. Admirable if you had the patience for it. If I had loved that record more it would have been a fine time. But my dissatisfaction with it, along with the fact that my opinion didn't seem to be carrying any weight, was really bothering me. In looking back on it, *Magic People* is a fine record. Could it have been better? Yes, I think so, but it's still a pretty good first effort. Nonetheless, I started thinking it was time for me to move on. I couldn't shake the thought that I had done all I could for the band and I needed to get back to Toronto and into something else. It was a difficult decision, certainly the toughest of my then still-young life, but I decided to quit working with the Paupers.

So, during one of the recording sessions one evening, I told the band I was leaving. I think they were all genuinely disappointed and we had a long discussion about me possibly staying on, but in the end I couldn't be persuaded. I did love the Paupers, and I owed Skip and the rest of the band a tremendous debt of gratitude for giving me a real chance to prove myself. I certainly did not mean them any harm by leaving when I did and I wished them only the best. As much as I was disappointed by some aspects of the recording, I still firmly felt they were going to become a major act. And leaving them with Albert was not exactly like leaving them at the five-and-dime store!

The next day I told Albert of my intention to quit. He wasn't too happy about this, as I think he expected me to lead the way with the band and also saw in me the potential to take on other responsibilities inside his company. Now that I have the benefit to see it all in hindsight, it's clear that I was walking away from a great opportunity. Representing Dylan would be enough alone to put him at the epicentre of the entire music business. But at the time, making the break with Albert seemed like the right thing to do, so I did it.

I worked out a deal that had Albert buy my 50 per cent of the management contract. Albert was going to give me $30,000. I would get $20,000 right away and the balance within a year. For a guy who had only been dealing with a few hundred dollars at any one time, that cheque for $20,000 was the most money I'd ever seen. Clearly, my frustration was not about money. It was about not being able to get things done the way I thought they should be done, mixed up with a homesickness for Toronto that was probably heightened by smoking just a bit too much grass.

To be truthful, I was surprised when Albert offered me the buyout. Thirty thousand dollars was a gift from heaven. I didn't expect anything, because I was walking out on him. Maybe, though, Albert saw it as a chance to manage on his own a band that he thought had the potential for great success. In any event, I took my first installment of twenty grand and headed back to Toronto. Despite my conflicted feelings, I was excited about new possibilities. Shortly before the Paupers had first performed at the Café Au Go Go, I had met a young singer-songwriter from Sault Ste. Marie named Keith McKie. Keith had an impressive voice and a handful of very fine and original songs. I had had a few meetings with him and we had started talking about the possibility of putting together a band. For the time being, the idea was placed on the back burner. Now that I was ready to take a good look around and decide what to do next, I thought about Keith and that band we'd talked about.

There isn't really that much that I regret when I look back at my career. No doubt there are many things I said and did that I might choose to say or do differently if given the chance, but when it comes to the main events I'm pretty satisfied with the outcome, even if the things I tried didn't always work out. I don't regret leaving the Paupers when I did (although it did leave a little hole in my heart at the time), though I can't help but think that my life would have taken a whole different turn had I stayed on. For starters, I most likely would have moved to New York. Whether or not things would have worked out better for the Paupers or for me I'll never know. Certainly it would have been a different, although not necessarily better, path.

It's worth looking at what happened to the Paupers after I left. *Magic People* came out in mid-1967. In November it peaked at 178 on the *Billboard* charts. Although the record had a modest success, it didn't do as well as we'd hoped. Yet charting in the States was an accomplishment, and a rare one for Toronto bands at that time. The Paupers performed at the Monterey Pop Festival as planned, but sadly, according to all reports, they had a very problematic performance. I suppose that was the beginning of the end for the band. They recorded another album, *Ellis Island*, but by then I was long gone.

Although I lost touch with Denny Gerrard and Chuck Beal, it was great to see both Skip and Adam go on to make important contributions in music. Adam had a successful career as a songwriter with many fine credits to his name. Skip was one of the founding members of Lighthouse, a Toronto band that had some very successful international hits, including "One Fine Morning" and "Sunny Days." Some thirty-three years later True North Records reissued the long-neglected Lighthouse *Greatest Hits* CD, and we went on to sell many thousands of copies for them, as well as to help refocus the spotlight on that very fine band.

Oh yeah, one other lesson I learned. Albert never did pay me that remaining $10,000. In the music business it's always best to be paid up front. However, over the years I did occasionally run into Albert, usually at MIDEM, the international music conference held each January in Cannes, France. Albert liked to go there and cook with Roger Vergé, who owned the famous Moulin de Mougins, a place where I had many fine meals myself, outrageously great seven-course dinners served with the best vintage wines. I would often see Albert at the restaurant where he liked to help out in the kitchen. He was always cordial but we didn't really have much to say to each other.

I have had occasion to meet Albert's wife, Sally, at various times. The first was while doing a satellite radio broadcast of a Bruce Cockburn show in 1991 from the Bearsville Theater in Woodstock, New York. Bearsville was the recording complex built by Grossman that featured state-of-the-art studios as well as a couple of fine restaurants. The studio had been used by everyone from the Band and Bob Dylan to Foreigner and the Rolling Stones.

Albert died of a heart attack while aboard a plane flying to MIDEM in 1986. Sally became the owner not only of the theatre but of the whole of the Bearsville recording complex. Albert was buried behind the Bearsville Theatre, and I thought of him quite fondly during Bruce's broadcast.

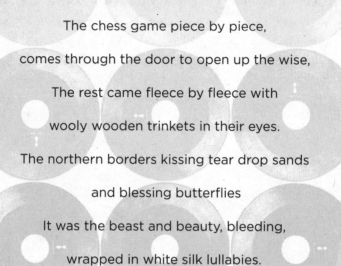

The chess game piece by piece,

comes through the door to open up the wise,

The rest came fleece by fleece with

wooly wooden trinkets in their eyes.

The northern borders kissing tear drop sands

and blessing butterflies

It was the beast and beauty, bleeding,

wrapped in white silk lullabies.

"Side I Am"
(Keith McKie and Gene Martynec)
Kensington Market

CHAPTER SIX

By early 1967 rock music had become the dominant force in modern culture and albums had supplanted singles in importance. In a big change from previous generations, both men and women now said the first thing they would do after getting married was buy a record player, even before purchasing fridges, stoves, and other trappings of middle-class existence. The music being made to play on all those record players was often groundbreaking. The Beatles were creating a trio of tremendously influential records: *Sgt. Pepper's Lonely Hearts Club Band*, *Magical Mystery Tour*, and *The White Album*. Bob Dylan had made a huge artistic statement with *Highway 61 Revisited* and would soon release his early masterwork *Blonde on Blonde*. The Doors were riding high on the charts with "Light My Fire," and two remarkable, and very different, Canadian groups were about to have a big impact on pop culture. The Band would release its debut album, *Music from Big Pink*, in July 1968, and a year later, Winnipeg's Guess Who would have commercial success with "These Eyes" and "Laughing."

I returned to Yorkville and looked up Keith. It was time to get back to work.

Yorkville itself was always on the edge of turmoil and often it boiled over with street protests and sit-ins. With the Vietnam War raging in the background, the street was crowded with draft dodgers from the States, and hippies, bikers, dealers, artists, poets, and loads of musicians. Revolution was in the air. Dropping acid was becoming an everyday, ordinary occurrence for many of the area's denizens, me among them. The expression *far out* came to mean exactly that. Many of the people on the street went so far out that, sadly, they never came back. In the middle of all of this I set out with Keith to put together a band. It was my hope that this band would be able to take off and go beyond where I had been with the Paupers.

The first person we approached was Eugene Martynec, the lead guitarist for Bobby Kris & the Imperials, one of Toronto's leading R&B bands and a good one. But the marketplace for blue-eyed soul had pretty much been replaced by the one for psychedelic sounds from bands like the Paupers, the Ugly Ducklings, and the Sparrow. Gene, a prodigiously gifted musician, was looking for something different, so he threw in his lot with us. In those early days, neither Gene nor I could have imagined that our musical association would endure for so long. Gene would produce many of the early albums for True North Records, including Bruce Cockburn's *Dancing in the Dragon's Jaws*, containing the single "Wondering Where the Lions Are," one of our biggest-ever international hits. But all that was still more than a decade away.

Keith and I had heard of a sixteen-year-old drummer named Jimmy Watson who also played sitar, one of many exotic instruments becoming popular in the sixties. (It was only after Jimmy joined the Kensington Market that we found out he was Van Morrison's first cousin.) Finding a bassist turned out to be more difficult than we'd thought. After searching around the Toronto area and further afield without luck, Keith suggested Alex Darou, an old friend from Sault Ste. Marie. Alex was living in New York and playing with David Clayton-Thomas. To our surprise, he agreed to come to Toronto to check us out. After playing a little with Keith, Gene, and Jimmy, he liked what he was hearing. Although he wasn't necessarily keen on leaving David and the security that came with that job, the Market represented a chance for Alex to be an equal member of a band, and one that he had a hand in creating. Alex brought a whole other vibe to the group. A little older than the rest of the members, he'd had some experience in other types of music, like jazz. Alex was also a bridge player, which seemed like a very complicated game to a poker player like me.

Originally the band was going to be a quartet, so with the addition of Alex they were set to go. We settled on the name Kensington Market in homage to the oldest running market in Toronto. Situated on several narrow streets not far from downtown Toronto's Chinatown, Kensington was a colourful collection of outdoor food stalls and rundown shops that sold some of the best and cheapest food and clothing around. It had started around the turn of the century as a Jewish market and there were still stores with windows bearing Hebrew writing. Over the years the market has evolved and just about every new immigrant community that has settled in Toronto – including Portuguese, Italians, Jamaicans, and Eastern Europeans – has left its mark there.

The band started rehearsals at my place off of Pears Avenue and quickly found their sound. They had a very musical take on folk-rock and loads of new ideas. The players tended to lean to the soft side of rock but nevertheless ended up somewhere near the edge with a real pent-up energy. As fine as they were sounding, it soon became obvious that another voice would be a good idea.

One of the great bands in Yorkville at that time was Luke & the Apostles, featuring lead singer Luke Gibson and a gifted guitarist named Mike McKenna. The Apostles were a band without rival on the local scene; they combined blues and R&B with rock in a style that made them a predecessor to Cream and Led Zeppelin. They managed to get an American recording deal with the mighty Elektra Records in 1965 but only got to record one single, a song called "Been Burnt."

The story behind the Apostles and their record deal illustrates the times. One night, Paul Rothchild, house producer at Jac Holzman's Elektra Records, heard the band at the Purple Onion in Yorkville and got Luke to sing the song on the phone to Jac, the man who had signed the Doors, the Paul Butterfield Blues Band,

With the Kensington Market at the El Patio (Frank Grant)

and the Stooges, among others. Jac was impressed and the band headed off to New York to record. Unfortunately, disaster would strike the band. Shortly before the single was to be released, Rothchild was arrested in the States for pot possession and given a one-year jail sentence. The release of the single was delayed and, in the end, never made commercially available. Jac Holzman is reported to have said, "The Luke & the Apostles record was the greatest album I never got to make." This kind of thing is not that rare in the record business, especially at the bigger companies. It usually happens when the person who signs you to the company leaves, or is let go, and you find yourself orphaned there. Still, losing your producer because of a pot arrest probably wouldn't have happened before the sixties.

At the same time that Luke & the Apostles signed with Elektra, San Francisco promoter Bill Graham booked them to do a week's worth of shows, from July 31 to August 5, with the Jefferson Airplane and the Grateful Dead at Toronto's O'Keefe Centre (now the Sony Centre for the Performing Arts). It was billed as "Bill Graham Presents the San Francisco Scene in Toronto." As promotion for the week of shows, Bill booked the Airplane and Luke & the Apostles to play what would turn out to be Toronto's most important free outdoor show up to that time – an afternoon concert at Nathan Phillips Square on July 23 that drew more than 50,000 people. It's been said that it just about put an end to the rivalry between the greasers and the hippies over which type of music would be dominant in Toronto. The rock scene had won out, and that seminal concert seemed to be the tipping point.

The Market had started playing as a quartet, mostly at the Red Gas Room, which was housed on the second floor of a building on Avenue Road just above a room called Boris's where Luke & the Apostles often played.

All the bands on the street knew each other and their secrets. Despite some of the good things going on with the Apostles it was apparent that there were tensions among the members. Luke had heard we were looking for a fifth member and approached us about joining the band. We were blown away that he would want to do this; not only did he write some pretty good songs, and sing like nobody else, but he was a showman of unparalleled excellence, at least in our circles. We immediately said yes, and shortly after their triumphant week at the O'Keefe, Luke left the Apostles and joined the Kensington Market.

The addition of Luke immediately made the band the most popular group on the street and crowds were now lining up to take in their shows. It also brought another kind of energy to the band and the show began to move away from a softer folk-rock format to something else again. With two lead vocalists, an infusion of blues, and great showmanship, the Market was becoming the band we had hoped it could be.

Coincidentally, a few years later Luke & the Apostles were to finally put out a single. The band was a newly formed version, reuniting Mike McKenna and Luke, and this time the record was on my newly launched label. The single had two A-sides, "You Make Me High" and "Not Far Off." I produced both tracks, and they're high on the list of my best work as an actual studio producer. The record went to number 27 on the single charts in Canada, which wasn't too shabby, although it somehow didn't quite make up for the sad, short sojourn the band had with Elektra.

As the Market's popularity began to grow, I felt the time had come to make a record. I also decided I should do it on my own. It still hadn't occurred to me to start my own record company; I just liked the idea of not having to work with people other than the band. With some of the money from the Paupers' deal I rented

Art Snider's Sound Canada studio in Don Mills, where we recorded four songs. (The A-sides were "Mr. John" and "Bobby's Birthday.") Art, who was one of the pioneers of Canadian music and always treated me well, was famous for having recorded "Live at the Village Corner" by a group called the Twin Tones, but is best remembered today for one member, Gordon Lightfoot. The Sound Canada studio was mostly home to country musicians like Dick Damron and Gary Buck, but we felt quite comfortable there and cut two pretty good singles. They were released on Stone Records, a small, independent company operated by Bob Stone. While they were scarcely number-one hits, both received a little airplay on radio as well as positive feedback from the press and fans. And shortly after Luke joined the band we went to Montreal to write and record the soundtrack for Don Owen's movie *The Ernie Game*, the follow-up to his highly acclaimed film *Nobody Waved Goodbye*.

There was an enthusiasm felt throughout Canada in 1967. More than half of the population was under thirty and Pierre Trudeau was our daring, stylish prime minister. It was also Canada's centenary, with a world's fair, the 1967 International and Universal Exposition – more commonly known as Expo 67 – taking place in Montreal. Working for a week in that city, at the National Film Board, it was hard not to feel pride and excitement about being Canadian, as well as an awareness that Canadians were increasingly interested in all things Canadian. Of course there was still the small matter of being able to make a living from my job. But somehow that felt secondary to me; I was just focused on the excitement of being involved in Canadian music.

Other things were changing around us as well. Albums were now overtaking singles as the way to get music across, and at the same time a new style of radio, on the FM dial, became dominant among young people. This new format, still in its infancy, was called "underground," "progressive," or "free-form" radio. On these stations, DJs chose their own music from album tracks that had become more experimental, less geared to commercial top-forty singles. It was a wonderfully creative time for both music and radio, and the marriage of a free-flowing style of radio with musicians who wanted to remove the barriers in pop music couldn't have been more perfect or timely. Suddenly you could hear all kinds of album tracks on the air. DJs would program sets of music where the ideas of the songs were strung together to tell a story in the mind and ear of the listener. Some of the early Canadian stations pioneering this kind of radio were CHUM-FM in Toronto, CFOX in Vancouver, and CHOM-FM in Montreal.

There was an eager audience waiting. It was an audience that couldn't get enough of the music and was ready to go on a sonically adventurous trip with the disc jockeys. And why not? After all, you could get a contact high just by walking down the street in Yorkville. You didn't have to smoke a joint at all. All you had to do was breathe in the air. It was this world that the Kensington Market strolled into.

My New York exploits with the Paupers had not gone unnoticed. An entrepreneur named Bud Prager had teamed up with record producer Felix Pappalardi in a Manhattan production company called Windfall Music. I knew a little about Felix, as he wasn't a complete stranger to Toronto. He had played bass guitar with both Ian & Sylvia and Buffy Sainte-Marie and had done a few recordings with Fred Neil, one of the all-time great singer-songwriters. (Do yourself a favour and find his CD *Bleecker & MacDougal*. You'll be happy you did.) Felix was given to wearing loads of turquoise jewellery and leather pants. He was a bit of a dandy, at least compared to us Yorkville types, but a musician and producer of the first rank. Bud was a tall man with prematurely grey hair who dressed somewhat like a banker. Both men were likeable and able, and would go on to have amazing careers, although Felix's would end in tragedy. At this time, they were just getting started with their new partnership. As it turned out, an Ian & Sylvia sideman, guitarist David Rae, had spoken to Felix about the Market. Felix and Bud were impressed by the band and had been enjoying our two singles.

My first encounter with Bud was one afternoon when I received a phone call from him and we immediately hit it off. He said that if we could work out an agreement between us he would be able to guarantee a two-album deal for the band with Warner Brothers in Los Angeles. Bud and Felix agreed to come to Toronto to hear the band as soon as Felix was back from England. Felix was putting the finishing touches on a new album from Cream, which featured Eric Clapton, Jack Bruce, and Ginger Baker. Cream had already released one album, the brilliant, underappreciated *Fresh Cream*.

Two weeks later, Bud and Felix arrived in Toronto and were so impressed with the Market that we began working on a contract. While we were taking care of our details, Felix treated us to the inside scoop on doing the record with Cream. The album was *Disraeli Gears*, one of the most influential records of the era. (In 2003, *Rolling Stone* listed it at number 12 on its "500 Greatest Albums of all Time.") The lead tracks on that record were "Sunshine of Your Love" and "Strange Brew." Both landed in the top twenty, although "Sunshine of Your Love" became the band's only gold single. Felix would go on to produce Cream's final two records, *Wheels of Fire*, which was the first-ever double album to be certified platinum, and *Goodbye*, released after Cream had disbanded.

It was hard not to be impressed with Felix, who was a first-class musician and producer. And the same was true of Bud – he was a straight shooter who really knew his way around the large record companies. Not only did I sign a production deal with them for Kensington Market but they also became my partners in the management of the group. Bud and Felix delivered the contract with Warner Brothers as promised and we left for New York to make the record.

In early 1968, we booked ourselves into the Earle Hotel in Greenwich Village and started recording at Century Sound, a studio owned by Brooks Arthur, whose engineering credits included such classic hits as "Chapel of Love" by the Dixie Cups, "Leader of the Pack" by the Shangri-Las, and "Brown Eyed Girl" by Van Morrison. Van's masterpiece and second solo album, *Astral Weeks*, also came out of Century Sound. Heady times indeed.

We travelled back and forth between Toronto and New York during the making of the record. When in Toronto, I continued to spend my time mostly at the Upper Crust Café, just hanging out with the band and taking in the scene, which continued to be a never-ending show. I was introduced to Bart Schoales, who was to become a lifelong friend of mine and who made many important contributions to True North Records. Bart was an artist, a painter of some note in fact. Although he had been having exhibitions, he thought the Toronto art world was constrictive, and soon found himself drifting more and more toward the world of rock 'n' roll.

We were introduced by one of those great Yorkville characters, Hugh Petrie, who called himself "the Cosmic Visitor." Hugh was a tall, lanky guy with long, long white hair. He could easily have been a character right out of Tolkien's *Lord of the Rings*. Hugh had opened a store on Yorkville called the Cosmic Visitor. I was never sure of what he sold there but it was a neat place and he had put a tent-like structure in the basement with carpets on the floor beneath it. It wasn't unusual for the regulars on Yorkville to retire to Hugh's basement and sit around inside the tent, smoking some outstanding grass and hash. Hugh had the best stuff around and it always led to long rambling discussions about this world and others. It all seemed real to me. Indeed, there was an otherworldly feeling of transformation in the air, a hint of danger, music in the cafés, and a sense of endless possibilities.

We all immediately liked Bart. When we told him we were just finishing the first album and starting to think about the cover art, he enthusiastically volunteered to design it and do the photos. I couldn't see any reason not to let him take a crack at it.

We had already decided to call the album *Avenue Road*, which was the name of the street that marked the western end of the Yorkville area and also where Boris's and the second-floor Red Gas Room were located. These were the two clubs where the Market did most of their live shows in Toronto. On one of our trips back to Toronto during the recording of the album, Bart took the photos for the cover on a day when, coincidentally, it started to snow. Little did we Canadians know what a stir this would create with Warner Brothers.

Avenue Road is an unusual album in many ways. It was somewhat softer than the band sounded live but at the same time it contained some interesting complexities. The highlight of the record for me was a song called "Aunt Violet's Knee," which was not only a great song but done with a tremendous seventeen-piece orchestra, arranged and conducted by Felix Pappalardi and featuring, of all things, oboes backing Keith on solo guitar. I think it still holds up today.

The first single from the album was called "I Would Be the One," which we had originally recorded with an entirely different arrangement as the B-side of the "Bobby's Birthday" single. The new version was not only different but now had horns and

Jimmy Watson on the sitar. The single did get to number 59 on the Canadian top 100 but not much else happened with it.

Getting on Canadian radio remained a real obstacle, not only for us but for just about everybody. To say there was no support at all would be wrong, but in the end there wasn't nearly enough. It seemed that you might well be good enough for the public on both sides of the border, even good enough for the press (well, maybe not always), certainly good enough to record, but when it came to radio you were found lacking, somehow seen as inferior. It was getting to be a real problem and there were rumblings of a change coming. Some of the people I knew in the business were talking about the federal government enacting "Canadian-content regulations." These could have the effect of waking radio up from its slumber and its coziness with the American charts, tip-sheets, and consultants. We needed the radio bosses to listen to the music that was being made in their own country, and to treat it with some seriousness and dignity. I was extremely interested in this potential development but for the time being I was stuck with the hand I'd been dealt, and I suppose it could have been much worse. Kensington Market had an album coming out on one of the world's largest labels, and we were working with a producer, Felix Pappalardi, whose other project, Cream, was the hottest act in music. Even better, we were about to embark on a mini-tour tied to the record's release and promotion in the States.

But before all this would happen I was off to Los Angeles to present the artwork for the album to Warner's brass. This trip wasn't my first to L.A. I had been there with the Paupers and really enjoyed it. I could never quite get over how easy and indolent life seemed to be there. You never had to park your own car. Freshly squeezed orange juice seemed to be running out of the water taps and it never truly got cold no matter what time of the year you were there, and if it rained, well, I didn't see it. On an earlier visit I had seen the Doors in a small club on Sunset Strip and I had brought home their first album and played it for everyone who would listen. This was just before the release of their single "Light My Fire," which went straight to number 1 on the *Billboard* Hot 100 chart. Los Angeles did indeed look a bit like the land of milk and honey – at least until our meeting started.

The meeting was with Joe Smith. He, along with Mo Austin, would eventually build Warner from a minor player in the rock world into one of the world's powerhouse labels, eventually navigating the company through mergers with Ahmet Ertegun's Atlantic Records and Jac Holzman's Elektra into the behemoth WEA. Joe had brought in a few of his senior marketing people, and we got down to work. The music had been making its way out to the Coast cut by cut. Apparently Joe and others at Warner liked what they'd heard so far, but they were concerned about a couple of other things. First, they didn't like Bart's picture. They thought a group standing in the snow just wasn't going to work and might even be confusing. At one point they even said that if we must have snow, why not have the band come out to the Warner Brothers movie lot and they'd arrange for a more convincing snow shot, Hollywood style. Truth is always stranger than fiction, at least in the music business.

More disturbing, they really didn't like the title of the album. *Avenue Road*? It made no sense to them. After all, didn't those two words mean the same thing? What *did* the title mean, anyway? Besides that, they argued, the title, when coupled with the band's name, meant there would be a strong chance that people wouldn't know if the band's name was Avenue Road and the album title *Kensington Market*, or vice versa. This boiled over into quite an argument. I explained that the title, representing a street associated with Yorkville, where we lived and worked and which was the source of the music, was at the heart of the record. The album would have felt incomplete without that title and, to me, keeping that title mattered more than money or any other issues that often come into play when you deal with big record companies.

As the saying goes, I may have won the battle but I lost the war. Not that I hadn't compromised anyway. For the U.S. release, I allowed the Warner Brothers art department to reduce the size of the photo on the cover and put a kind of psychedelic-inspired, pop-art border around it. In Canada, the album was released the way we wanted it. I ended up quite liking the U.S. cover, but never as much as I liked our original artwork. But I did convince Joe to retain the album's title and, even more importantly, no one messed with the music.

In fairness to Joe Smith, whom I would get to work with later when he was running Asylum Records, expressing his concerns about the album's title, design, and photography was his way of keeping the band's best interests in mind. Was he right? The album didn't sell the way we hoped – although I doubt that it had much to do with the title or artwork. Either way, this was now my second disappointing experience dealing with large record companies. Although I was able to weather the storm – and it did often feel like a storm – these modest, but to me traumatic, engagements would influence my future direction. Given that I had placed the band's future – and my own – into the hands of the record company executives, I had to take their suggestions and criticisms seriously, no matter what I thought about the ideas they were presenting. You don't have to be a rocket scientist to know that arguing with your record company on the eve of the release of your album isn't the most productive way to spend your time.

Still, we ended up largely with what we wanted and it was time to put this behind us and move on.

Meanwhile, back in Yorkville, the streets continued to overflow with people from all over, but the summer of love had ended and the previously optimistic attitude was starting to change to something darker. The clubs were still jammed but many local acts were either breaking up or leaving for the U.S. Many Canadian musicians who'd moved to the States a couple of years earlier were now reaping the rewards of relocation to the larger marketplace. Neil Young and his bandmate, Bruce Palmer, had disbanded the Mynah Birds only to re-emerge just a short time later as members of Buffalo Springfield. The band's first single, "For What It's Worth," became a big hit after its January 1967 release. The former lead singer in the Mynah Birds, Ricky James, ended up in Detroit as a songwriter and producer for Motown Records and would, a little later, hit it big with a string of very successful funk records as Rick James. Another fixture on the Yorkville scene, the Sparrow, had also left the city for Los Angeles, and by August of 1968 Steppenwolf was topping the charts with "Born to Be Wild." Joni Mitchell released her first album and was working on her breakthrough record, *Clouds*, which included the hits "Chelsea Morning" and "Both Sides Now."

But while artists like these had left Canada, there were also many staying behind trying to figure out how to make things happen without being forced to leave their own country. To leave or to stay? There was no right or wrong way to make a career out of music, just a burning desire to do it.

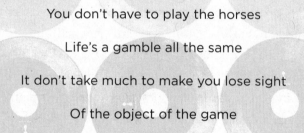

You don't have to play the horses

Life's a gamble all the same

It don't take much to make you lose sight

Of the object of the game

"You Don't Have to Play the Horses"
Bruce Cockburn

CHAPTER SEVEN

In early 1968 I met a character who was, in his way, having as large an influence around the city as any musician, politician, or artist. His name was Brazilian George and, as his name suggests, he was originally from Brazil. He had told us, and we had no reason to doubt him, that he and his brother Tony had left Brazil after one of that country's many political upheavals. He was from the town of Manaus, he said, deep in the heart of the Amazon where the Negro and Solimões Rivers met. He claimed to have walked out of the jungle when he left Brazil, then ended up settling in the Toronto area and gravitating to Yorkville.

George was a big fan of the Market. He was dealing, mostly soft stuff like acid and grass, but also starting to get involved with a hallucinogen called MDA. They used to call MDA the love drug because it had the tendency to make you feel rather blissed out. MDA, a phenylethylamine, was, in chemical terms, a forerunner to Ecstasy, a recreational drug that became popular in the late '80s in gay dance clubs and then spread into straight clubs.

George was at the heart of the distribution hub for MDA and he was doing it rather well.

I'll say again that in hindsight I'm not always proud of my early connections to the world of drugs. Yet those were the times, and my involvement was always limited to soft drugs, nothing hard and nothing that required needles. Drug use was an inseparable part of the world I inhabited and, honestly, it didn't seem wrong at the time. I don't apologize for it but in the end I was lucky to get out alive. Some of the people I knew didn't. Would I do it again? Maybe. Further down the line I did step away from all drugs other than the odd toke now and then. But I was young and it was a big part of the culture and certainly a big part of the music scene, so I threw caution to the wind and got involved in it with abandon.

Brazilian George was an appealing person and we became fast friends. You might say he was the nicer side of the Tony Montana character played by Al Pacino in the movie *Scarface*. He and most of the band members hit it off. It wasn't unusual to see George and his pals at our shows and the band spent plenty of reciprocal time at his house. MDA was becoming a popular drug in Toronto and money was never in short supply around George's house. Many in George's orbit passed the time blasting the latest albums on his very expensive sound system, doing MDA, and partying into the early hours of the morning and even well into the next day, sometimes for several days in a row.

Plans were proceeding for the Market's first tour of the U.S. We were to open with four days in New York at the Bitter End, which was right across Bleecker Street from the Café Au Go Go. We were scheduled to do shows at several of the famous ballrooms across the country, including a three-day stand at the Fillmore West in San Francisco, September 5–7, where we were on a bill with Chuck Berry and the Steve Miller Band. There would be stops in L.A., Chicago, and Detroit, and then a headlining concert back in Toronto at the Rock Pile (today the headquarters of MTV Canada).

Bart Schoales had become our de facto tour manager and he was making the arrangements to get our equipment shipped to New York. At this time, we were using some pretty high-tech gear made in Toronto by a company called Wire. I'd been told that Kensington Market was one of the loudest bands anyone had heard. I don't know if this was true but I'll take people's word for it. What I do know is that the amps were very large and well made, and literally weighed a ton. I know this from helping to move them around – part of the glamorous life of a manager in those days.

By the time we played the shows at the Bitter End, the record had received a favourable review in *Rolling Stone*. (In Canada, music journalist Ritchie Yorke had already written in the *Globe and Mail* that it was "probably the finest album ever cut by a Canadian group.")

On the evening before we were scheduled to fly to San Francisco, Bart told the band they should get rid of any drugs they had before getting to the airport. In other words, use it or flush it. We were all so inexperienced that we somehow thought there would be a customs search at the airport, even though the domestic flight we were on was between New York and San Francisco. Live and learn. The next morning everybody got rid of their drugs all right, but instead of throwing them away, we took them all. Bart recalls being so high that the airplane disappeared while he was sitting in it somewhere over the Grand Canyon. I'll have to take his word for it as I can hardly remember the flight at all. What I do remember is Keith McKie, carrying a metal suitcase, walking right through the plate-glass doors of New York's

Gorham Hotel. He'd swung that suitcase in front of him and shattered the glass into thousands of tiny pieces but kept right on walking as though nothing had happened and stepped calmly into the cab waiting to take him to the airport. I heard later that Warner Brothers had picked up the cost of replacing the doors.

When the plane arrived in San Francisco I had finally reached the city of my early dreams. Only four years after moving out of my parents' house in Downsview with a vague idea of going down the road, I found myself in the city of Jack Kerouac's novel *The Dharma Bums*, and of Allen Ginsberg's poetry, only now it was also the city of the Grateful Dead and Jefferson Airplane. Our temple would be the Fillmore West rather than Lawrence Ferlinghetti's City Lights bookshop, although I took it all in and happily spent an hour or two at the store. It was there that I bought my first copy of the *Whole Earth Catalog*, a magazine that was to come in handy just a year or so later. But for now, there couldn't have been a better place to be than San Francisco. It was loose, free, and vibrant. Everything seemed to be happening there.

We made our way over to the Fillmore on September 5, the afternoon of the first show. Bill Graham, easily the most famous rock promoter in the world, was there to greet us. Bill could be a pretty tough guy with a no-nonsense attitude – you didn't want to cross him. (I remember an article where he was quoted as saying that he knew things were over with the Jefferson Airplane when the band made it seem like they were performing a ballet when they were simply crossing the road.) He was also an extraordinarily hard worker, which I really admired. Here he was, helping us unload our truck and set up our amps. Talk about high-priced help!

I had met Bill in New York during the Paupers' shows with the Airplane and again in Toronto for the free City Hall concert at

Nathan Phillips Square, which had featured the Dead, the Airplane, and Luke & the Apostles. Bill operated three of the most influential venues in America – the Fillmore West and Winterland in San Francisco and the Fillmore East in New York. He had helped to popularize both the style and the look of the movement with the wonderful posters being designed for the shows he was presenting. (Today, the wildly imaginative imagery and hallucinatory typography of these posters, by artists like Wes Wilson and Stanley Mouse, have made them valuable collector's items.) Even though the show was being headlined by Chuck Berry and included another notable act, the Steve Miller Band, Bill had commissioned a poster dominated by a Canadian moose done up in full psychedelic style. It was a tribute to the Market and I thought it a great honour.

That night, the Steve Miller Band opened the show, with the Market performing next and then Chuck Berry playing last, backed by the Steve Miller Band. Chuck didn't carry around his own backup musicians at that time. The show had been sold out for weeks and the house was packed. People were sprawled all over the floor, with some standing at the back and along the sides. An overpowering smell of hash, grass, and incense filled the air. The house light show, which included plenty of strobe lights flashing constantly, was almost like having a fourth act on the bill. Everyone who came to the show was given a poster on the way in.

Felix Pappalardi and other top Warner people had flown in from New York, and were hanging out with the entire San Francisco branch. Backstage, it felt more like a carnival than a dressing room area, and everyone was smoking some of the strongest pot I'd ever had. To say we were all getting stoned would be an understatement of the highest magnitude. Brazilian George was there along with many of our other friends. He was handing out MDA to everyone backstage, calling it a gift in return for the generosity of Owsley Stanley, who was the first to manufacture large quantities of pure LSD. He gave away tabs of acid by the thousands throughout the Bay area, leading some to say he was responsible for psychedelic music, if not the entire hippie movement.

At one point during the evening, while Steve Miller was onstage, Chuck Berry joined us for a backstage toke. Chuck was wearing one of those waiter-style jackets he was famous for and George, not recognizing him, assumed he actually was a waiter and politely asked him for a Coke. You'd think Chuck Berry would have been insulted but instead he simply got George his Coke. Later that evening, when Chuck was onstage, he gave George a wave and a wink. I think Chuck got pretty high that night along with the rest of us.

Kensington Market at the Fillmore West

It was time for the Market to take the stage. I went out into the audience and joined Felix, who was sitting in the middle of the ballroom, and the band hit the stage. How were they that night? I would say they alternated between great and bad but were consistently really loud. As the show built, I could feel the band and the audience getting higher and higher. In some ways it was a completely free-style performance. Sometimes it seemed like they were all playing different numbers simultaneously, and every once in a while the music seemed to be soaring to new heights. I don't think that even this thoroughly hip, music-savvy San Francisco crowd had ever seen or heard anything quite like it before. When the band played its last number, a song called "Ring On Good Times" (a number they unfortunately never did record), Keith's performance was so intense that he actually bent the mike stand while leaning on it, slowly bending over and outwards towards the audience. Try bending a mike stand sometime. It's no easy feat. I know that I can't do it.

Felix was astounded and kept telling me that this was awful and great at the same time. Of course, he wasn't exactly straight either. I think on balance it was a show where the band just got too stoned, and the combination of the adrenaline rush with the over-the-top psychedelic atmosphere of the Fillmore completely overwhelmed them. I'd have to call the evening a draw. At the next two shows, calmer and clearer heads prevailed, and they had fine concerts.

Then it was off to Los Angeles for shows September 12–15 at the Whisky a Go-Go, the mecca of rock. Located along the Sunset Strip, which was always lined with cars, the club was jammed with people throughout the night. It was the home of the Byrds; the Buffalo Springfield; Arthur Lee and his band, Love; and the Doors. The Whisky was also where the great Otis Redding had recorded his famous live album two years earlier. The club had given its name to the mid-sixties go-go craze, personified by the Whisky's house artist, Johnny Rivers.

Before going to the club, we checked into the Tropicana Motel, L.A.'s equivalent of the Chelsea Hotel, only with sunshine, on Santa Monica Boulevard. The Tropicana was owned by the greatest left-handed baseball pitcher of all time, Sandy Koufax. He had been a hero of mine when I was a kid and a rabid Brooklyn (later Los Angeles) Dodgers fan. I don't know which made me more excited, to be in Sandy's motel or to be in a room right beside Sly Stone from Sly & the Family Stone. The Tropicana, which was a few storeys high and built in a square surrounding a kidney-shaped outdoor pool, was notorious. Jim Morrison lived there off and on and record companies booked out-of-town bands in its rooms, which were often trashed during all-night parties. Sadly, it was also the motel where Janis Joplin was found dead just a few years later.

The Tropicana was home to Duke's Coffee Shop, which became known as a musician's hangout. Its regulars included Tom Waits, Janis Joplin, Jim Morrison, and Rickie Lee Jones, along with many local and out-of-town musicians and groupies staying at the hotel. Duke's was known as a place where you could get anything you wanted, not the least of which was the best freshly squeezed orange juice and breakfast in the world.

We had a day off so we were hanging around the pool taking it easy when our old friend Nick St. Nicholas, the bassist from Steppenwolf, appeared. Nick asked us to come to his room so he could play us a new song he had just finished writing. There, we lit a joint and he pulled out his guitar. We could barely hear him over the sound of the air conditioner but then we realized that the new song he said he'd written was Bob Dylan's "Blowin' in the Wind." When he finished, he asked us what we thought. Unsure whether Nick was having fun with us or really believed he'd written it, we told him it was great and he should think about recording it. That night, we all went down the road to Barney's Beanery for dinner but the subject of his new song didn't come up again. Given the times, it all seemed like just another normal day on the road.

For our three nights at Whisky the headliner was Spooky Tooth, the British group whose first album had just been released, and the opening act was the Chicago Transit Authority, a band that had recently moved from Chicago to L.A., signed with Columbia Records, and released its first album. Chicago Transit Authority was, for a while, the house band at the Whisky. Later the name was shortened to Chicago, and it became among the most successful and long-running pop-rock groups in history. At the time, though, the band seemed quite ordinary to us, though its members were nice people to work with. The Market performed well but the guys were underwhelmed by the crowd, which was large but rather subdued. Keith McKie thought the majority of the audience members were on Quaaludes and he may have been right. It's also possible that it was just an ordinary audience and the members of the Market were spinning at a faster than normal speed.

Joe Smith came to the club one night and was quite encouraging about the band. He also regaled us with stories about working with the Grateful Dead. I understood his message: he was letting us know that no matter what we might throw at him, he could handle it. I learned a lot just by listening to Joe's stories. Incidentally, remember the brouhaha about the Market cover photo in the snowfall? Well, we did go out to Warner's studio lot and finally did a photo session with fake snow falling and a giant wind machine blowing it around the set. Who knows, it might have been the same snow they used in *White Christmas*. The pictures looked kind of nice but never did get used.

Next stop, Chicago. The Kensington Market was there for almost a week doing multiple nights at Aaron Russo's Kinetic Playground, then did a show in Evansville, Illinois, with the Paul Butterfield Band and an in-store record-signing session at a plaza in suburban Chicago. Aaron Russo was the Bill Graham of the Midwest, looming large over the area's music scene. The Playground was another psychedelic rock palace with strobes, a light show, tons of incense, and all the other accoutrements of the era. Aaron would go on to manage Bette Midler and the Manhattan Transfer as well as to produce movies like *The Rose* and *Trading Places*.

Because we were going to be in Chicago for a week I had time to look around, and for reasons that now entirely escape me, I bought three suits. They were on sale, but given that I never wore suits – I was working in rock 'n' roll, not banking – I'm not sure what I had in mind. Perhaps an image change of some kind. Maybe New York and L.A. were rubbing off on me. Or maybe I was getting tired of always having to explain who I was and what I was doing, which was not uncommon in the late sixties. If you looked like a hippie you were always under suspicion. It was mostly long hair that brought this on, but clothing raised its share of problems as well. In any case, I bought the suits, picked them up the day we were leaving Chicago, and put them in the equipment truck for transport back to Toronto. That was going to be our next stop before going back across the border to Detroit for what would turn out to be a memorable gig at the Grande Ballroom. I guess I just wasn't meant to wear suits, at least not then, because the truck caught on fire just outside of Toronto. Although most of the band's equipment was undamaged, my suits were nothing but ashes. A sign of things to come.

Although the gigs in Chicago went well enough, the record-store signing was a complete bust. Nobody showed up and it was so frustrating that our guitarist Gene Martynec, a critically important part of the band, quit and just took off. We did find Gene later that day and convinced him to stay with the band so we didn't have to cancel any of the Chicago shows. Still, Gene's reaction illustrated the cracks that were beginning to show in the foundation of the band. What with the copious amounts of drugs, the roller-coaster nature of performing and touring, and being constantly away from home, it's not surprising that nerves were becoming frayed. Even though everyone had agreed they weren't in it for the money, we were all constantly broke and it just wasn't always as much fun as it had once been. Still, we soldiered on and did what had to be done. After the week in Chicago we returned to Toronto, where we would be headlining a two-night stand at the prestigious Rock Pile.

The Rock Pile was Toronto's Fillmore. Located at the corner of Yonge and Davenport in the old Masonic Temple building, it was on the same circuit as the other ballrooms we had been playing in the States, complete with light show, a permanent haze of smoke, and room for 1,400. (The building now houses CTV and MTV Canada.) The Who were following us by a few days and Led Zeppelin were on their way too. The Market was one of the few Canadian bands that could headline a show there, never mind sell out two. At this point, we had become such nomads that we stayed at the Regency Hotel on Avenue Road, even though Toronto was our hometown.

There was a lot of anticipation among the sold-out crowd when the band took to the stage. And the band delivered. The audience loved them. There was no doubt that the Market was getting louder and louder, maybe too loud, but to my ears they had a great two-night stand. At times it seemed as though the sound didn't even bounce off the back wall; it seemed to be pinned there as successive waves of sound came blasting off the stage. The show received mixed reviews from the local press; some of them loved it and some hated it. But the Market had managed to do what no other local band had yet done – headline the Rock Pile for two nights. It was an exciting few days in Toronto, followed by our next gig in Detroit, where we would learn the true meaning of loud.

Our show in Detroit was at the Grande Ballroom, the historic dancehall run by DJ Russ Gibb who worked with local legend John Sinclair to bring in psychedelic bands from San Francisco as well as international acts like the Who, Cream, and Pink Floyd. The bill was the Kensington Market with the Pacific Gas & Electric and MC5. Until hearing MC5 I always thought the Market was the loudest band in the land, something with which I was never too comfortable. But when the MC5 took the stage I really came to understand the meaning of loud. Led by Wayne Kramer, the MC5 became famous for their live record *Kick Out the Jams* recorded at the Grande. I can't say I was a big fan but I admired the band's anti-establishment politics that were far to the American left, almost all the way to anarchism. For me it was an introduction to what was later to become punk or heavy metal, depending on where you were coming from.

While we were in Detroit we got a call from Toronto informing us that our friend the Cosmic Visitor had been arrested for throwing a garbage can through the front window of one of the stores on Yorkville Avenue. When he was caught, he was wearing a cape and claimed to be a direct descendant of Jesus Christ. He was also demanding a jury of twelve angels. Things were constantly in flux on Yorkville and there had been a lot of unrest on the street. The drugs were moving from soft psychedelics like pot, LSD, and psilocybin to amphetamines and crystal meth. There was also a growing biker population, along with more and more discontented people, although it was still a street for the most part dominated by hippies and an atmosphere of social revolution, expressed through both music and dialogue. The Cosmic Visitor was one of the many getting caught up in the sweeping changes that few truly understood, and, as in all social movements, some people became casualties.

The talk of government action on Canadian radio content was picking up steam. Around this time, musicians and those working in the music business, both young and old, were starting to feel that no matter how hard they tried they weren't going to get a fair shake on Canadian radio and that something had to change. I had heard rumours that the federal government was open to legislating Canadian-content regulations for radio, and although I didn't feel that I knew enough about it, I began to think that this might indeed be the way to go. As a manager, I would sometimes be asked to comment on the possible regulations, and even though I felt my bands had been treated well enough by local radio, it was also true that the amount of Canadian music being heard on the airwaves was minuscule. Despite all of my time spent in the U.S. and travelling around North America, I wanted to work in Canada, with Toronto as my base, and it seemed not only advantageous for my acts and for myself but beneficial for all Canadians to hear their own artists on local radio. Why not? I knew from experience that Canadian acts were as good as, and sometimes better than, American or British ones. This attitude would shamefully cost me plenty later in my career, as it wasn't uncommon for some broadcasters to punish you by withholding airplay for speaking out too loudly about Canadian content. But I'm proud of my role as an early advocate on this issue, and if I had to do it over again I wouldn't change any of my actions. Canadian content clearly, at least to me, was and is a policy that worked and continues to work. I may not have bought into all aspects of the peace-and-love social revolution during the sixties, but I was an unabashed supporter of the cultural revolution that I could feel building in Canada.

Returning to Toronto after the Detroit shows with the MC5, we started to think about doing another album. The new songs were stronger than the material on the first album and both Felix Pappalardi and the executives at Warner were ready to record once again. But first we had the idea of adding another member to the group.

Bart Schoales had introduced us to a Toronto-based mixed-media group called Intersystems whose four members were sculptor Michael Hayden, architect Dick Zander, poet Blake Parker, and musician John Mills-Cockell. John played the most astounding new instrument, called a Moog Synthesizer.

I remember the first time I heard John play his incredible machine. Intersystems operated out of a large loft on George Street at Adelaide. It was an amazing place with all kinds of weird and wonderful stuff spread out all over the studio, everything from schematics to paintings, but nothing was more amazing than John's Moog. The Moog was the first electronic music machine and was being manufactured right across Lake Ontario in Rochester, and John had managed to get his hands on one of the few that were commercially available. We had never heard anything like it before in our lives. Not only did it sound amazing, it looked amazing. The Moog was right out of a science fiction movie. A large machine, it stood almost six feet tall, with a keyboard, a vertical panel of blinking lights, and a jungle of electronic cables that John would plug and unplug while playing. Our imaginations ran wild at the possibilities. Yes, there had been some electronic music in rock, but no band had ever included a musician playing a Moog. Determined to be the first, we asked John to join the Market and he said yes.

We told Felix about it and he seemed interested but he wanted the band to come to New York as a five-piece without John. He had booked a sixteen-track studio, a technology that was only in its infancy then, and we could only record there for two days. Getting the sixteen-track studio was a bit of a coup and he didn't want to spend time getting to know a sixth musician – especially one playing something as far out as a Moog. We would then move back to Toronto to an eight-track studio, and it was there that he would have the time to check out the Market as a six-piece with the Moog.

We headed down to New York to begin work on the album that would eventually become *Aardvark*. Why the title *Aardvark* you might ask? Well, we had noticed that the Warner's catalogue was listed alphabetically, so the Market's first album, *Avenue Road*, was near the top. We thought it was a noble goal to be first in the catalogue the next time around. Besides, we thought it was a cool title on its own and seemed to suit the proposed content of the album.

And indeed we did get to be first in the catalogue when the album was released. The graphics for that album were very special and quite intriguing. They featured the album title written in an Art Deco–inspired font and an aardvark on stage on the front cover, and on the back, the same aardvark, sitting by a window looking out to sea with a telescope. The artwork was done by Bruce Meek, who later designed some pretty amazing covers for Procol Harum, among others, but then left Toronto for Amsterdam, where he became the art director for the European edition of *Vogue*.

In New York the band recorded "Side I Am," a truly strange and mysterious song that took full advantage of our newfound wealth of sixteen tracks. This meant the band and Felix were able to do lots of overdubbing. Although some of the ideas were clearly influenced by the Beatles, much of it remains breathtakingly original even when heard today. We tried a few other things during our brief stay in the sixteen-track studio but soon returned to Toronto and took up residence at Eastern Sound, an eight-track studio located on the corner of Yorkville and Bay. It seemed appropriate that the Market would be recording right on Yorkville.

John Mills-Cockell joined the band in the studio with his Moog and it blew Felix away. He couldn't believe the sounds that John could produce from the synthesizer. There is no doubt that some of the *Aardvark* album was miles ahead of its time. Although many Canadian critics and music historians missed this, or have forgotten about it, for those who were aware this record was truly cutting edge, a harbinger of what was to come with the marriage of rock 'n' roll to synthesizers. A great example was the song "Help Me," which was written during the studio sessions by Luke Gibson and Felix Pappalardi. It features a throbbing Moog bass line that triggers other haunting sounds from the synthesizer while drummer Jimmy Watson plays along with the Moog and Keith and Luke provide soaring vocal harmonies. Another pioneering track on that album is called "Half Closed Eyes," a marvellous union of folk-style guitar and Moog that at times is almost otherworldly.

It was during the *Aardvark* sessions in Toronto that I was first introduced to cocaine. Felix had brought some into the studio and late one night he asked me to join him down the hallway. Felix always wore a beautiful, hollowed-out whale tooth on a chain around his neck, where he kept his stash of cocaine along with a little silver spoon for measuring it out and making lines. On this night, he laid out several lines of the white powder for the two of us to snort. I'd heard about coke but didn't really know much about it; however, we had introduced Felix to MDA, which he liked, and now he said he wanted to return the favour. In some ways an unfortunate marriage, but not one I blame Felix for. If it wasn't then, it would have been somewhere with someone else. I did survive the experience, although it took several years before I finally stopped using it. By the early seventies coke had become endemic in the music business and there's no question that it threw many people off track. I don't recommend it, but it was readily available and I got involved. In the end, luckily for me, not much turned on it.

After he finished recording *Aardvark*, Felix returned to New York and formed the band Mountain with guitarist Leslie West. Mountain's first album, *Climbing!*, included a top-forty hit now considered one of the all-time classic rock tracks, "Mississippi Queen." The group's second album, *Nantucket Sleighride*, dealt with the lore of whales, which the pendant Felix always wore around his neck also evoked. I always liked Felix, and although there were problems with the records he produced for us, it wasn't because of a lack of passion for the projects. He was especially effective on *Aardvark*, to which the band had brought an unwieldy and ambitious musical landscape and that Felix handled with aplomb.

One day Felix and I were walking through Greenwich Village when we ran into an old friend of his, the drummer and co-founder of Blood, Sweat & Tears, Bobby Colomby. Bobby told us that the band's other co-founder, Al Kooper, had just quit a few days earlier and they were looking for a new lead singer. I told Bobby about David Clayton-Thomas, whom I had always admired and thought of as one of the greatest white rhythm and blues singers. David was now back in Toronto and performing in the Yorkville area. Thinking of the blues and R&B influences of Blood, Sweat & Tears, I figured David would be a perfect fit for the band. Bobby followed up on my recommendation and the rest is history, as they say.

Tragically, Felix was shot to death by his wife, Gail Collins, in 1983. They say drugs were the cause but I don't really know what happened, other than that the world lost a fine musician and producer and someone who had had a strong influence on me.

The Market began playing live shows again with John and his Moog Synthesizer as part of the band. While the Moog could be sensational, it was also a bit of a technical challenge. The synthesizer kept going in and out of tune and there wasn't much you could do about it other than wait for John to retune it. This was not conducive to dynamic, fast-paced shows. Fortunately, audiences were forgiving once they heard the sounds coming off the stage, to say nothing of the pure spectacle of seeing the Moog's many red lights flashing on and off in sequence to the music. It had a certain magical quality and looked like something out of a science fiction movie. But despite this revolutionary new instrument in the band and the very fine album that was about to be released, things weren't going all that well.

One night at a show just outside of Toronto, Jimmy Watson showed up with his head completely shaven. Backstage he started painting his shoes blue. Midway through the concert he grabbed a mike and started to berate the audience for wearing leather shoes. The band managed to complete the show, but it was taking all of our combined abilities just to keep the group together. No one was making any real money and there wasn't any infrastructure in the Canadian business to help you out. Basically you were on your own. Today you have programs like FACTOR (Foundation to Assist Canadian Talent On Record), MuchFACT (to provide assistance when making music videos), the Radio Starmaker Fund (which helps artists and record companies invest funds to market their music and tours), and the Canadian-content regulations, which can give you some comfort as well as a leg up, as you make your way through the morass of the business. But back then, you were on your own. We were hurting for many reasons, some of our own doing and some that were completely out of our control.

Anyway, *Aardvark* was finally released, and although it was enthusiastically greeted, the record really didn't seem to have the commercial hook that was going to give it and the band traction. Not that any of us were thinking all that commercially, but perhaps we should have been. Maybe things would have turned out for the better.

I could see that the band was at the breaking point, and I would be the first to leave. I found myself increasingly worried about the amounts and types of drugs I was taking, a worry further compounded when I woke up one day with a girl on one side of me and a small but lethal bag of pure meth on the other. I decided right then that it was time for a change. Yorkville was also in the throes of radical change. There was the so-called hepatitis epidemic that was supposed to be sweeping through Toronto and thought to be centred in Yorkville. I'd heard rumours that the street would be cordoned off and quarantined.

One day I went to have coffee at the Lothian Mews along with a few members of the Market and rock journalist Larry LeBlanc. The Mews was known for its "European-style" outdoor patio and espresso, and although we never really thought of it as a real part of our Yorkville, it was close at hand, located between Cumberland and Bloor. We sat at a table on the patio and waited and waited for service. Finally after what seemed like forever, a person who must have been the café manager came over and told us they wouldn't be able to serve us. The reason: we were hippies and might be contaminated with hepatitis. When he asked us to leave, I was outraged and we all flatly refused to go until we'd been served. A few minutes later, no fewer than fifteen cops arrived. They ran into the Mews courtyard like a scene from an old silent movie where the police are chasing bank robbers, the only difference being that these cops were looking seriously mean. They told us that if we didn't immediately vacate the café they would arrest us. Well, we decided that discretion being the better part of valour, we'd leave, but I've got to say if I had it to do over again I would stay and let them try to lock me up. It would have been interesting to hear the charges. I can see it now: Bernie Finkelstein, you are charged with having hair that is too long, how do you plead? But we left.

Of course, the hepatitis epidemic turned out to be a hoax completely trumped up by the city and the vested real estate interests, the idea being to clear the area of hippies and other undesirables, and to drive up the value of the real estate so it would be safe to sell overpriced purses, wallets, and jewellery to the kind of people who had just too much money on their hands. There were very few cases of hepatitis ever found despite the many medical alerts sent throughout the city, and by no stretch did those cases add up to an epidemic. It seems that almost everything will revert to form given the opportunity, and the natural form for most of the population is to be straight and uptight. The Yorkville I had known and loved was now in its death dance. It would hang on for a few more years – in fact I would become partners with the owner of the Riverboat a few years later, and that club managed to stay open until 1977 – but for all intents and purposes the street as I knew it was dead.

In early 1969 I came to the conclusion that it was time to get out of Toronto. It was more a move of self-defence than anything else. I felt if I remained in the city I was going to possibly die, and I could see that the Market was on its last legs, so I decided to quit before the group broke up. I was not particularly happy about this, much like I wasn't happy about leaving the Paupers, but it was still early days for me, and I was doing what I thought was best for the bands as well as for myself. Later on it would take a nuclear blast to make me leave anything.

About a year earlier I had gone up to Killaloe, a town just south of Algonquin Park, with my lawyer and friend Buzz Chertkoff. There was a hippie community around Killaloe and Buzz was doing some legal work for a commune, as strange as that may sound, started by a fellow named Dalton McCarthy. I had really enjoyed the weekend up there. I felt it was one of the world's loveliest places. The countryside is full of rolling hills with plenty of lakes, rivers, and streams and it's about as wild as you can get and still have roads where you can drive around in a regular vehicle. I decided that's where I'd head after leaving the Market. I even thought I might quit music and maybe just live off the land in some manner. This was 1969 and I was now twenty-five. It had been an action-packed seven years. There had been some good times and some bad times.

Unquestionably on the good side I had been involved with two great bands that had seen some success, but on the other hand, despite their accomplishments, neither had broken through in any significant manner.

It's important to know that "making it" in the traditional sense was never my main goal, in fact I'd have to say that until the time I headed for the country, I really didn't have a personal goal. Of course I wanted my bands to succeed. After all, there is no sense doing this kind of work if you're not going to be in it to win, but to win, you've got to know the game, and I can assure you, at this time I really didn't know the game. Though, as Albert Grossman had pointed out, I might have known as much as anyone else, I was also aware that I was making most of it up as I went along. I had done a few smart things, the main one being to work with some very talented musicians, and I'd been keeping my ears open for great ideas and encouraging those ideas to flourish when they crossed my path. As well, I had hooked up with some of the world's leading music figures, Albert Grossman, Bud Prager, Bill Graham, and Felix Pappalardi.

I had to face that the careers of both bands had come crashing down around me and that I had to shoulder some, if not most, of that responsibility. In both cases there had been a lot of frustration in dealing with the big record companies. And it wasn't because they weren't good at what they did – they were. And it wasn't because they weren't nice people – I liked almost everyone with whom I had worked. Still, when the chips were down they didn't have to listen to me, and I was finding that hard to take. Not because I think I'm always right – I know that not to be true – but mostly because I thought I had a better vision of the future and it felt fatal for me to have to put that on the back burner.

I also think that I was still operating on a built-in clock from my years of being an air force brat. My family had moved just about every two years, and strangely enough I had quit both bands after exactly two years. Later on, I would watch out for this tendency, almost to a fault.

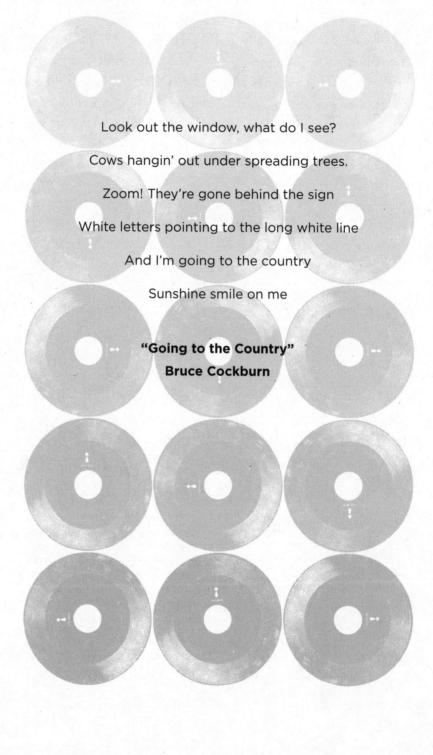

Look out the window, what do I see?

Cows hangin' out under spreading trees.

Zoom! They're gone behind the sign

White letters pointing to the long white line

And I'm going to the country

Sunshine smile on me

"Going to the Country"
Bruce Cockburn

CHAPTER EIGHT

One afternoon, shortly after I'd left the Market, I ran into Luke Gibson on Scollard Street. He told me that the band had just broken up – which didn't surprise me – and we sat down to have a coffee and talk about it. I told him about my plans to visit Dalton McCarthy's commune outside of Killaloe and that I was hoping to leave Toronto in a week or so. The next day I ran into him again and this time he asked if he could come along with me. Having some company would be great, and I'd always found Luke to be an easy guy to be around. But I still had to find a way to get up there.

Besides Bart Schoales, the Market had another roadie, named Mick Brigden, an amiable lad from England who was really the prototypical roadie. He wanted to get things done and knew how to do them well. He had worked for the British band Procol Harum before coming to Toronto and we had all felt lucky to have him with us. I approached Mick with a proposition: if I rented a car, would he drive us to Killaloe, drop us off at Dalton's place, and return the car to the rental office in Toronto? Mick agreed, so

Luke and I bought a couple of small tents, an outdoor stove, some buckwheat noodles, and a few other items. Then we packed the rental car and headed for the country.

Killaloe is about 300 kilometres northeast of Toronto, roughly a five-hour drive away. Located in the Madawaska Valley not far from Algonquin Park, the town is just a few kilometres from the lovely and aptly named Golden Lake. The area was settled by the Irish, French, Poles, and Germans, but the first inhabitants were the Algonquin, who continue to have a large land claim moving slowly through the Canadian justice system. Although it has always been a very difficult area to farm, farming was the other main occupation besides lumbering. Originally known as Fort McDonnell, it was renamed Killaloe Station, for the train station that served the local railway carrying passengers and lumber between Ottawa, Arnprior, and Parry Sound. In 1968, just shortly before I arrived, the station was torn down.

Killaloe's landscape is beautiful, but for its inhabitants, making a living from the land proved more than just daunting, it was close to impossible. The soil and the climate made farming a meagre proposition for all but the most industrious. By the late 1960s, incomers found that land was selling at reasonable prices, because there was a constant migration of the children of the original settlers out to the towns and cities of the surrounding area. Due to Dalton McCarthy's desire to see his old hometown gain some new popularity as well as some new inhabitants, Killaloe was becoming not only the part of Ontario most identified with the back-to-the-land movement but also the central nexus for several sprawling communes. In 1967 Dalton, with Erika Neuman, had bought the Doyle Mountain Farm that originally belonged to Dalton's relatives. Even today some of these same communes are operating in and around Killaloe. The most prominent of these,

Morning Glory Farm, was just getting going around the time that Mick Brigden dropped us off at Dalton's Doyle Mountain Farm.

We were greeted by about twenty or so men and women including Dalton, Erika Neuman, and Erika's partner, Mario. Believe me, it was really hard to tell if we were being met by a group that was standing at the edge of history or the survivors of an apocalypse. Some of them had been on the farm for quite a while and they were more than a little suspicious of three strangers from Toronto showing up at their door. The Killaloe area was pretty isolated but Dalton's farm was even more out of the way than the rest. It was spread out over several hundred acres with a house that was surrounded by at least seven or eight outbuildings, including a pretty large barn. Everything was made of old, grey, weathered barn-board. I doubt that there was anything there that hadn't been built at least a century earlier. There were acres of forest as well as empty fields and the land ran gently down towards a lake that sat on the commune's property. However, the closer you got to the lake, the steeper the descent became.

Dalton seemed glad to see us and told the assembled group who we were. Many knew of Luke, so news of his fame had clearly made its way to Killaloe. Seeing it was so close to dinnertime, we were invited to join the members of the commune for the meal, where we could explain to them what we were doing at their farm. We all sat outside, on the ground in a circle around a small fire. But before we could eat, a loaf of freshly made bread was passed around. Each person held it upright on the palms of their two hands like it was an offering, smelled it, paused for a few moments of what appeared to be a deep and private contemplation, then passed the loaf along to the next person. When it reached me I did my best to imitate everyone else without breaking out laughing. I knew which side my bread was buttered on, although today I look

back and believe they were really into something good, and quite
ahead of their time.

When we were asked to explain why we were there and what
we were looking for, I took the lead and told them that our band
had just broken up and we were trying to get away from the
scene in Yorkville. We hoped that it might be okay for us to stay
for a while until we got our bearings. If we were allowed to stay,
someone asked, what could we contribute to the community? We
told them that we weren't necessarily looking to join the commune but thought we could be productive, plus we had tents
with us and would be self-sufficient and keep well out of their
way. To be honest, I couldn't think of a single thing I could do
for them, but I volunteered that Luke could play and that it
wasn't that often people would be fortunate enough to have
someone as great and well known as Luke playing for free. (Once
a manager, always a manager.)

Everyone in the commune seemed to think it was a pretty
good idea, so Luke, being the good sport he was, pulled out his
guitar and played a couple of numbers. After he finished, the group
asked us to go for a walk and come back to the circle in around
twenty minutes, at which time they'd have made a decision. Being
a betting man, I figured our odds were pretty good. When we
returned and had resumed our seats around the fire, Dalton
announced we were welcome to stay. We could pitch our tents down
by the lake, but we couldn't hang around the house without permission. We would also have to provide our own food, and every once
in a while Luke was to come up to the house and sing some songs for
them. Also, they were working on the long road that led to the
farmhouse and requested that we help them with that project.

After we agreed to the terms, they began serving the meal,
which turned out to be a runny, greenish kind of thing served

over brown rice. Again, looking back, I think they were far ahead of the game, but I was really just a sandwich kind of guy in those days. I struggled through the meal, and then, as it began to get dark, we said our good nights, got back into the car with Mick, and he drove us down to the lake. When we got there, a light rain began to fall. We found a spot on a small ledge about twenty-five feet from the shore and started to pitch our tents. Within moments the rain got heavier and the mosquitoes started buzzing around in full force – whole battalions of them. Looking at us skeptically, Mick said he really had to get back to Toronto, that he wanted to head out before it was completely dark so he wouldn't get lost just trying to find his way off the farm. We waved goodbye as Mick drove off and I suddenly felt both complete dread and over-the-top excitement. This was what it meant to be a Canadian.

Much later, Mick admitted that he'd thought as he sped away that he might never see Luke and me alive again, and that he felt a bit guilty leaving us behind in the rain with two pup tents surrounded by millions of bugs, though there was no way he wanted to stay there a minute longer than he had to. A word about Mick might be appropriate here. After he got back to Toronto, Mick received a call from Felix Pappalardi, who had just started his band Mountain and needed a roadie. Mick took the job and eventually found himself working with Bill Graham in San Francisco. Mick became the co-manager of Eddie Money, and later managed multi-Grammy-winning guitarist Joe Satriani. He's still Joe's manager at the time of this writing.

We woke up the next morning to our new life on the side of a lake. Nothing to do but jump into the water. To our amazement, we saw a couple of the girls from the commune taking a swim just a few hundred feet away and, yes, they were also naked. This was beginning to look like a not too unpleasant experience. The days came and went slowly and lethargically. From time to time, we would go up to the farm where Luke would play some songs and I'd stand around chatting about life on the road and my past life in the music business, if you could call it that. Sometimes we would help out with the road construction – mostly we were moving rocks and timber around, kind of like they did in the Gulag, but at least nobody was making us do it, and I actually started to get into reasonable shape, both physically and mentally. But many days I did absolutely nothing. I had brought a few books and often spent the better part of a day hanging off a log in the water reading, waiting for the girls to come down to the lake to go swimming, which happened just enough to keep me happy.

I started getting quite friendly with Dalton and told him that I was beginning to like it up here enough that I wondered if he would show me around the area. He told me that he would be happy to do that and we started taking drives throughout the area from Barry's Bay to Clear Lake. He also told us that the group was ready to invite us to become full members of the commune, but we gently declined. Both Luke and I were just too anarchistic for group living. The more we drove around the area, the more I liked it. The vistas were breathtaking, all rolling hills, forest as far as you could see, big skies, clear fast-running streams that were clean enough to drink from. I decided that I wanted to buy something here of my own. I liked Dalton and really appreciated his hospitality and willingness to help me out, but again it was time to move on.

The first thing I did was buy a vehicle. I found a blue 1959 Chevrolet Apache panel van on a used car lot in Barry's Bay and bought it real cheap. Man, I loved that truck. It was a bit of a wreck but it was *my* wreck, and it had loads of space in the back. Luke and I had decided to buy a farm together and now, with the

Apache in my possession, we started to look in earnest. One day, we found a wonderful place up on a hill about five kilometres outside of Killaloe Station. It was one hundred acres with a century-old house and some great outbuildings, and it was selling for under $10,000. True, it didn't have indoor plumbing, water, or heat, but it did have electrical service. So we bought it.

We drove back and forth to Toronto in the Apache to pick up our belongings and then began settling into the farm. The first thing we needed was a wood-burning stove. We bought a huge, old, slightly rusty monster that had a combustion chamber large enough to take logs that would burn right through the night and

The Killaloe farmhouse (Photo courtesy of Wendy Sebert and Luke Gibson)

keep the whole house warm. Even after a night's sleep the fire would still have lit embers when we awoke in the morning. We drew water from a well located near the barns for drinking, cooking, and washing. It was pretty rudimentary but great.

Occasionally we would have girlfriends come and join us for a few days at a time but few of them appreciated our housekeeping abilities or our enthusiasm for the back-to-the-land movement, especially the part that involved using an outhouse. My friend Brazilian George gave me a twelve-gauge double-barrelled shotgun when I bought the farm and every once in a while I would take it out and shoot it against the side of a barn just to make sure it was working. It had a tremendous kick, and I didn't really enjoy using it that much, but it was comforting to have it around. Bears roamed the area, and though I am very thankful that I never had to use the gun on a bear or any other animal, it was wild country, and you never knew what might happen.

Sometimes, when we were driving around, we would see the odd person sitting on a hill with a gun, just staring off into the hills. I would wonder if they were, say, escaped drug dealers awaiting retribution for a misdeed from their past. But I didn't know for sure. Around Killaloe, you didn't really ask people what they were doing or why they were there. You pretty much left everyone to his or her own life, which was just fine by me.

I continued to help out at Dalton's place but now I could come and go as I pleased, and I started spending a lot of time sitting on my porch in an old rocking chair and thinking about what I had been doing and what I wanted to do next. One thing we did have in the house was a record player and it was the time of Van Morrison's *Astral Weeks*, the Band's first two albums, Dylan's *Nashville Skyline*, and Neil Young's *Everybody Knows This Is Nowhere*. But maybe most impressive to me was

Winnipeg's the Guess Who, who still lived in Canada but were making a big mark on the charts around the world with their wonderful hit singles "These Eyes" and "Laughing." That was extremely encouraging. I started thinking about re-entering the music scene.

I kept reflecting on what had gone wrong with both the Paupers and the Market. Sure, they had done well enough that I actually landed on the cover of *Saturday Night* magazine in May of 1968, and indeed both bands had made some terrific and innovative music. Still, in the end, things just weren't going the way they should have. It was obvious to me that if you wanted to really be successful you were probably better off being in New York or Los Angeles, at least if you were on the business side of things, but that just wasn't an option that I was ready to consider. I wanted to stay in Canada.

In contrast, doing the Market's first two singles before we had signed to Warner Brothers seemed so simple. Even though I had given the records to another company to distribute, its only responsibility had been sales; all other decisions were left with me. It was all easygoing

On the cover of *Saturday Night* in 1968

with no team of marketing experts and A & R (artists and reper-toire) people to have to please. I wanted the artists I worked with to be successful but I wasn't so sure that success was going to happen if I couldn't have a stronger say in what was going on both inside and outside the studio. I felt I could easily leave the music to the musicians, but I didn't particularly want to leave the business or the production decisions to the record companies. At the same time, my taste in music was making a shift. Since I had taken over the Paupers I had been working in rock 'n' roll, but the sounds I now liked were decidedly more acoustic, even folky. No doubt it was being influenced by where I was living and by many of the re-cords I was listening to, but I also think it's fair to say that after four years of working with some of the loudest rock bands in the world and hanging around the backrooms of most of the greatest rock clubs in North America, I was ready for a change.

I also realized that I wasn't exclusively interested in hit sin-gles. There was more to music, I thought, and my own interests might not lie in chasing after the dollar. While contemplating all this, I admit part of me considered just staying put on the farm. True, I was beginning to run out of money, but I thought that I might be able to make a living by just driving around the area in the Chevy panel truck, buying items for one price and selling them in Toronto and other urban centres for a few dollars more. That sounded appealing, an easy enough life that would keep me out of trouble. Still, I kept being drawn back to the idea of returning to Toronto and doing something new in music.

Early on the morning of July 20, 1969, Luke and I were expe-riencing a bit of cabin fever, so we decided to go to Ottawa. The Chevy had been acting up, so we agreed we'd walk out to Highway 60 and then hitchhike to Ottawa to visit my old friend, Harvey Glatt, who ran Le Hibou, where the Market used to play.

The highway was about five miles from the farm and it was a hot day, so every once in a while we'd pass a stream and jump in for a quick swim to cool off. We cut across several fields and through several woods and eventually made it to the highway just outside of Wilno. This town has one of the more interesting stories in Ontario. Legend has it that Wilno was inhabited by vampires, and there were people in the Killaloe area so certain that the legend was true that they would swear on a bible that they had seen them. I'm guessing these vampire stories originated with the early Polish settlers and, over time, they became deeply ingrained in the lore of the area. I never believed the stories myself, but on the other hand I avoided Wilno in the evening, and both Luke and I wanted to make sure that we were well past the town before it got dark.

After a few hours' walk we made it to the highway and stuck out our thumbs. It didn't take long before a car stopped. A few minutes later, the driver put on the radio just in time for us to hear that man had made it to the moon. Yes, it was July 20, 1969, and we had been so isolated that neither of us even knew the mission had left Earth. I realized that I was falling completely out of touch with the world.

Hours later, when we finally made it to Ottawa, we tried checking into the Holiday Inn downtown. The desk clerk took one look at us and told us we couldn't stay. I could see their point. There was little question that we were looking pretty strange. Probably something like Ontario's version of mountain men. Unwilling to take no for an answer, I told the clerk that we were music producers in town from New York and that this was the way we dressed in our business. After a brief meeting held behind the front desk between the clerk and the hotel manager they bought my story and let us check in. We went down to Le Hibou, checked out the music, had a few good meals, and then headed back to the farm several days later.

One evening, while I was sitting on the porch watching the rain approaching the house from across the valley, the idea of what to do next came to me almost as if it were at the leading edge of that storm. I would start my own label. I'd call it True North and it would become a home for acoustic music. Well, maybe not acoustic music exclusively, but certainly that would be the immediate emphasis of the label. As far as I knew nobody else was doing this in Canada and I was aware that there were a lot of talented singer-songwriters around who weren't getting a chance to record and market their music to a wider audience. Everyone in the business was obsessed with getting hit records, but singer-songwriters weren't thought of as artists who produced hits.

I don't really know where the name came from. It just popped into my head while I was sitting on that porch. Maybe I was looking at Polaris, the North Star. The words were also, of course, from the Canadian national anthem. And true north was the constant north relating to the geographical north, rather than the magnetic north on a compass. It was a name that seemed to say it all. It indicated a direction that was both real and true and it was also very Canadian, and if I could get it off the ground, this label would be both of those things. I was especially interested in the notion of being "constant" too, constancy being something I thought I'd been somewhat missing up to this time.

Still, the days and nights went by. I loved the Madawaska Valley and the life I was living there and it was hard to imagine just picking up and leaving. I also had a small problem: I had perhaps two thousand dollars to my name at that time, plus the farm. Enough to stay put in Killaloe for a while, but not enough to start a record company, even on the cheap.

One weekend Luke and I invited a couple of girls from Toronto to the farm for a few days. We were having our usual good time when one of the girls pulled out of her pocket a few tabs of psilocybin, a synthesized version of magic mushrooms. Since moving to Killaloe, I had only smoked some grass and not even much of that, but Luke and I didn't hesitate to give the psilocybin a shot. Before long the drug kicked in and I embarked on an amazingly strange trip. The girls decided it was time to head back to Toronto, and I'm happy to report they made it home okay. With psychedelics, you sometimes experience a strange, or even bad, trip and, at least for Luke and me, this was one of them. Once the girls had gone we became frozen on the porch. For some reason the house seemed alive, and I didn't want any part of going inside. There were strange noises coming from in there, and the noises outside didn't seem any better, but nonetheless we both felt safer on the porch. Finally, by dawn, the drug had begun to wear off. The first thing that hit me when that experience was over was that it was time to get out of Killaloe. My adventure in the country was coming to an end. It was time to go to Toronto and start True North.

I don't know what would have happened had I not taken that psilocybin that evening. I think eventually, possibly within months, I would have left Killaloe and gotten back into music anyway, but you never know. One thing is sure – for reasons I can't entirely explain, that bad trip hastened my re-entry into the business of music.

Singin' don't you want to keep on moving

Don't you want to get undone

Don't you want to change from losing

Don't you want to have some fun

"Down by the Henry Moore"
Murray McLauchlan

CHAPTER NINE

At dawn Luke and I grabbed a few things from the house and hopped into the Apache. But the damn truck was barely running so we limped into Killaloe, barely making it to the local gas station. The mechanic took one look and told us it was going to take a while and that maybe it wasn't worth fixing at all. I told him we had to get back to Toronto and he agreed we could leave it on the lot for a few days until I called to let him know what I'd decided to do with it. Still somewhat high, we walked across the road to the greasy spoon. Never in my life did sausages, eggs, and toast taste so good. I just felt incredibly lucky to have survived the previous night and now everything was looking up to me.

We checked the bus schedule. There wasn't one due until the evening so we decided to walk out to Highway 60 and hitchhike. After a while it became apparent that no one was going to pick up the two of us, so we split up, and eventually I got a ride back to Toronto. It took Luke a few more days to make it back home. He just couldn't get a ride and stayed the night with friends who lived outside Killaloe.

I ended up at Brazilian George's place, just outside of Bolton, where I began hatching my plan for the label. I spent most of my time in Yorkville, which was already becoming a ghost of what it had been just a short year earlier. The hepatitis scare had done its job for the city fathers, and now developers were prepping to create Toronto's own swell version of Rodeo Drive. Too bad. The Yorkville of 1967 was a thousand times more interesting and a hundred times better for the city, at least the way I see things. With George now living outside Toronto, I decided to look around for somewhere to live that would be closer to downtown. Someone I knew had a place in the north end of the city on Carson Crescent, just off Yonge Street and only a few blocks south of the 401. It was a fairly large house and they were trying to rent the place on a short-term lease. Although I had never imagined myself living that far north in Toronto, the place would be easy to handle, so I took it. I rented a car to move around with and started thinking about how to get my new company off the ground.

As it turned out, word was spreading that I was thinking about starting a label. One day I got a call from Gene Martynec. I'd always thought of Gene as the most impressive musician in Kensington Market and indeed as one of the most talented guitarists I had ever heard. This was pretty much common knowledge among the Toronto music community. It was Gene who brought to the Market most of its musical discipline, as well as many of the outside-the-box arrangements the band had become known for. He was also the least comfortable with the lifestyle choices the band had been making and was quite happy to be out of the rock 'n' roll circus. He wanted to become a record producer and had been out looking for artists and record companies to work with him.

Gene told me that he had been talking to an Ottawa singer-songwriter named Bruce Cockburn who was looking for a way to make his first solo record. He had recorded before as a member of a few Ottawa bands, and had spent a short stint with 3's a Crowd, a folk-rock band whose first album, *Christopher's Movie Matinee*, had been co-produced by Cass Elliot of the Mamas & the Papas. Although Bruce didn't join the band until a year later, three of his songs appeared on that album.

I had met Bruce once before when he was a member of the Children, an Ottawa group that was opening for the Lovin' Spoonful at Toronto's Maple Leaf Gardens. I had gone backstage to say hello to my old friend, Zalman Yanofsky, the Spoonful's lead guitarist. Zal and I had gone to Downsview Collegiate at the same time and even though he was a few grades ahead of me we'd become friendly. Later, we ran into each other quite often in Yorkville, before he went to New York where he hooked up with John Sebastian and formed the Spoonful, which remains, to this day, one of the best groups of all time. Some time after Zal had left the band and was operating Chez Piggy, his very fine Kingston, Ontario, restaurant, I called him to see if he would do a special guest spot in a video we were making with a Kingston-based band signed to True North Records called the Hell Billys. Zalman was glad to do it and we had him play a butcher in the video. He did his usual fine job. The day Zalman died was one of the few times I cried over a death. I thought the world had just become a worse place with his passing.

Beyond the brief introduction to Bruce backstage at the Spoonful show I knew little about him and I wasn't familiar with his music at all. However, I always listened very carefully to what Gene had to say and he was very enthusiastic about Bruce. So I decided to meet him at the opening night of a two-night stand Bruce was doing at the Pornographic Onion, a coffee house on the campus of what was then called Ryerson Polytechnic Institute, today's Ryerson University.

The Onion, which held about two hundred people, was located downtown, at the corner of Victoria and Gould Streets. It was one of several coffee houses around the city catering to the popularity of folk music at this time, including the Riverboat, the Penny Farthing, the Bohemian Embassy, the Fifth Peg, the Village Corner, the Gerrard Street Coffee House, and Club 71. The Pornographic Onion got its share of the better artists working the city, including Joni Mitchell and Murray McLauchlan.

The club was about half full the night I went to see Bruce, and it was clear that he had some fans as well as friends in the audience. After a brief introduction, Bruce walked onto the stage. At that point in his career he sat down on a stool when he performed, so he didn't really create an imposing figure. He played hunched over his guitar, and from the opening number it was obvious that he was intense about his music. But to be truthful, I was listening mostly for the songs. I had grown up listening to songs on the radio and that was the yardstick I used that night in assessing what I thought of Bruce. For me, the song is always the fundamental building block upon which the whole of the music business is built. I don't see where that has changed much, even in today's music business, although these days you can disguise almost anything. Still, in the end, the song is king. I knew that I wasn't looking for the next Guess Who, but it was never far from my mind that a good song could transcend almost all other problems.

Bruce played and I listened. I was impressed with a couple of the songs, in particular "Musical Friends," which Bruce performed at the piano, and "Going to the Country." It struck me that these songs could become popular and had a universal appeal. It's funny how these things work. I wasn't wrong about those songs; their popularity has lasted a long, long time. "Musical Friends" was recorded by Anne Murray and ended up on the same album as

"Snowbird," and the song title, "Musical Friends," has become part of the lexicon for describing musical events. "Going to the Country" has likewise had many covers and uses in movies and television and it came to be strongly identified with the whole back-to-the-land movement, although that was not Bruce's intention when he wrote it. But neither one would become a hit. It would take nine more albums and nine more years for that to happen with "Wondering Where the Lions Are."

But that evening at the Onion I was interested enough to go backstage and meet with Bruce. I invited him to come up to my house on Carson Crescent to talk things over. Bruce arrived with Michael Ferry, who was giving Bruce advice – not quite functioning as a manager but giving him the benefit of his experience in the music business. Michael was better known as Lee Jackson, from Jon & Lee & the Checkmates, one of Toronto's greatest R&B bands. At one point they gave the Mandala a pretty good run for their money as the most popular blue-eyed soul band in the country. Later, members of the Checkmates would join Rhinoceros, a "supergroup" (a band formed of members from other bands that had already had some fame) signed to Elektra Records, which would go on to be heard around the world.

I enjoyed my meeting with Bruce. After I told him about my plans for True North, he impressed me with his very focused idea of how he wanted his first record to sound. The thing that seemed to be mostly on Bruce's mind was that he wanted his album to be recorded solo. He had no interest in embellishing his songs, whether with a simple band or an elaborate orchestra. He also wanted to do any necessary overdubs himself. He might want a bass player on a cut or two, but that would be about it.

From my point of view, this was both good and bad news. The bad news was that there was no way any of these songs was going to get airplay on the AM radio stations that still made the hits. There just weren't stations of that type playing solo recordings. Before I go to the good news, let me just back up a minute. Though I loved hit songs and certainly would have enjoyed getting my piece of that lucrative pie, it was already evident to me that you could put out music that wasn't hit driven and still sell records. There was the new FM radio embracing album tracks and new sounds, as well as a burgeoning underground that would spread the word on good music even if it wasn't being heard on the airwaves. This was the way I was thinking True North should go. Less hit driven and more music driven. Still, combining both, that might be the ideal, especially if the singles sounded like they really belonged to the album and not formulated exclusively for airplay. Strangely enough, I had it in my head during that meeting with Bruce that he had that very opportunity although recording "Musical Friends" and "Going to the Country" solo wasn't going to make that especially easy. Well, it took about ten years, but my instinct did turn out to be correct.

On the other hand, the good news was that I didn't have that much money. I had made a deal with George that he'd back my launch of the label, but even with his help I was sitting on only $4,000. From this, I would have to not only make the record but also have the cover art done, design a record label, and pay the rent. George had promised me more money but it hadn't yet materialized (and, as things turned out, it never did). So here was Bruce sitting in front of me, telling me in no uncertain terms that he wanted to record solo. All I could think of was that old line from the Uncle Remus stories, the one where Brer Rabbit says to the fox, "Please don't throw me in the briar patch." After all, recording Bruce's album solo, or nearly solo, was going to be cheaper than using a band. So I agreed, despite my misgivings about missing a potential opportunity for "Musical Friends" and "Going to the Country" to become commercial hits. I told Bruce I would guarantee that he could record his album in any manner he wanted. And that's how I became an enlightened record man.

We worked out the details and signed a contract to make Bruce's eponymous first album. TN 001 became Eugene Martynec's first job producing an album and Bruce's first recording under his own name. We booked Eastern Sound, the studio where two years earlier Felix Pappalardi had furthered my education both musically and otherwise, and in October 1969 we embarked on making our first album. The sessions were finished in just three days and it was then that I became truly aware of the depth of Bruce's talent. I had entered into the agreement thinking the deal was all about those two terrific songs, but it turned out the real story was unfolding with songs like "Thoughts on a Rainy Afternoon," "Man of a Thousand Faces," and "Spring Song." I was also blown away by Bruce's astonishing guitar playing, something I had completely missed when I saw him at the Onion. As an artist and a songwriter, he seemed completely original. Certainly an artist worth fighting for.

While we were recording the album there was much more going on, and not all of it was good. George, who was always a reckless driver and had a special love for very fast Mercedes-Benz roadsters, wrapped one around a concrete lamppost and nearly killed himself. Fortunately he survived, but he was never to be the same person again. During his long recovery George was understandably unable to come up with the money he had promised to invest in the label. So I found myself on my own with very little cash. Also, even though I was making the label's first record, I didn't have a deal in place to get it out into the marketplace. In other words, True North didn't have a distribution contract.

I started to make the rounds in Toronto, going from company to company explaining my idea of having a label that would

specialize in Canadian singer-songwriters and that the first release
would be by an unknown named Bruce Cockburn. Mostly I was
met with stony stares and little or no enthusiasm. It's fair to say
that I had pretty much exhausted all distribution possibilities,
when finally a ray of light came from a most unexpected source.
One day I got to talking with John Williams, the head of A & R
at CBS Canada, at a club in Yorkville. I told John what I was up to
and he looked interested, even after I told him that I'd been unable
to get anyone from CBS to return my calls. John informed me that
there had recently been some changes at the company and that he
was looking to take CBS further into the business of recording
and promoting Canadian music. John brought me up to their
offices at Leslie and Eglinton, where he introduced me to Jack
Robertson, the vice president of the company.

There couldn't have been two more apparently different
people than Jack and me. He was nattily turned out and played
golf. I looked like a rejected version of Pancho Villa, and the
only golf I had played was on a pool table. But we hit it off right
away, and they offered me a contract on the spot. Maybe it was
because Jack liked Bruce's music; maybe it was because he was
trying to encourage John, who was very enthusiastic about working with us; or maybe it was because Jack was born in Scotland
and Bruce is of Scottish heritage a few generations removed . . .
Whatever it was, the offer was on the table.

There was just one hitch, and it was a big one. The offer
wasn't that good, and they weren't going to sweeten it. CBS was
prepared to give me $15,000 in return for six albums by artists of
my choice, one of them being Bruce's debut album. I would own
the records, but they would have the distribution rights for five
years, plus an option to distribute the records outside of Canada,
provided they released the records in the States within a year of

their initial release in Canada. CBS would also pay all promotion and marketing costs.

In simple terms, I would receive $2,500 to deliver a finished record, including artwork, ready for manufacturing, which CBS would handle. Even with an album as simple as Bruce Cockburn's first, I was spending more than $2,500. Of course, there was always the chance that I would be able to sell enough records to earn back the $15,000 advance, but still, on paper I was going from being on the hook for one record to being on the hook for six records. However, on the up side, they were prepared to give me an immediate $9,000 up front and a further $1,000 as I delivered each successive album. Listen, when you have no money in your pocket and someone offers you a $9,000 cheque as well as the means to promote your first record, and the company making the offer is CBS, you jump at it. Everyone else had turned me down and this was my shot. What was the worst that could happen? Well, you might say, if you don't deliver, you go bankrupt and you fail. In hindsight, all real possibilities, but when I took that cheque none of those options even crossed my mind. I was going to succeed and that was all there was to it.

From the day I signed that contract to the day I started to write this book, I've lived close to the edge when it comes to money, and that original contract with CBS Canada was only the beginning. Barely a day ever went by, even when I was on top of the world, when money wasn't an issue, but I never really let it bother me. The music business is not a place for the faint of heart. I remain grateful to both John Williams and Jack Robertson for giving me a chance back in 1969. Although it took some doing, that deal with CBS Canada worked out, and for the next twenty-five years I operated under that same, original contract, even though the terms were modified and improved many times as I moved forward.

A few years before the CBS contract I had met a singer-songwriter named Murray McLauchlan. Murray used to hang around the Upper Crust when I was managing the Kensington Market. We all liked Murray. Even then it was clear he was very talented. One day during the summer of 1968 as I was walking up Avenue Road to my place on Pears Avenue, Murray came running up behind me and asked if I would work with him. He told me he would make me a million dollars. I should have listened to him then. But instead we stood around and chatted and got to know each other a bit, but I was far too stoned and far too deeply involved in rock 'n' roll just then to care much about acoustic music. So I let it pass, but I always remembered that promise of Murray's. After I signed Bruce I started to see Murray around a bit more, as he and Bruce and their wives, Patty and Kitty, were sharing a flat on Queen Street West.

One snowy night just before Christmas in '69 I heard a knock on my door at Carson Crescent and there stood Murray and Patty, quite drenched and needing a place to stay. I was happy to have them at my place, which I was sharing with three girls, and even though it was already full of people and dogs, there was still room for two more, especially given that some of the people at the house would soon be going home for Christmas.

Murray had fallen on hard times but he still had a great spirit and I really enjoyed having him and Patty around. On Christmas Eve they went out and found a Christmas tree that had been abandoned by the merchant selling them and brought it back to the house. That's how this Jewish kid from Downsview had his first Christmas tree. I don't think I have ever had a nicer one.

While Murray was staying at my place we talked a lot about his struggle to get his career off the ground. Once again he asked me to work with him, but at that point I was very concerned about finances; after all, I hadn't even put out my first album through my new, but as yet untested, distribution deal with CBS. I then made what could have been the worst decision of my career: I advised Murray to move to New York. I can't tell you how lucky I am that he returned and that I was finally able to put together a deal with him. A great talent like Murray doesn't come around too often, and the fact that I turned him down twice and still got another chance to work with him makes me one very lucky guy. But that Christmas, even though I wasn't that smart, I was honest. I told Murray that if you wanted to make a movie you go to Hollywood and if you wanted to make a record you go to New York. I'm happy to report that I never told anyone that again, but at that time, given how much I liked Murray, and how great his songs were, that was probably the best advice I could give.

New York was pretty good to Murray. He fell in with Tom Rush, who is often credited as the guy who ushered in the era of the singer-songwriter by covering songs written by Joni Mitchell, James Taylor, Bruce Cockburn, Jackson Browne, David Wiffen, and many others, among them an unknown artist named Murray McLauchlan. Tom recorded two of Murray's songs – "Child's Song" and "Old Man's Song" – which made people sit up and take notice. Fortunately for me, Murray didn't like living in New York and came back to Canada about a year later. I went to see his gig at the Riverboat and he was better than ever, playing not only the two songs Tom Rush had covered but others like "Honky Red" and "Sixteen Lanes of Highway." Not about to make the same mistake a third time, I signed him to both True North Records and to my management company. Sometimes being lucky is better than being smart.

By the time I signed Murray, I had already released Bruce's first record. Although Bruce wasn't setting the retail world on fire, the album was being noticed. Soon Bruce began selling out the Riverboat and other clubs around the area. When I first signed Bruce, it was only to the record company; I had decided I didn't want to be a manager again. However, as Bruce's record became more successful I began getting loads of calls to my new office on Scollard Street, in Yorkville, regarding shows for Bruce. Nobody knew how to reach him since he didn't like giving out his number, so all the calls were coming to me. It was becoming apparent that the only way for his record to grow was for Bruce to be doing the right shows at the right time. So one night, in the Riverboat dressing room, after he had sold out the club for four days running, we decided that I would become his manager. We didn't sign a management agreement then and still haven't bothered to this day. Not long after that, Murray became the second act with whom I became involved in the big three areas of the music business: management, recording, and music publishing.

Between signing Murray and releasing his first album, the offices of True North became a busy little place, to say nothing of the fact that I was also living on the second floor of the building. Bruce's first album was released in the U.S. and we were starting work on his second album, *High Winds, White Sky*. Meanwhile, before I signed Murray, I decided to release an instrumental album by the electronic music trio Syrinx, led by the Moog synthesizer player John Mills-Cockell (who'd been part of the Kensington Market), along with Doug Pringle on horns and Allan Wells on percussion. Syrinx was an outgrowth of the Intersystems group that Bart Schoales had introduced to me earlier. To say they were ahead of their time is an understatement. The music was both exotic and psychedelic, not unlike the eletronica that would become so popular decades later. It put its listeners into a trance. This was a long way from acoustic music but it made sense to me. It was my hope to put out the best music I could find and afford. Little did I imagine that I would actually get True North's first chart-topping record from Syrinx.

By 1970, I also realized that Canadian-content regulations were going to be introduced, soon. I was not just in favour of this but had been active in lobbying for this kind of legislation, although mostly in the background. From time to time I was called upon by government officials or members of the media to comment and I never hesitated to add my voice as loud as I could in favour of the regulations. In fact, I made more than one trip to Ottawa with small groups of music producers to actively lobby the government to move forward on the content regulations, although we kept our actions as quiet as possible because we were all concerned about reprisals from radio broadcasters, who vehemently opposed the rules and had made it clear those who supported them would suffer. Amazingly, being seen to support Canadian content was dangerous if you wanted radio to promote your new records. But, for many of my colleagues, it didn't matter, since you couldn't lose what you didn't have: airplay. It was clear to me that Canadians were never going to hear homegrown music on Canadian airwaves as long as radio could import ready-made hits from America and elsewhere. Why take a chance on playing an unproven Canadian artist's record when you could have a full playlist of hits handed to you on a silver platter just by looking through the U.S. record industry bible, *Billboard* magazine? Not to mention how easy it was to pick up a phone and hire an American radio consultant to provide you with all the programming ideas you needed. No fuss, no muss, no worry.

Were there exceptions among radio broadcasters? Of course. There were talented people in radio with great ears who were dying to play Canadian music, and they did so whenever they could get away with it. But overwhelmingly, the executives in charge of radio in Canada, a big business, weren't interested in taking chances, plain and simple. Low ratings meant no job, and for some misguided reason the powers in radio had decided that Canadian records meant low ratings. Secretly, many people in radio were entirely in favour of the Canadian-content regulations, but their voices were muted in fear of losing their positions.

In 1970, at the same time as the Canadian-content regulations were being formed, I received the sad news that Alex Darou, the former bassist for the Kensington Market, had died in his flat above the Grab Bag on Yorkville. The circumstances surrounding his death were mysterious. Alex had locked himself away behind his apartment door although he did respond to people talking to him through the door, among them me. He had said he was on a fast to cleanse himself and didn't want any company. Alex was a kind and gentle person and a very fine musician who, among other things, taught me how to play bridge. Many a sunny afternoon we played sitting on the patio at the Upper Crust, interrupted only when I had to make or take a call at the corner pay phone. We had all been worried about Alex, but he had kept assuring us, from behind the door of his flat, that he was well and would see us soon. Sadly, it never happened. Some say that he had stopped his fast and started to eat, but that he had made himself so weak that just the act of digesting had a terminal effect on his body. The cause of his death was never fully established, at least to my satisfaction. Alex was just twenty-seven when he died.

I had just recently taken on Bruce Cockburn's management when he was offered the opportunity to do the score for a movie. The film was being directed by Don Shebib and was tentatively titled *The Maritimers* (its final title was *Goin' Down the Road*). Bruce took the job and came up with a handful of great songs, including the theme. The film has become a Canadian classic; it's rare to hear a discussion about Canadian movies that doesn't include it.

Don wanted us to release the soundtrack and perhaps in retrospect we should have, but Bruce was concerned that he would become overly identified with the film. At this time, Bruce's main interest was ensuring that people got to know his work from his first album. Bruce saw a real difference between the writing he had done for the film and the direction his recording career was taking. I had some misgivings about this decision from a business point of view, since I was sure that "Goin' Down the Road," as Bruce had recorded it, could have been a hit. But I understood Bruce's artistic goals and I supported him. This would not be the last time Bruce would ignore commercial opportunities in favour of artistic ones, but that's part of his genius. Even after all of these years, people continue to perform and record that song.

It was now time for Murray McLauchlan to begin recording his first album. Once again, we selected Gene Martynec as the producer. Gene had done a great job on Bruce's recording and it was no surprise to any of us how adept he was in the studio, because of not only his masterful musicianship but also his interest in the sonic side of producing. He could talk the talk and walk the walk with the best of the engineers. We were happy to have Gene on board.

Murray's first album is one of the great joys of my career. The songs were startlingly good and we knew right from the beginning that something great was happening. Murray didn't want to make just any folk album. He wanted it to be raw and rough around the edges, and his idea of how to achieve this was unusual. He surrounded himself with some of the finest musicians in North America but he asked our mutual friend Jay Telfer to play drums, instead of hiring a real drummer. You might recall Jay from earlier in this tale. He was the lead singer and guitar player in A Passing Fancy, not the drummer. Yes, he could play a little, but he was far from a professional on the kit. Murray was looking for something simple and not too slick and that's what he got. It wouldn't be the last time Murray would make decisions in the studio that ran contrary to standard recording methods.

To record the album, we booked Thunder Sound, a new studio in town. It was located on Davenport Avenue near Yonge Street and about a hundred feet from my office and home on Scollard. The studio had been built by David Briggs, who had worked with Neil Young. Neil had owned at least part of Thunder, although now it was about to be taken over by a very young Moses Znaimer. Thunder was a wonderful studio with some eccentricities such as a downstairs sauna. I ended up owning the original speakers from the studio, two huge, wonderful wood-encased JBL Studio 100s. I still have them in my office. We made a lot of fine music in Thunder using those speakers, and I have many great memories from those times.

Having successfully used Bart Schoales for several projects, I had decided I wanted to use him as often as possible to do our artwork, or at least to advise us on how to get it done. Murray's photos for his debut were shot in Kensington Market. He's looking though a chicken coop containing a single chicken waiting for the chop, although at the time this subtlety was lost on me. Murray says he identified with that chicken from time to time.

He needn't have worried. *Song from the Street* was met with very favourable reviews, and because FM radio was growing in importance at this time the record also received its fair share of airplay, although nothing on the powerful AM side where all the hits were still being made. It didn't really matter to us as there was little question that an important new songwriter had emerged on the scene, and I knew it was only a matter of time till Murray would attract a large audience. Murray's record signified a new turn in the Canadian folk scene. Until *Song from the Street*, most of the great Canadian folk songwriters had strong references and often direct links to the more pastoral side of the country. Murray put himself smack dab in the middle of urban Canada, specifically Toronto, with songs like "Honky Red" and "Sixteen Lanes of Highway." His album cover reflected this and strongly identified him as that "kid from the city."

In December of 1970, around the time I signed Murray and was starting Bruce's second album, I attended a meeting called by Stan Klees at the Inn on the Park, a hotel right next to CBS Canada in suburban Don Mills. Many of the country's top producers were in one room together for the first time. Guess Who producer Jack Richardson; Terry Brown, who at that time was riding high on the worldwide charts with "When I Die" by Motherlode and who would later go on to produce Rush and Blue Rodeo; Frank Davies, who had just started Daffodil Records, a company that would sign Klaatu, Crowbar, and Tom Cochrane; artist-producers Tommy Graham (former member of the Big Town Boys) and Paul Clinch, both of whom had been making or producing records for Stan Klees's labels Tamarac and Red Leaf Records; and Art Snider, a true pioneer in Canadian music. Snider's independent label, Chateau Records, got off the ground in 1956. Talk about getting there early. As if that wasn't impressive enough, Allan Macmillan and Ben McPeek, Jack Richardson's partners in Nimbus 9 Productions, were in the room. It was Ben, along with Doug Riley, who had produced the original demo for the Paupers, the one that helped me get my first U.S. record deal with MGM. Walt Grealis, the publisher of *RPM*, Canada's music business trade paper, and Ritchie Yorke, the journalist who would document so much of the early history of Canadian music in his breakthrough 1971 book,

Axes, Chops & Hot Licks: The Canadian Rock Music Scene, were invited in to observe the proceedings.

The principal issue that had brought us together that day was that the radio broadcasters had announced, in response to the coming Canadian-content regulations, that if they were going to be forced to play Canadian records they would start their own record companies. In other words, they planned to play their own records on radio in order to make at least some of the money that was going to be made from playing Canadian music. One broadcasting company, CHUM, had already started a label, Much Records, and had hired two very able record industry figures in Bob Hahn and Brian Chater. Much had already signed April Wine, Michel Pagliaro, and a few other acts.

Naturally we were all alarmed. Not only was CHUM against the regulations and very, very down on having to play Canadian music, but they were now saying if they had to play Canadian records they would play their own. These were public airwaves. It's one thing to play the music you own, but when you add that to the threat of boycotting everyone else's records, then, it seemed to me, we had a problem. The situation was so serious that even though two journalists were present at the meeting, both of them had agreed not to report on who was in the room. The threat of reprisals against anyone who would dare to speak out against the broadcasters was a real and present danger, the possible punishment being that your own records would not get played on those very same radio stations – a truly fearful situation if your business was making and selling records, especially in those days. Sadly, this sorry state of affairs continues in many ways even now.

Thinking there would be safety in numbers, we decided to form a trade association that day. It would become a kind of watchdog to look after the greater good of the then-fledgling Canadian independent record business. And that's how the Canadian Independent Record Production Association, or CIRPA, came into being. CIRPA is still going strong today and has been in the forefront of many of the important issues affecting Canadian music, from funding to copyright. CIRPA has since changed its name and is now known as the Canadian Independent Music Association (CIMA).

Jack Richardson became the first president of CIRPA, and I was on the board from the beginning. Ironically, Brian Chater, who in 1970 was working for CHUM's Much Records, ended up becoming the executive director of CIRPA in 1987 and fought many battles with radio, albeit always with dignity and good manners. Brian has made a valuable contribution to the Canadian music business, and along the way he was responsible for being the first person in the business to recognize the talents of not only April Wine but also Bryan Adams. Much Records was quietly wound down in 1975. In reality it had not been very active since the early seventies, after CIRPA and others let CHUM's executives know that it would not go unnoticed if they played their own record label's music at the expense of others'.

A further irony. Along with Moses Znaimer, I helped start VideoFACT, an organization that funded music videos in 1984. It was at first funded entirely by MuchMusic, which was wholly owned at that time by CHUM Radio. (Later in the book, I will elaborate on VideoFACT and how I came to be involved.)

There is a certain tragedy here and it's one that all of us should feel some shame about. There never should have been an environment in which music producers felt threatened for speaking out publicly about issues affecting their industry, especially when it came to Canadian content and government regulation. It's my own feeling that we ourselves were somewhat responsible for letting this happen and that it still continues to this day. We all should have gone to the CRTC right from the start and spoken out loud and clear about these threats, which were constantly being aimed at us simply because we were asking for a level playing field. Had we spoken out, we might have been helped by the regulator and the landscape might have changed for the better. So even though in the end we publicly addressed all of the issues affecting Canadian content, our fear of the broadcasters remained a dark and dirty secret. And we were mostly on our own. The multinational record companies had little to say about the issue, as they owned the remaining 70 per cent of radio's playlists and couldn't see too much in the Canadian-content regulations that would directly benefit them. As time went by and the broadcasters consolidated and became media behemoths, speaking out would become an even harder proposition.

Back then, at least you knew you had a fair chance to speak your piece in the printed media. Today, all too often, the same corporations own not only the radio stations but also the TV stations and the newspapers. Not a climate to foster healthy debate. It became clear to me that to some degree the CRTC was being held hostage by these giant organizations, and had allowed, even encouraged, them to grow. As time went by, the idea that the regulator would listen to us seemed to grow more remote and naive. So, yes, we should have spoken out right from the beginning, but who can blame the independent record companies? They were truly Davids against Goliaths. They had to make a living not only for themselves but also for their artists and, in the seventies, radio was just about the only way to do that.

Still, despite the often tense relationship between the broadcasters and Canadian record-company owners, our records were in fact now being played. Radio was finding out that spinning Canadian music wasn't going to put them in the poor house and was sometimes downright satisfying. Many of us were making very good friends among the people on radio's front lines, the program and music directors. The hits were coming, so other than those problems that our trade organization was charged to deal with, we often just let the issue of threats and blacklisting sit on the back burner.

Eventually the issue of Canadian content cooled out and radio's incursion into music production ended, leaving most of us able to get along well enough and to look for the common ground we all shared. Namely, the making and playing of great music. But as an industry we were always aware of just who was holding the proverbial sword of Damocles over our heads, as we still are and perhaps always will be, as long as there is regulation of the airwaves. In my opinion, one thing is certain. The Canadian-content regulations worked and Canadian music began to thrive in this new environment. The Internet may soon render the whole argument moot, as radio's grip on the manner in which music is heard and consequently sold is slowly loosening. The role of record companies, large and small, is also in flux. It seems this flood will spare no animal.

I'm happy that this world of backroom politics only occupied a small part of my time. Meanwhile, Gene Martynec had evolved into a wonderful and creative producer. His work on Bruce's second album, being readied for release, was a great example. It remained a largely solo acoustic record but it included an experimental instrumental ensemble piece done with two members from the group Nexus, who went on to become one of the most lauded progressive music groups in the country. Late one night, in the main room at Thunder Sound, John Wyre and Michael Craden, from Nexus, had set up all kinds of percussion instruments. They went into an extensive jam session with Bruce, and out of it came a beautiful, free-form instrumental. Bruce wasn't sure what to call the piece but that was settled when he threw the

I Ching and came up with the title "Ting/The Cauldron." The album also contained the song "One Day I Walk," which continues to be one of the most covered songs in Bruce's repertoire. Among the best known is k.d. lang's version, recorded on her much-loved *Hymns of the 49th Parallel*. The Syrinx album was surprisingly well received and Murray McLauchlan was beginning to sell out all of the clubs on the folk circuit, a sign of his rising popularity.

We were also beginning a recording with Luke Gibson, who had a collection of songs that were particularly poignant for me as they largely dealt, at least atmospherically, with life in and around Killaloe. The songs became the album *Another Perfect Day*. Around this time, I got to know Moses Znaimer better. He was a larger-than-life character and we hit it off. Moses had taken over Thunder Sound from the previous owners and was operating it for a venture capital company. He had a lot of interesting ideas, some of which he explored with me. Moses suggested that we become partners and bring together under one roof Thunder Sound and True North and then take a look at buying Quality Records, which at that time was the largest Canadian-owned record company, with both a distribution and manufacturing division. It was an interesting idea and one that I perhaps should have pursued, but I was having too much fun. Maybe I'm just not ambitious enough, then or now. The music I was involved in seemed more important to me than empire-building, but I always liked Moses and we kept in touch over the years. In 1983, we finally did some real work together when he started the Canadian music video channel MuchMusic and I assisted him at the CRTC hearing where we gave birth to VideoFACT.

This was a loose and wonderful time. Both Bruce and Murray were starting to hit their stride and they regularly performed at a circuit of clubs in Toronto, Ottawa, and Montreal. I would always be travelling with one or the other of them and there was only one way to go: train. Planes were too expensive and cars too laborious. I got to know the dining car stewards and we'd sweet-talk our way into the dining car the moment we stepped onto the train and not leave until we were a few minutes from our destination. There were two separate dinner sittings during the trip, so there was a time limit on how long you could stay at your table, but our friends the stewards looked the other way. We were blessed.

The dining cars on the trains were sensational. All gleaming wood, shining silver, and freshly pressed linen. The tables were set with a red or white carnation floating in a heavy glass goblet placed in the middle of each table. The silverware was ornate and heavy. The menu was pure Canadiana: Alberta beef or Atlantic salmon. With the countryside sweeping by the large panoramic windows we were in heaven. We'd easily go through a bottle of cognac before reaching our destination. It was during these journeys that we worked out the problems of our respective careers, and for good measure the problems of the country, and the world. If we were going to Ottawa, when we got off the train we took a five-minute walk to the Grand Hotel. As our careers improved, we'd take a five-minute walk in the opposite direction to the Château Laurier. From either hotel we were less than a ten-minute walk from Le Hibou, the club we'd most often be playing. I still take the train as often as I can but it just isn't the same without those fabulous dining cars.

Sometimes you find success in the most unlikely places. By 1972 I had released six albums on True North, two by Bruce Cockburn, one by Murray McLauchlan, one by Luke Gibson, and two by Syrinx. The second Syrinx album was called *Long Lost Relatives*. It is an amazing record, distinguished by the symphonic suite "Stringspace," which took up most of the album. Tucked away inside the recording was a short, bouncy, upbeat instrumental number called "Tillicum," which was the theme for the half-hour TV show *Here Come the Seventies* on the CTV Network. We decided to put out the track as a single, hoping to take advantage of the national TV exposure. The album was True North's fifth, and so far, even though we had been receiving terrific support from the few FM progressive stations across the country, we had not yet had any appreciable airplay on the top-forty stations, where the real sales action was.

To be honest, I knew we weren't exactly making the most commercial music at True North, but at the same time I never put out a single that I didn't think was going to be a hit, so I was getting disappointed a lot. Not that I felt discouraged – far from it. I just kept thinking it would be the next one. Optimism and denial are two important qualities to have if you're going to live a life in the music business, but even so, never in my wildest dreams could I have known that I was about to have my first legitimate top-forty hit single since beginning with the Paupers in 1965.

"Tillicum" started on CHED radio in Edmonton, where it hit number 1 thanks to the hard work from the local CBS sales and promotion team. Then it spread to many other parts of the country and, although it didn't go top ten, it did hit number 38 on the single charts. Our first top-forty hit. And then, less than a year later, we got our first national top-ten single ("Farmer's Song"), and that one got played everywhere across the country, and I mean everywhere.

In the early seventies a group of about twelve radio stations put together a panel that would meet weekly to judge the current week's Canadian record releases. The panel was known as the Maple Music System. No doubt this idea was conceived with the best of intentions, but the net result was that only one record a week was judged worthy of airplay and the rest were more or less relegated to the nearest dustbin. Even in sports the second-, third-, and fourth-place teams get into the playoffs, but in the early seventies this system identified only one winner. Without even looking at the quality or the qualifications of the judges it's obvious there was something wrong with this project. I took a particular dislike to it and wasn't alone in my assessment of the Maple Music System. It too faded away in time.

In 1969, during a trip to New York Bart Schoales had introduced me to the famous American designer and artist Ed Schlossberg. Ed was just getting started and had yet to make his reputation as one the world's most innovative thinkers. Nor had he yet married John F. Kennedy's daughter Caroline. He was a friend of Bart's, liked the Kensington Market, and invited us to accompany him to Andy Warhol's studio, The Factory. Not that much happened during our visit, the most notable thing being that Andy was very nice and seemed happy to have us there. We smoked a joint or two and enjoyed ourselves, quite captivated by the studio.

What I did take away from that encounter with Ed and Andy was a saying that Schlossberg had written on a piece of silver Mylar. It was a quote that I decided to use in our first-ever advertisement for the True North label, and it was subtly aimed at the Maple Music System. The ad had pictures of our first six album releases by Bruce, Murray, Syrinx, and Luke. The copy read, "If all the weeds on all the world's beaches got together to elect a king, the tide would still come in."

That's how I viewed the Maple Music System. They could do all the voting they wanted but we were still going to make it one way or another. Supreme arrogance on my part, I suppose, but it was a tough world that we found ourselves in, and you had to be at least a little cocky to survive.

Sometimes the best map will not guide you

You can't see what's round the bend

Sometimes the road leads through dark places

Sometimes the darkness is your friend

"Pacing the Cage"
Bruce Cockburn

CHAPTER TEN

By mid-1971 I began to feel that I truly had a record company. We had six albums in the market and had just gotten our first small taste of a radio hit with Syrinx's "Tillicum." Bruce's *High Winds, White Sky* was now in stores and it was pretty obvious that it was going to be bigger than his first release. Murray was off to a great start with *Songs from the Street* and Luke's album was getting lots of interest. On the management side, things were even better. Both Bruce and Murray were drawing strong crowds wherever they played, and I was beginning to think that Bruce could move into theatres if I could put all the pieces together properly.

Around this same time I was approached by a young man from Vancouver named Shelly Siegel. Shelly was a few years younger than me and may not have weighed much more than one hundred pounds. He told me he had been watching my label and thought I should open a West Coast office, a move that would have been unprecedented for a small independent label in Canada. I immediately liked Shelly. Although small in stature he had a big, passionate enthusiasm for music and the music business, as well as a compelling pitch for why I should hire him to work for True North in Vancouver.

I was always interested in being seen as a national company, but money was tight, and also I had the local CBS promo reps looking after things for me in the West. Still, it was clear that Vancouver, along with Calgary and Edmonton, was the future. If I wanted to be successful in what was the fastest-growing area of the country it would be important to have more control over what was happening several thousand miles from Toronto. Shelly was willing to come on board for next to nothing, which was about all I could afford, so I made a deal to hire him and open an office in Vancouver. Shelly would become True North's West Coast promotion man.

The move paid off right away. Shelly tipped me to a tour that was about to happen throughout British Columbia and Alberta with two great groups: the Everly Brothers and Commander Cody & His Lost Planet Airmen. The tour promoters were looking for another act and expressed interest in Murray. I jumped at the opportunity and quickly closed the deal, not only for Murray to do the tour but also to travel on the tour buses that the Everlys were using. This was one tour I was going to have to go on. The Everly Brothers were heroes of mine, and their records were indelibly imprinted on my mind: "Bye Bye Love," "Wake Up Little Susie," "All I Have to Do Is Dream," and "Cathy's Clown," among others. No way was I going to miss this. I was also quite interested in Commander Cody, who was riding the charts with his novelty hit "Hot Rod Lincoln," as fine a song about a car as you will ever hear.

The tour turned out to be both an amazing and an enlightening experience. I was surprised to discover that Don and Phil Everly not only didn't speak to each other, they wouldn't even stay in the same hotels. They even had separate tour buses. These weren't the elaborate tour buses we associate with rock stars today. They didn't have bunks, kitchens, couches, toilets, and TVs. These were just plain old coaches, the kind that Greyhound uses to move travellers from town to town. Still, any kind of bus beat crowding into a variety of cars — the kind of transportation I had become accustomed to since getting into music management. In the sixties, it wasn't unusual for the members of a band to squeeze into a station wagon, jam a few amps and instruments in the back, travel from Toronto to Ottawa to play a gig, and then drive home the same night.

So for the entire tour, day after day, I would watch the Everly Brothers go their separate ways, then each evening hit the stage, give each other a big hug, and proceed to play some of the most amazing songs ever recorded. Their harmonies, which had even influenced the Beatles, gave me and the audience goosebumps every night. The shows were magic, and the fact that they made it onto the stage each night without killing each other was even more astounding.

The pianist in the Everlys' band was Warren Zevon, a fine songwriter who would go on to have his own solo career and a huge hit single with "Werewolves of London." Murray and Warren became fast friends during the tour. Warren loved Murray's song "Honky Red," and Murray was very fond of Zevon's "Carmelita." They agreed that as soon as they had the opportunity, each would record the other's song. A year later Murray recorded "Carmelita" on his self-titled album, and as far as I know he was the first performer of any stature to record a cover of one of Warren's songs. Warren never recorded "Honky Red," but I did have the pleasure of hearing him play it on the tour.

During the time that I hired Shelly Siegel and Murray joined the Everly Brothers' tour, I started thinking about Murray's second album. CBS in the U.S. had an option on Murray, with the right to release his next album there as part of True North's deal with CBS Canada. I thought he had the right stuff to make it in America and I was determined to give it my best shot. I started to put big pressure on CBS Canada to live up to the option I had given them and they responded. With their help I got in touch with Epic Records, the American label in the CBS family that was often used to release non-domestic acts. I had meetings with Walter Yetnikoff, head of CBS International; Ron Alexenburg, head of Epic; and Don Ellis, VP of A & R. All three seemed ready to work with us. The main topic of conversation was picking a producer for the new record. My goal was to make the American company a part of the process so it wouldn't feel like we were just dropping a finished record on their already full laps. Nothing had been decided but we were well ahead of the game, seeing how Murray wasn't quite ready to start recording in any case.

One day not long after the Everly Brothers tour had finished, I got a call from Shelly. From a jail in Vancouver. He'd been busted for marijuana possession. In those days, if you had more than a single joint the police would charge you with trafficking, and that was what they were going to do to Shelly. I arranged to pay his bail but his days working for True North were drawing to a close by his own choice. He was a wonderful person and I would have gladly kept him on, but he was totally consumed with his possible criminal conviction and wanted to spend as much time as possible fighting the charges. I was a bit shocked by the whole episode. It made me examine my own conduct more closely and although I didn't change my behaviour right away, I became somewhat more circumspect when it came to drugs.

As disappointed as I was about Shelly deciding his True North days were over I was secretly relieved. As little as I was paying Shelly, it was still more than I could afford. I didn't replace Shelly, but I certainly had a new love and respect for the West that I owe in part to my close relationship with him. I stayed in touch with him and we remained good friends. On trips to L.A., which is where he eventually moved, I would often stay at his place. He did eventually beat the drug charge and went on to have a very successful career in the music business. He was one of the original founders of Mushroom Records, which signed several great bands including Chilliwack and Heart. With Heart, led by Ann and Nancy Wilson, he had three consecutive international hit singles in 1976: "Dreamboat Annie," "Magic Man," and "Crazy on You." I like to think that while I was learning from Shelly, he was picking up the odd thing or two from me. Shelly's career tragically ended in 1979 when, at only thirty-two, he died of a brain aneurysm.

By early 1972, the time had come for Bruce to play larger halls across Canada, the so-called "soft-seaters" like Toronto's Massey Hall, Vancouver's Queen Elizabeth Theatre, and the National Arts Centre in Ottawa, all of which had capacities of around 2,500 seats. But it's one thing to decide it's time to make the move and another to figure out how to make it happen. With both Murray and Bruce consistently playing and selling out the Riverboat, I had been spending a lot of time with the club's owner B. C. (Bernie) Fiedler, whom I'd known since the sixties. Bernie knew how successful both of my artists were becoming because he was often the one at the door selling the tickets! It was impossible to spend any time in Yorkville and not know about the city's most famous folk club and its owner. Both were local institutions. Going back to my time with the Paupers and Kensington Market, I would frequently pop my head into the club to check out the acts playing at the Boat. They were always great. I knew Bernie was promoting many of Gordon Lightfoot's concerts, so I approached him with the idea of presenting Bruce at Massey Hall. One thing led to another and the talk turned to doing a cross-Canada tour. Bernie came up with the idea of involving Marty Onrot, who was at this time one of Canada's top concert promoters. Together they cooked up a proposal that covered the right cities and right venues, as well as appropriate artist guarantees, percentages, and promotion. I liked what I saw, so we worked out the details for a tour that would hit most of the country during November of 1972.

At the same time, Bruce was putting together the songs that would form his third album, *Sunwheel Dance*. We would eventually do ten albums in nine years; the tenth, 1979's *Dancing in the Dragon's Jaws*, contained the international hit "Wondering Where the Lions Are." Not that Bruce really needed a hit single to have a successful career, but it certainly made my job a lot easier, although maybe just a bit harder as well. But that's a different story and was still eight years in the future.

During the time I was working out the tour details with Fiedler and Marty, Fiedler had started talking to me about possibly getting involved in my management company. I was interested. As well as things were going for me, when you come right down to it, I didn't really have an organized business. Sure, I had an office, but I was always chronically short of money, and certainly didn't have a clue about accounting and bookkeeping. I was just plain disorganized – and I knew it. The important things were being done and I was even ahead of the curve when it came to the music and artists, but when it came to banking, financial records, and other items that a growing business required, there was no question that I needed help. I could also see that the headlining concert business, at least for my acts, was where we had to be pointed, and with all the things I had on my plate – from managing artists to music publishing, in addition to running a record label – I was more than just a bit busy. I also loved spending time in the recording studio, which meant there were plenty of nights when I just didn't sleep. It wasn't unusual for me to spend all day working in my office and then all night in a studio watching Gene produce our records and making whatever contributions I could to the recording process, requested or not.

So when Bernie said he wanted to get involved, I was intrigued by the idea. When he offered me some money, I became even more interested. My arrangement with Brazilian George had gone completely off the rails and I was ready to try something new. I decided to wait and see how the tour went. If it was successful and I enjoyed working with Fiedler, then I would take him up on his offer and form the partnership.

The tour went off without a major hitch. Not every show was a sellout but we did extremely well in all the right places, including a sold-out show at Massey Hall. I was impressed with the abilities of both Bernie and Marty. It wasn't lost on me that Marty Onrot seemed to be doing much of the work, but that was part of Fiedler's charm and also a trait that really appealed to me. What counted was the ability to bring good people into the picture who could get things done, not who actually did the heavy lifting. With the tour over I sat down with Bernie and we started to work out the details of our proposed partnership. Fiedler was to be represented in the final negotiations by a lawyer named Bernie Solomon. Later we would collectively be known as the Bernies, since Solomon became our company's lawyer and the three of us would spend lots of time together. We would not throw everything into the same shared pot but in the end we'd have a lot of ground covered under one roof: artist management, concert promotion, a record company, music publishing, and the Riverboat, the leading club in the country for our kind of music. It promised to be a sweet arrangement if we could pull it off. On top of all that, Bernie was also going to give me $10,000. Money that I sorely needed.

But things in the music business are never straightforward. It's not a business for the faint of heart. (Have I already told you that?)

Two incredibly distressing things happened almost simultaneously. First, Brazilian George served me with a lawsuit stating he was my legal partner. Second, the tax department claimed that Fiedler owed a significant amount of money in unpaid taxes. I had to move quickly to decide what to do under these extraordinary circumstances. I ignored whatever caution I had left in me and went forward with the deal with Bernie. I remember thinking right after we signed our contract that I wasn't really sure whether Bernie and I had become partners or whether the government of Canada and Brazilian George had just become partners. Either way, things were changing once again and I leapt into the void. I never once regretted the decision to join forces with Fiedler, although we had our share of stormy times before our partnership ended in 1982. But it was a great ten-year run.

One of the things that came up almost immediately was that Bernie was now unable to come up with the full ten thousand. I took five with a promise to receive the other half later. I never did get the other five but that was my choice. I let Bernie off the hook one day when we were playing chess in our office. By then it didn't matter much to me as things were moving along quite nicely.

Our management company was called Finkelstein-Fiedler and our first two clients were Bruce and Murray. The first thing we did was take Murray to New York for meetings with CBS. Our plan was to finish the work I had started with them, notably finding a producer for Murray's next album. Until then, I didn't have a contract with Murray, but Fiedler wanted our new company to have one and I could see how it was a prudent move. Although the details had been worked out and approved by Murray before we left Toronto, New York was the first opportunity we had to be together, so we signed the contract at a pharmacy in Manhattan, where we had it notarized. (It was not unusual for pharmacists to be notary publics in New York.)

The drugstore was just around the corner from the Russian Tea Room, where we were to have lunch with the three senior executives from CBS, Walter Yetnikoff, Ron Alexenburg, and Don Ellis. At that time in my life, the Tea Room was one of the most beautiful restaurants I had ever been in. I loved it. The decor was spectacular and the food was great. For many years, if I happened to be in New York on a Wednesday, I would go there for lunch, as it was the only day of the week that the restaurant served pelmeni, a Russian delicacy. Pelmeni, Russian Tea Room–style, are little dumplings served in a chicken broth into which a liberal dollop of sour cream and mustard have been blended. For my money, this is one of the great dishes in the world.

But pelmeni wasn't the only thing cooking at lunch that day. We had been kicking around the idea of hiring Ed Freeman to produce Murray's album and now the idea seemed even better, seeing as how Ed had just produced Don McLean's "American Pie," a single that had been number 1 in the U.S. for four straight weeks and would turn out to be the record of the year. Ed was interested and he was available to start work on the project right away. It seemed like a great opportunity, providing the chemistry between Ed and Murray was right.

Walter Yetnikoff was one of the true characters in our business. He had a reputation for being ruthless and capable of erupting at the drop of a hat, and for having a ferocious drug habit. None of these things seemed like a problem to me, and my own experiences with Walter were always positive.

Just after Murray's second album was released in the States we encountered problems crossing the border on our way to a show at Passim, a famous coffee house located in the heart of Cambridge, Massachusetts. In those days we never had proper visas. This was entirely out of ignorance of the procedure and it was usually easy enough to just go through American immigration and customs. It was nerve-wracking but I just didn't know how to approach getting the job done properly. A failing on my part for sure, but so far so good. We'd never had a problem although from time to time it was a bit of a nail biter.

On this occasion, after we landed at Boston's Logan Airport, Murray was thoroughly questioned at the immigration office, located just inside the terminal. He gave them our usual story — he was just visiting friends and would be in town for a few days. Although the immigration officer finally let him into the country, he issued Murray a BI visa for only two days. The visa would then have to be stamped by Canadian customs authorities upon his return. Our problem was that Passim was a four-night engagement. I had cleared immigration ahead of him, and when Murray and I met up at the luggage carousel we decided not to risk having a run-in with the U.S. government.

I sent Murray immediately back to Toronto and I did something I rarely ever did during my career: cancel a show. The owner of Passim, Bob Donlin, understood and was even sympathetic (and Murray would play at the club several more times in the future). Then I got Walter on the phone and explained the situation. I knew he was a lawyer and thought he might be able to help us. Walter was willing to see me the moment I arrived in New York.

A few hours later I was sitting in his office. Walter called in Gary Baker, one of CBS's in-house lawyers, and said, "This schmuck needs a visa, give him a hand." Gary explained the visa process to me and started a petition for us to get one, sponsored by CBS. About thirty days later, Murray had a visa. I ended up using Gary Baker to do visa work for me for many years. From that time on I made sure that my acts always had the proper visas, not only for America but for every country in which they toured. Today there is information on the visa process readily available and the Canadian Federation of Musicians will help artists get them. But back then, the Canadian music industry was still in its infancy and these kinds of legalities were hard to figure out. The real point of the story is that Walter was there when I needed him. Although we were never close friends, I have fond memories of him and I'd take him, with all his excesses and his fearsome reputation, over many of the people posing as music industry professionals in the business these days.

Murray's second album, simply called *Murray McLauchlan*, turned out to be a good one. While in New York recording the album Murray was inspired to write "Farmer's Song." The recording was pretty much finished by the time he wrote it and it could easily have been left off the album, but fortunately he and Ed Freeman decided to give it a last-minute shot. It was the simplest recording on the album and was about as close to a solo number as you could get without it being just guitar and voice. "Farmer's Song" would go on to be the biggest single of Murray's career, selling well over 50,000 copies in Canada alone, which in those days made it a gold record. The funny thing is that it wasn't even the A-side of the single. For those who may not remember, singles were seven-inch records with two sides. The A-side was always the song intended to be the hit, while the B-side was often just a throwaway number. Sometimes artists and record companies deliberately put another potential hit song on the B-side, hoping for a "two-sided hit." That's because occasionally DJs, music directors, or program directors would flip over a single and play the B-side.

Here's our story. The first single was picked after much consultation with CBS in Toronto and New York. We decided it would be a song called "Lose We" with "Farmer's Song" on the B-side, a decision I fought hard for. I thought that maybe after "Lose We" became a hit, we might be able to get some mileage from "Farmer's Song" on country radio. Even though Murray wasn't a traditional country artist, I thought commercial country radio programmers might like the song and the natural country twang in Murray's voice.

With the benefit of hindsight, it's easy to wonder what was wrong with all of us, especially me, that we didn't make "Farmer's Song" the A-side from the start. Or, if you're more charitable, you might marvel at how smart we were to have made "Farmer's Song" available, despite the fact that our record distributors on both sides of the border didn't have any interest in it. Well, there's an old saying that goes something like this: "If I said yes to everything I'd said no to, and no to everything I'd said yes to, things would turn out just about the same."

Let's just leave it at that, but the B-side was there by choice, and it turned out to be the best B-side of my career. "Lose We" was getting a bit of top-forty AM radio airplay, which was an improvement over anything on Murray's first album, but it wasn't exactly lighting up the phones. Finally we began to pay more attention to "Farmer's Song." I was all over the CBS Canada promo staff to get radio programmers to listen to the B-side and I started working the phones myself, calling everyone I could get hold of at country radio. Our first break came after a DJ named Ted Daigle at Ottawa's leading country station started playing it and reporting loads of requests. It didn't take long to spread the record to more stations, although there were certainly lots of holdouts at country radio, especially from those programmers who were into image, as opposed to music. By that I mean they were into playing the artist, not the song — no matter how good the record was, they just weren't going to play a folk singer from Toronto on their stations.

But things really began to take off in Canada when a few top-forty pop stations started playing the record and listeners began requesting it, as had happened at the country stations. Soon plenty of people were going into their local record stores and buying both the single and the album. "Farmer's Song" was off and running. Murray had his hit, and I was over the moon. The record went top ten on all of the big three radio formats of the era — country, top-forty, and adult contemporary. True North had its first-ever gold record. We would end up with over forty of them before it all ended, but for me none ever felt as sweet as this one.

Murray would go on to have many other hits, even though making hit singles wasn't really his game. And you could say the same about True North Records. But we all liked hearing our music on the radio.

Sadly, I couldn't break "Farmer's Song" in the U.S. After Epic released "Lose We" with little result, the company pretty much gave up on the album. When "Farmer's Song" began climbing the charts in Canada, I flew down to New York for a morning meeting at Epic, to ask them to consider working "Farmer's Song" for us. This was during the time of Epic's major involvement in Gamble and Huff's wildly successful label, Philadelphia International, the home of the O'Jays and Harold Melvin & the Blue Notes. They were having number-one records, one after another, with songs like "Backstabber," "Love Train," and "If You Don't Know Me by Now." Not only was radio full of these Epic recordings but it was also the time of the Spinners, who were in the middle of a run of great songs like "I'll Be Around," "Could It Be I'm Falling in Love," and "One of a Kind (Love Affair)." I loved all of these records, and it certainly wasn't lost on me that I was not exactly going to be the guy to fill the pipeline with more of the same. In other words, it wasn't the best time to be sitting with a successful, hard-nosed record executive in his Manhattan office telling him that he should get excited by a record called "Farmer's Song" that wasn't exactly pop, rock, or country. Which, to record executives, means it's neither fish nor fowl. Still, I was going to give it my best shot.

When I walked into Ron's office that morning, he had his Gucci loafers up on his desk with the sound system at ten playing "Love Train" by the O'Jays. Ron was likeable but he could also be abrasive. Before we could get into a real discussion about my reason for being there he took a call and abruptly left to attend a meeting upstairs. We agreed to meet again at two that afternoon. With a little time to kill I did what any respectable person would do. I went to the Gucci store around the corner on Fifth Avenue and bought my first pair of Guccis, in brown suede, which I wore back to CBS. When we reconvened in his office at two, I put my new shoes on Ron's desk. He burst out laughing and asked what he could do for me.

Ron didn't feel that he could do much with "Farmer's Song" out of the New York office without the help of their country division in Nashville. He agreed to set up a meeting for me with the top country label executives and we would decide the next move based on the results. I flew to Nashville that same evening.

Epic's Nashville division was the home of the great country artist Charlie Rich, of "Behind Closed Doors" fame. The guys in

Nashville were courteous and seemed to be interested but I could tell this was going to be an uphill battle. Murray's style just wasn't going on in Nashville at that time. The "Americana" sound, as it would come to be known, would take another thirty-odd years to come to Nashville and was at best only a distant rumour during my meeting there. Murray was truly on the cutting edge of something new and exciting. A mix of country, folk, and rock, but Nashville wanted lots of twang. Epic gave the song a modest shot but nothing really came of it.

Still, Murray did have his first hit in Canada and his reputation started to grow in the U.S. Looking back, it saddens me that I was unable to get that record off the ground in the States, but then, if the music business teaches you anything, it's to be prepared for disappointment even when you're having some success. So, even while we were receiving our gold single in Canada, I was feeling let down by what seemed like an obvious failure to get that song charted south of the border.

Nothing worth having comes without some kind of fight

Got to kick at the darkness til it bleeds daylight

"Lovers in a Dangerous Time"
Bruce Cockburn

CHAPTER ELEVEN

Bernie Fiedler turned out to be a good partner, and by 1974 our company was moving along at a great clip. Both Murray and Bruce were regularly touring across Canada, playing many of the biggest theatres in the country, such as Toronto's Massey Hall, Montreal's Place des Arts, Vancouver's Queen Elizabeth Theatre and the Orpheum, and the Jubilees in Calgary and Edmonton. There's something quite wonderful about these venues. They are all loaded with a mystique that comes from hosting so many great performing artists from so many disciplines on their stages over the years. The feeling I used to get with a sold-out house in these places, and still do, is very special, and the pay isn't to be sneezed at either.

Let me explain the concert business a bit. Using rough figures, let's say the theatre has 2,000 sellable seats at $50 a head. That's $100,000 coming in for a full house. There are all kinds of deals out there but, to make it simple, let's say the performer's take from the show amounts to 60 per cent. That's $60,000. The other $40,000 goes toward the costs, including the hall rental, advertising, staff and crew charges, catering, the promoter's profit, and . . . well, the list can be endless. A manager might be taking somewhere between 15 and 25 per cent of that $60,000. Keep in mind, too, that to get to that venue your artist may have been performing for many, many months or, in some cases, even years, in circumstances where the split amounted to pennies. In the end, if you're in the music business for the money, you're in the wrong business. Still, it could pay, and when it did, it paid out quite nicely, thank you very much.

In the mid-seventies we hired a young man named Rob Bennett to come in and help us with our burgeoning concert business. Rob was the music editor for *The Varsity*, the University of Toronto's student newspaper, and on the side was running shows on the campus with some regularity. He was also a friend of Liz Braun, who was our assistant at the time. Liz went on to become a journalist and is still at the *Toronto Sun*. Liz is fond of reminding me that I didn't want to hire her because I didn't think that anyone with a university degree should have to work for a high-school dropout, especially in the music business.

Aside from the shows we were doing with Bruce and Murray, Finkelstein-Fiedler was regularly promoting shows for outstanding acts such as Harry Chapin, Joni Mitchell, Tom Waits, Leonard Cohen, James Taylor, and John Prine. Often Fiedler would book artists into the Riverboat and just a few months later they'd be riding the top of the charts and back in Toronto selling out a concert hall. For example, I recall hearing James performing "Fire and Rain" to a half-full late show at the Riverboat in early 1970 and then, in what seemed like only a matter of weeks, "Fire and Rain" was a top-ten hit and he was back in town playing Massey Hall.

With or without hit singles, the early to mid-seventies was the era of the singer-songwriter and we were right in the middle of it. As I had guessed earlier, putting all of the elements under one roof – concert promotion, management, publishing, and record label – turned out to be a good call.

We rarely did a show without throwing a party afterwards, more often than not at Fiedler's place. For a while we all lived in the same building on Alexander Street right behind Maple Leaf Gardens. At one point, Murray, Lightfoot, Fiedler, and I were all living there at the same time. (On top of that, we also had a separate suite that was a dedicated office where we housed all our companies.) The parties were always good, plenty of booze, drugs, and women. Fiedler knew how to throw a party, something I enjoyed but had no real aptitude for. Our partnership was a perfect yin-yang while it lasted. Bernie Fiedler was the social director and I was the friendly neighbourhood socialist. Well, not really, but working was more fun than partying as far as I was concerned, not that I didn't enjoy those evenings.

In 1973 we got a call from Elliot Roberts, Neil Young's and Joni Mitchell's manager. Elliot was partners with David Geffen and we had become friendly with both of them. The company had been promoting shows on behalf of their two Canadian stars in Ontario for some time. Both Joni and Neil had started off at the Riverboat well before I had become associated with Fiedler.

The previous year, Neil's album *Harvest* had become a huge hit. The best-selling album of 1972, it included the worldwide number-one hit single "Heart of Gold." Although Neil was selling out arenas, he was now going to do a special tour called *Tonight's the Night* and wanted to open it in Canada. Elliot asked us to look into booking three shows, which of course we were more than happy to do. At this same time, despite the fact that

Murray had just had his hit with "Farmer's Song," it was unclear to us if he was ready to sell out Massey Hall. We didn't want to book him there unless we were confident it would be packed to the rafters. There just wasn't room for empty seats during your Massey Hall debut.

So we suggested to Elliot that Murray could open up the *Tonight's the Night* shows in Ontario. A day later Elliot called back and told us that Neil thought it was a good idea and we were set to go. What a tour it turned out to be. Neil Young was sitting on top of the world after *Harvest*, yet still taking chances, pushing the envelope. Each night the roadies prepared the stage with props, including a life-size drugstore Indian. Neil was accompanied by his band Crazy Horse and playing the songs from his yet-to-be-released album. Many of the songs were about one of his roadies, Bruce Berry, and Danny Whitten, a former member of Crazy Horse, both of whom had died from drug overdoses. These were seriously great songs played with more emotion than I had ever heard in live music up to that point. The energy and music were so powerful that even now it still reverberates in my mind. I feel my life is better for having had the experience of being on that tour.

The match-up between Murray and Neil was perfect, and Murray was extremely well received during the Ontario tour. By the last show, he had been invited to continue on the tour through the U.S. For the American leg, the shows were to be opened by Nils Lofgren with his band, Grin, followed by Murray accompanied by his bassist, Dennis Pendrith. Then Neil would hit the stage with Crazy Horse, including Nils on guitar. It was a wild tour with every show sold out. Most of the halls held around 3,000 people – even though Neil probably could have sold 20,000 tickets in each market – so the lucky ticket-holders brought a feeling of near-pandemonium to the auditoriums. But the U.S. tour was sometimes difficult for Murray. Though he was well-received some nights, on others his experience was miserable. One night, a contingent of fans just kept on yelling "Neil, Neil" all the way through Murray's set. Murray was a bit shaken by that but things lightened up when Neil came into his dressing room and said, "Don't let them get you down." And, he added, "Watch during my show and you'll see the same people yelling the same thing, *even when I'm onstage.*" We watched and, sure enough, it was true.

Still, it was a wonderful tour and Neil deserves every single bit of praise he's ever received. His shows and songs were mighty and still are, and I for one was glad to see him finally release the album *Tonight's the Night* a few years later.

We started the tour riding on Neil's bus. Like the transportation for the Everly Brothers tour, Neil was using an old-fashioned day coach with bench seats. On the first day of the U.S. segment I met Neil's tour manager, a very young Irving Azoff. Elliot Roberts had done the Canadian shows but had sent Irving out for the American dates. Today, as chairman of Azoff Music Management, Irving is one of the most powerful people in the music business, representing many acts, including the Eagles, Josh Groban, Steely Dan, and Christina Aguilera. In those days, Irving was just getting started. He was more than pleasant to work with and treated Murray and me well. There was something in the manner that Irving handled things that made me think that I would be hearing more from him. As indeed we all did.

Starting with the release of True North's first album in 1970 I had set out to learn as much as I could about how the record business really worked. I considered any hour that I wasn't talking to someone about the business to be a wasted opportunity. Apart from being able to spot and work with talented musicians and songwriters — and that remains for me the most important part of the business — there was a whole world of disciplines to learn. And unlike my days in school, I was voracious in my studies.

I was constantly on the phone with people from radio, retail, and the press. When I wasn't talking or hanging out with these folks I was speaking to anyone who would take my call at CBS, our Canadian distributor. It didn't take me long to understand that no matter how sincere people were regarding their commitment to your records, in the end the only person you could really rely on 100 per cent of the time was yourself. CBS had offices across the country and when we had an act going into these markets I would call everyone at the branch to make sure they were doing everything they could to help us out. Whether it was getting people out to the shows, moving larger quantities of the albums into the stores, or pushing for more airplay and media coverage, I was always in their face. I thought it was my job and I enjoyed it.

I would constantly visit radio stations, meeting with their music directors, program directors, station owners — just about anyone who would talk to me and listen to our music. I did the same at retail, meeting the buyers, the owners, and even the people working in the warehouses. I especially enjoyed meeting the guys and gals who worked the front of the stores. They were the people in contact with the public and on the front lines. I had a lot to learn from them. Yes, they were being told by their bosses what records had to be on the front racks, but I knew they had some discretion and I wanted some of those prime spots. I also wanted them to chat up the casual buyer about this new great record that had just come in from True North. I did exactly the same with the press. I was continually inviting them to drop into the studio while we were recording so they could get the inside track on the work being done there. My life started to consist of never-ending travel from coast to coast meeting anyone and everyone I could, but it wasn't a hardship. I was truly enjoying it.

Almost everyone I met wanted to help out in one way or another, and seemed to genuinely enjoy hearing the music before it was released to the general public. Many of the people I visited weren't used to spending time with someone who was actually involved in getting the records made. I found that I could talk and talk about my artists and no one ever walked out on me, although I'd bet that there were a few who wanted to. I was constantly buying lunch and dinner for the people I was meeting with and it wasn't unusual for all of us to get high and then listen to a record that True North was about to release or was still working on.

I understood that many of the records we were releasing weren't necessarily commercial enough for the big radio stations, so I would convince the local promo reps to work with the smaller stations, as well as with the smaller newspapers. Nothing was too small for True North. Keep in mind that CBS was releasing thousands of records every year and many of them were huge hits by major international stars. To get them to pay attention to some of the stuff we were releasing, and then to devote time to dealing with the smaller media players, was not always easy, but I was lucky to have some real believers inside the company helping me out in important ways. Not only do I owe many of those people a great deal of gratitude but I also have to thank them for teaching me the ins and outs of the record business and consequently how the music business worked from the inside out. There was a genuine curiosity about the growing Canadian music business and I always had time to talk about it. I think it was a two-way street. Everyone had something to teach me and I had something to give back to them.

At the same time as Murray earned his gold single for "Farmer's Song," Bruce continued to put out a quiet stream of great albums, each one doing better than the last. A friend of Bruce's, singer-songwriter David Wiffen, had landed a contract with United Artists in the U.S. and it looked like he was in for some real success. Bruce had worked with David in 3's a Crowd during the time they were both living in Ottawa. David was clearly one of the most talented songwriters of his time, and he was blessed with a deep baritone voice. His songs could tear your heart apart, but sadly so could his life. He was troubled and had turned to the bottle. United Artists was a large American label and the executives there were not pleased with the progress being made on David's album. The project had started with Brian Ahern at the helm but it just wasn't working out. Ahern was a very talented producer who had worked on Anne Murray's *Snowbird* and who would go on to produce and marry Emmylou Harris, but the circumstances surrounding the recording sessions had become as troubled as David himself.

One day I got a call from Wiffen's manager, Harvey Glatt, informing me of the situation. There was a very real possibility that David was not going to be able to finish the album in the state he was in. Harvey told me that as a consequence Wiffen could possibly lose his recording contract with UA. Harvey had the idea that Bruce might be able to step in and finish the album with David.

Bruce has never really wanted to be a producer although the few times he tried he was good at it. It just wasn't something that appealed to him. But the opportunity to help his friend David was not one he could easily ignore, so he reluctantly agreed to take on the job. Bruce assembled a crackerjack band consisting of Dennis Pendrith on bass, Pat Godfrey on piano, John Savage on drums, and himself on lead guitar. Some nights the sessions would move along fabulously well, but other nights David would be unable to proceed. At these times, Bruce would play David's rhythm parts, doing his best imitation of David's style, and then go back into the studio and overdub his own lead parts. In some ways, it was a traumatic experience for Bruce, but during those sessions he decided that it was a waste to have this good a band standing around doing nothing, so he began to put into place the pieces for his next recording, *Night Vision*, which would become a break-through album for him.

After completing David's album, called *Coast to Coast Fever*, which turned out to be a remarkable record, Bruce immediately started to record the tracks for *Night Vision*. Enlisting the same band and recording at Thunder Sound, he called in Gene Martynec to co-produce and ended up making a very special album. Released in 1973, it became the first gold album for both Bruce and True North.

Apart from the music, the record was notable for several other reasons. Over Christmas, just prior to the recording sessions, Bruce had received a book of paintings by Maritime artist Alex Colville. One day while leafing through the book we stopped at a painting called *Horse and Train*. It's a beautiful but ominous image of a horse galloping at full speed down a railway track, heading right towards an oncoming train. The viewer is left with the lingering question of what is about to happen – will the horse jump off the tracks or collide with the train?

It seemed to sum up the feeling of the album Bruce was making. *Night Vision* was no longer Bruce Cockburn fully rooted in the folk genre. It contained a mélange of styles, including rock, blues, and jazz. We decided that we would try to get the rights to use the Colville painting. The album's art director, our friend Bart Schoales, tracked down the painting, which was on display at the Art Gallery of Hamilton at McMaster University. Off we went to see it. It was perfect. Now all we had to do was get Alex Colville's permission to use it. I found his number and gave him a call at his home in Wolfville, Nova Scotia. He was gracious but not too sure how he felt about our idea, and asked me to call him back in a few days.

I decided that Bruce and I should fly out to Wolfville to meet him regardless of what his answer was going to be. The next day, I called Alex and he said he had been talking to his kids, who were fans of Bruce's music, and he was inclined to say yes to our request. I told him that we wanted to come out to Nova Scotia to meet with him anyway, so, a few days later, we flew to Halifax and drove a rental car to Wolfville to spend a great day with Alex. We visited his studio and then went for lunch in a small café in town. Alex gave us permission to use the painting even when he found out it was going to be folded into a gatefold-style jacket. Bart had come up with an innovative way to use the painting so that it kept the work's integrity but still made a wonderful and compelling cover. *Night Vision* won for Bart and True North the 1974 Juno Award for best Album Graphics. In the folk category that same year, both *Night Vision* and David Wiffen's *Coast to Coast Fever* were nominated for album of the year. With Murray's *Day to Day Dust*, an album that I co-produced, True North had yet another nomination in that category. However, none of these albums won. That honour went to Gordon Lightfoot for *Old Dan's Records*.

A bit of non-musical trivia that arose from *Night Vision* could be found in the liner notes. Bruce had thanked several people for their inspiration, among them Samuel R. Delany, the great African-American science fiction author, for his book *Driftglass*. Later, in 1976, Delaney published his Nebula-nominated book *Triton*. Set in the distant future on one of the moons of Neptune, the story has one character singing several of Bruce's songs, including "Mama Just Wants to Barrelhouse All Night Long" and "The Blues Got the World," both of which are on the album. I'm a science fiction fan who believes Samuel Delany is one of the masters of the genre, so for me, this was one of life's wonderful small pleasures.

So now True North had its first gold single, "Farmer's Song," and its first gold album, *Night Vision*. No one was getting rich, but we were all doing fine.

Murray had made one album with Gene Martynec as producer and one with Ed Freeman, who had worked with Tom Rush and Don McLean. Now Murray thought it was time he should be producing his own records, but he still felt he could use some outside help. When he asked me whether I'd co-produce with him, I said, sure, why not? There certainly was no one else around who had heard Murray's songs and performances as many times as I had and I believed that what would eventually distinguish Murray would be the feel of the music, not the technical perfection of his recordings. Besides, we would have a first-rate engineer in the studio with us, so I took the job. What this meant is that while Murray was recording, I would be in the studio all night, then I'd go to the office, usually quite early in the morning, and work all day. Then I would return to the studio to do it all over again. Seemed like a reasonable schedule to me. The first album we did together, *Day to Day Dust*, wasn't bad but in hindsight probably not one of Murray's best. Those were still to come.

The sessions for *Day to Day Dust* were distinguished by the copious amounts of drugs – of all descriptions – in the studio. We had assembled a terrific band for the sessions, including ace guitarist Amos Garrett who was famous for his legendary guitar solo on Maria Muldaur's hit "Midnight at the Oasis." One of the strongest tracks on *Day to Day Dust* is a song called "Golden Trumpet." One night, we had done several takes of the song, with each one sounding entirely different from the others. The song was very spacey on its own, but that was magnified by the fact that everyone in the studio was stoned. With Murray playing on the studio floor, it was my job to sit in the sound booth and work with the engineer to ensure everything was getting on tape, and to identify the best takes and generally move things along, always looking for ways to maximize the impact of the song. Mostly it came down to whether it instinctively felt right to me, something that I did think I had an ear for.

I'd had a chance to work with several great producers by this point – Felix Pappalardi, Rick Shorter, Gene Martynec – and later on I'd work with such notables as Bob Ezrin, Colin Linden, and Jon Goldsmith. Each great in his own way. Producers are noted for several things: their music arrangement skills, technical wizardry, and, in some cases, their ability to pull hits out of the air. Each of these was also an extremely fine musician with a terrific ear. I did not bring all of that to the table, but I was enthusiastic and confident that I could help Murray find a way to make terrific records.

As the evening rolled on we continued recording "Golden Trumpet" and everyone kept getting higher and higher. Finally, after innumerable takes, I heard a version that I thought nailed the song. I called Murray and the band into the booth for a play-back. As usual we had the speakers up about as loud as you could get them and not make our eardrums bleed. The song ended and I asked everyone what they thought. Amos said it was out of tune and that we should do another one. Murray asked to hear it again. As it was playing, Murray whispered in my ear, "Don't let the musicians ruin my record." This was Murray's way of saying he liked it and we shouldn't let a thing like tuning ruin a great take. In other words, "feel" first. At the end of that second playback I said it was a wrap and that it was time to move on to another song.

You know, Amos wasn't really wrong. But "we fixed it in the mix," as they say, and the take we kept holds up well even today, and it really does feel good. How could you not love Murray?

Me and Murray in the recording studio

As a production team, Murray and I got better as time passed. His next record was *Sweeping the Spotlight Away*, which included one of his most famous and enduring songs, "Down by the Henry Moore." Murray had asked a young violinist and mandolin player named Ben Mink to be part of the sessions. Ben later became well-known as k.d. lang's producer and more recently co-produced Feist's enormous hit single "1 2 3 4."

At this time, though, Ben had very little recording experience. Much later, he told me his impression of his first time in the studio with Murray and me. We were recording "Down by the Henry Moore" and Ben remembers sitting in a corner of the studio with his headset on learning his mandolin part, which, by the way, plays a very prominent part in the final recording. After a few run-throughs, he heard my voice through the headphones asking him to come into the booth. A worried Ben thought he wasn't getting the part down well enough and that he was going to be fired. Instead, he was shocked to hear me say, "I think we've got it, Ben." He tried to tell us that he was still learning the part, but both Murray and I thought it sounded just fine. Listening to the record now, it's hard to imagine his part being any better than the version we released. Ben later became an important part of Murray's touring band, the Silver Tractors, and made several other records with him.

With the success of *Sweeping the Spotlight Away*, Murray finally made his debut at Massey Hall and, as we had hoped, it was sold out. That was quickly duplicated in all the major theatres across the country. Now the Finkelstein-Fiedler Management Company had two acts travelling across Canada playing the best venues and selling out on a regular basis. Bruce had followed up *Night Vision* with a wonderful album called *Salt, Sun and Time*, which was a complete left turn from anything else he had ever done. It was an acoustic album featuring only Bruce and his producer, Gene

Martynec, on guitars, but unlike his earlier recordings, this one had a real jazz twist. Changing direction would turn out to be something Bruce would do often throughout his career. He was never satisfied to repeat himself; he always pushed his own limits with little or no concern for commercial matters. This strategy didn't always lead to greater success but it always led to interesting and often spectacular artistic results.

By 1975 True North had released fifteen albums, not a large number, but the record company was moving along at a clip that was manageable and the results were pretty satisfactory, particularly on the artistic side.

On June 15, 1976, around the time that Murray's single "Boulevard" was high on the charts, we received a call from a friend asking if we'd seen the evening's news. Apparently the assistant general manager of the Canadian National Exhibition, Howard Tate, who was also responsible for booking the talent at the CNE's grandstand, had just been on the CBC show *24 Hours*, saying that he would never book a performer like Murray McLauchlan. He was being interviewed by the show's host Bruce Rogers, and the other guest was a well-known city alderman named Ben Nobleman, who was a strong supporter of Canadian talent and thought the CNE should feature more of it. What really stunned us was that Tate had apparently said Murray was too lewd.

There was a CBC office right next door to our offices at Alexander and Church so we called some people we knew there and made arrangements to take a look at the broadcast. Here's a bit of the transcript:

Mr. Nobleman: Why didn't you ask Murray McLauchlan [to play the CNE]?

Mr. Tate: Because I don't want that kind of a show on the grandstand, Ben, and you know better.

Mr. Nobleman: How do you know?

Mr. Tate: Because I have seen the show.

Mr. Nobleman: He is one of the top pop singers.

Mr. Rogers: What is wrong with him?

Mr. Tate: Well, his language, his story, his show, the whole darn thing, Bruce. I mean . . .

Mr. Nobleman: What is wrong with his language?

Mr. Tate: Lookit, Ben, you want your eight-year-old sitting in that stands and listening to this guy?

During that same interview the following exchange happened:

Mr. Nobleman: What about Bruce Cockburn?

Mr. Tate: No. We haven't approached him.

Mr. Nobleman: You haven't?

Mr. Tate: No. But who is Bruce Cockburn?

A little later, this exchange occurred:

Mr. Nobleman: No. It is not. You admitted – you admitted you didn't even try to call Murray McLauchlan and Bruce Cockburn.

Mr. Tate: I will not. I told you before I wouldn't have that type of show on the grandstand or even on the grounds of the band shell or anywhere. I don't want that kind of stuff on our grounds.

Mr. Nobleman: But you haven't even tried.

Mr. Tate: I don't want to try.

I talked it over with Murray and Fiedler and although none of us were too pleased we just shrugged it off. We still lived in a world where being a Canadian act meant you were constantly looked upon with suspicion, so who really cared what the assistant GM of the CNE thought? The dogs bark, but the caravan moves on.

However, the next morning, while I was eating breakfast, I got a call from another friend asking me if I had heard that morning's CBC radio show. So once again I called my contacts at the CBC and listened to a tape of it. And once again, it featured Mr. Tate, this time being interviewed by Harry Brown, the host of CBC's *Metro Morning*. All this was happening just five days after Murray had performed, with Gordon Lightfoot, Sylvia Tyson, and Liona Boyd, at a sold-out benefit for Canada's Olympic athletes at Maple Leaf Gardens. The following is in response to Mr. Brown asking Mr. Tate why the CNE didn't book more Canadian talent.

Mr. Tate:	Well, you name them and we will try and get them.
Mr. Brown:	Well, you know —
Mr. Tate:	No. This is fine. It is so easy because we are the Canadian National Exhibition, it is so easy to sit back and criticize but nobody comes up with any sound reasonably good names of Canadian talent that we can put on the grandstand. I asked the same question of Nobleman last night and Ben came up and made up a whole bunch of things that you wouldn't want your children to — to sit and listen to and there is no way we are going to change our policy.

Mr. Brown:	Tell me the ones that Mr. Nobleman suggested that I wouldn't want my kids to sit and listen to?
Mr. Tate:	Well, McLauchlan – McLauchlan for example.
Mr. Brown:	Murray McLauchlan?
Mr. Tate:	Yes. And also –
Mr. Brown:	Why wouldn't I want my kids to sit and listen to him?
Mr. Tate:	Well, I don't think you would because Nobleman said that certainly he would have to change his act and I agree with him but I don't think that he would do that and after all –
Mr. Brown:	Well, just a minute. The kids could sit and watch him at the – at the Maple Leaf Gardens the other night?
Mr. Tate:	That's fine. But we are not going to do that down here because we feel that this is a family outing and it is the only place left really in Metropolitan Toronto where you can bring your family and enjoy it without being offended and you can't take your kids to the theatres and things like this nowadays and enjoy a theatre without the exception of a very limited number of movies that are produced for kids and this is our policy.

One more snippet from the radio interview is interesting:

Mr. Brown:	Yesterday the C.N.E. announced part of its lineup for this year's grandstand shows and only one Canadian artist will appear, the Bachman-Turner Overdrive. Yesterday we spoke with Alderman Ben Nobleman of York. He is quite outraged and

	today we have the Assistant General Manager of the Canadian National Exhibition, Mr. Howard Tate, with us. Good morning, sir.
Mr. Tate:	Good morning, Harry, how are you? Okay?
Mr. Brown:	I am very well. Only one Canadian in seven?
Mr. Tate:	That's all we can get this year.
Mr. Brown:	Why are we not getting any better?
Mr. Tate:	We are getting better but the talent in Canada is not getting any better. At least they won't play here. We have endeavoured to get as much Canadian talent as we can.

As it turned out, the man responsible for booking all the talent at the CNE, a man who represented one of Canada's premier showplaces and should have been familiar with current Canadian music, knew so little that he had confused Murray with another act called MacLean & MacLean who, indeed, were known for their risqué songs and live shows. Strange that no one corrected him on the days between the interviews. But none of this really surprised me. Ignorance of Canadian talent was the norm rather than the exception in the 1970s.

Then, as if his confusion and consequent maligning of Murray's character wasn't bad enough, Tate also disparaged the entire Canadian musical community with the comment, "We are getting better but the talent in Canada is not getting any better."

I just couldn't see how we could let this stand. Murray's reputation had been called into question on both CBC TV and radio. Furthermore, it was a symbol of the battle we were all fighting, not only in our own hometown but right across the country. Simply, how did you get respect for Canadian talent in an environment that seemed to only have time for imported music? Fiedler and I decided to draw a line in the sand. We would sue the CNE for defamation and libel. Once we let the media know our intentions the story began to pick up momentum, alarming the CNE's executives enough for them to ask for an immediate meeting with us. They were to be represented by Julian Porter, who was not only the president of the CNE at that time but by coincidence one of the top libel lawyers in Canada. We were satisfied to be represented by our good pal Bernie Solomon.

During that meeting a member of the CNE's staff reminded us that Howard Tate had a family. I went crazy when I heard that and just about jumped across the table, screaming that we weren't from Mars, and that we also had families and that maybe, just maybe, Howard Tate and the CNE should have thought about that, before being so cavalier and uninformed in public. I'm not sure why, but right after my outburst their side excused themselves and retired into a private room. They returned a half-hour later and asked us what it would take for us to drop the action. We had already decided well before the meeting that what we wanted was a public apology. We weren't really looking for money, although had we wanted it we probably could have got what would amount to a small fortune, given our circumstances. Instead, we worked out the following deal:

1. CNE would hold a press conference where they would apologize to Murray and further apologize to the whole Canadian music business.
2. Howard Tate would be relieved of his talent-booking duties for the CNE and the new bookers replacing him would include Sam Sniderman, the founder of the Sam the Record

Man stores and a strong supporter of Canadian talent. This would be the first and last time I would have the opportunity to get Sam a job.

3. The CNE would pay for both our legal costs and the press conference.

4. The statement of apology would acknowledge that during the same week of Mr. Tate's unfortunate statements the following events were happening in Toronto:

    a. Rush had just sold out three nights at Massey Hall, grossing $42,000, which for the time represented a record gross for a rock 'n' roll band;

    b. April Wine had also just sold out Massey Hall, grossing $15,000, and was on a Canadian tour that was grossing over $1,000,000

    c. *Crawdaddy*, one of the leading music magazines in the U.S., had just hit the stands with an article on Bruce Cockburn, declaring him one of the most important artists of the decade;

    d. Gordon Lightfoot had put on a benefit show featuring Murray McLauchlan, Sylvia Tyson, and Liona Boyd that had grossed $191,000 between gate and television receipts;

    e. The CNE would buy full-page ads in both *RPM* and *Record Week* based on material supplied by Bernie Finkelstein and again apologizing to the Canadian music business.

The press conference was held on June 28. Journalist Larry LeBlanc, a well-known Canadian music journalist, and publicist extraordinaire Gino Empry were brought on board as experts.

The room was packed with interested observers from in and outside the music business. Pretty much all of the media that mattered were there. Even MacLean & MacLean responded to our invitation and showed up. Julian Porter was quite eloquent and publicly apologized to both Murray and the entire Canadian music business on behalf of the Canadian National Exhibition. They also ran the ads as promised. The story received major coverage right across the country. The CP wire story that was printed in every major paper across the country concluded:

> Finkelstein, in an interview following the news conference, said he accepts Porter's comments and regards them as sincere. "I think an attitude has been exposed," he said, "I think in the future they [CNE officials] will become more aware of the Canadian music scene. Once people are aware, they will take advantage of it. It's good for business."

Did any of this really matter? Yes, I think it did. An attitude that had been the conventional wisdom in Canada was publicly exposed as having no basis in fact. And, from that time on, those who were in positions to help us were more inclined to show Canadian musicians the respect they had earned.

Personally, I had and continue to have nothing against Howard Tate. I never did see him after this event. I don't think he was being malevolent nor did he harbour any ill will towards Murray. But he did represent an attitude that was a searing constant in our collective lives. For me it always felt like a war getting any recognition for Canadian music. Today, it's history, a topic that's been analyzed to death, so I won't go further into it. But when the opportunity came to shine a spotlight on the issue, we took it. I think Mr. Tate was not so different from all too many people in influential positions during that time. The only difference was that Mr. Tate was in a position to say what he thought publicly, instead of behind closed doors. Unfortunately for him and the CNE, we simply weren't interested in being any-one's target.

What you dream is what you get,

anything can happen

Following the big beat

If your dreams haven't happened yet,

you just keep dreaming

Following the big beat

And they call me Yellowjacket

'Cause I never run away

"Yellowjacket"
(Stephen Fearing and Tom Wilson)
Stephen Fearing

CHAPTER TWELVE

By 1975 the time had come to expand the management side of our business. I sat down with Fiedler one day and told him it was his turn to find an act for us. So far our only two management clients were Bruce and Murray, both of whom I had brought to the company. Bernie was an important part of the equation but on a day-to-day basis I was looking after the majority of the details concerning them and their business. Bernie agreed with me, and when he did find the act, a short time later, it was a good one.

We had started celebrating our various sold-out concerts by taking everyone involved for a post-show dinner. More often than not we would end up at Noodles on Bay Street, where it wasn't unusual for us to spend a few thousand dollars on a dinner for ten to fifteen people. Sometimes we'd go back to Fiedler's apartment on Alexander Street and continue the festivities well into the wee hours of the morning. I was beginning to develop a taste for good food and especially for good wine. I recall being enamoured of a 1972 Pouilly-Fuissé, a wine that we'd often clean Noodles right out of. This was our version of "café society." We were having loads of fun, the conversation was good, the veal was great, and the world seemed right side up. Certainly we were excessive in our habits and we wore the joy of having achieved a certain degree of success right on our sleeves for everyone to see. Working and play- ing around the clock was the norm, not the exception.

Known to everyone as "the Bernies," our reputations as managers and concert promoters were growing. We began getting calls almost every day from acts of all kinds, some known, some not, wanting us to either record them, manage them, or promote their club or concert shows. But we were quite selective, even in our often-blurry state of mind.

Both Fiedler and I liked to play poker. Fiedler, in particular, thought he was good at it, and he was always hooking up to some pretty high-stake games. Every once in a while I'd join him at the table. One evening we went to a game at the Four Seasons Hotel on Yorkville. There were some pretty sharp players gathered around the green felt and by 5 a.m. we had lost around $2,500, a considerable amount in 1976, no matter who you were. We were pretty sure we were being cheated but we weren't sure exactly how. What we did know is that even when one of us had a full house, with, say, jacks on top, one particular player would end up with a similar hand but with kings on top. After this happened several times we packed it in. I hoped we would be able to find a way to get our money back, but I wasn't sure how.

One afternoon, a few weeks later, Fiedler called me from the Twenty-Two Bar at the Windsor Arms Hotel. The card player that we thought had cheated us – let's call him Terry – was there having a drink and Fiedler had engaged him in a conversation about cards and other types of gambling. Along the way, he convinced him to shoot pool with me. For money, of course. Now, Fiedler wouldn't have known how good Terry was, but he instinctively thought that I could beat him. He was anxious for me to get over to the nearest poolroom, which happened to be located on Bloor Street, and give it a shot. I hadn't been shooting that much pool since the music business had started to take up all of my waking hours, but to me it was a bit like riding a bike; I figured I could still shoot a pretty reasonable game.

The truth is, the last time I had played was in Chicago some six months previously. Murray and I had a night off during his engagement at the Earl of Old Town, an ancient and celebrated folk and blues bar in one of Chicago's more rundown – but totally cool – areas. We were with singer-songwriters John Prine and Stevie Goodman and had ended up in a pretty funky bar looking to shoot some pool. However, at this bar the only way to get a table and stay on it was to beat any and all challengers. I worked my way onto a table and proceeded to keep on winning. I guess I was focused on the game because after awhile Prine whispered in my ear that we would all be better off if I lost a game and we got the hell out of there. Apparently he had sensed the locals weren't too happy with me and there was a growing consensus to show me the wrong end of a cue. When it came to matters like this in Chicago, I trusted John and, at the first opportunity, lost a game, and we quickly left the bar and ended up in another joint for a nightcap.

So, I met up with Bernie and Terry at the poolroom near Bloor and Bellair. As we started the match I sized him up and could see that I should be able to beat him, although I'd have to be at my best, seeing how I was out of practice. As the night went on I finally reached the point where not only had I won back our $2,500 but I'd made an additional grand. I was pleased that one of the few skills I had learned during my high-school days had finally been put to good use.

One problem, though: when it came time to pay, Terry revealed that he only had $1,000 on him. He gave us a promissory note for the additional $2,500, payable in three days. Three days came and went with no word from Terry. This went on for a few weeks and finally Fiedler and I became really angry. After all, Terry wasn't paying up, even though he'd had our money in his pocket under questionable circumstances.

A little known fact about the Riverboat was that located right above it, on the second floor, was a company called Haitian Imports, whose owner Bernie had befriended. His name was Albert Volpe and he was alleged to have ties to the mob in Toronto. I don't know if the stories about Albert were true or not, but I do know that Albert used to give Bernie a hand from time to time during the day, doing odd carpentry jobs around the Riverboat. Just being neighbourly. So one day Bernie told Albert about our problem with Terry and asked if he could help us out. A few days later we got our money, and Bernie and I decided it would be wise not to ask how it had happened. We also agreed never to put ourselves in that kind of situation again. Sure, we continued playing poker, but we became more careful about who was at the table with us.

During this period, Fiedler was still keeping his eye out for a new artist for our company to manage. One night I got an excited call from the Riverboat. Bernie was over the top with enthusiasm and wanted me to drop everything and get right down to the club, which I was unable to do. However, the artist he wanted me to see would be playing the following night as well, and I told Bernie I'd be there for sure to see what the excitement was all about. Bernie had found his act.

The artist was a young singer-songwriter named Dan Hill. I'd been hearing him a bit on radio. He had a single out on the

GRT label that was making some noise, a rather beautiful song called "You Make Me Want to Be." The next evening I caught Dan's show at the club and knew that Bernie had found our next management client. Dan had something different from the more roots-based singer-songwriters who usually played at the Riverboat. His songs were more romantic, deeply rich in melody, and both he and his performance skills were entirely engaging. I said to Fiedler, "Let's do it."

We immediately made a deal with Dan to become his managers and started to work with GRT, his record company, to maximize the single and get the company to release the full album as soon as possible. Working with Dan was a pleasure. He had a great interest in the business side of the music industry, much more than either Murray or Bruce did. Dan liked following the charts and was eager to know how things worked from A to Z. I enjoyed that because I found the business, although it was slowly becoming just about all I had time for, so engrossing that it was the main thing I was interested in. As a client, Dan was a willing and enthusiastic partner.

By the time we got around to releasing his second album, *Hold On*, Dan's records were being released outside of Canada on the 20th Century Fox label, through a deal we had helped put together with GRT. In Canada his sophomore record had gone gold, and he was already playing the major theatres here.

By the middle of 1976 we were in an enviable position. We now managed three acts and they were all selling out just about every theatre in Canada and making progress around the world.

Aside from the management business, True North was on the rise as well. I had made a deal with Island Records to distribute the label in the U.S. Between that deal and our relationship with 20th Century Fox for Dan's record, I found myself spending a lot of time in L.A. There is no better city to be in if you're single, in the music business, have some extra change in your pocket, and are not overly concerned about tomorrow.

Life was easy there: valets parked your car and drugs were plentiful. An old friend of mine from the Toronto scene, Cathy Smith, would often be around the city and would always have some cocaine. I had met Cathy when she was living with Gordon Lightfoot. Murray McLauchlan had used her as a backup singer on the song, "Do You Dream of Being Somebody," from *Sweeping the Spotlight Away*, which I co-produced. Cathy had always treated me well and I really liked her. She was full of life and always seemed gracious and kind. Yet this was the same Cathy Smith who, in 1982, would be convicted and jailed for the murder of John Belushi. Maybe I got it wrong, but I saw her as more of a victim of the entertainment business's excesses than a criminal.

Bernie Fiedler, Dan Hill, and me

In L.A. I stayed at L'Ermitage Hotel on Burton Way, one of the finest hotels in the city. I was living the good life, sitting around the rooftop pool, drinking champagne and eating strawberries. I was spending money as fast as I made it but there was plenty of it coming in. Maybe not millions, but between our management business, the label, and concert promotion we were doing just fine. After years of riding around in the back of station wagons going from gig to gig I felt I could afford to live a little, or a lot, depending on your point of view.

Island was preparing to release Murray's new album, *Boulevard*, as well as Bruce's latest recording, *In the Falling Dark*. *Boulevard* was a terrific album, in my opinion the best he had done to date, and I felt similarly about Bruce's latest. Cockburn had outdone himself with this one. Even though it didn't have a single on it – a fact I was getting used to by then – *In the Falling Dark* contained some of the most powerful writing and playing Bruce had done, including the masterful "Lord of the Starfields" and the superb instrumental "Islands in a Black Sky." This was the album that established him as one of the leading innovators in the singer-songwriter field.

The albums by the three artists we represented – *Hold On*, *Boulevard*, and *In the Falling Dark* – went gold in Canada around the same time. In the U.S., all three of the records received very positive attention. Cockburn's actually charted on *Cashbox* at number 196. That's hardly a major breakthrough, but it proved that people were noticing him. I could feel we were all close to something big happening; it was just a question of when and what.

As it turned out, 1977 would be a landmark year. The year before I had met a woman I liked a lot named Ronney Abramson and we had moved in together. Ronney was a fine singer-songwriter, so it made sense that she would make a record for

True North. I hired Dan Hill's producers Matt McCauley and Fred Mollin and they helped her record *Stowaway*, Ronney's first True North album.

I went back into the studio with Murray to work on his follow-up recording to *Boulevard*, his first gold album and biggest seller to date. For months he had been touring Canada with his band, the Silver Tractors, which consisted of bassist Dennis Pendrith, drummer Jorn Anderson, Gene Martynec on guitar, and Ben Mink on mandolin and violin. This was one awesome band. Murray was at the top of his game. We had rented a GMC motorhome to do the tour and hired Bart Schoales as our driver and tour manager. It was like old times with the Kensington Market, only now my artist had a few hits under his belt and was playing to full houses from coast to coast.

Murray goes gold. We're smokin' in so many ways

Meanwhile, for the first time Bruce was able to sell out two shows at Massey Hall. We recorded them for what would become a live double album, *Circles in the Stream*, which was released in 1978.

In perhaps the most unlikely turn of events for Fiedler and me, 1977 was the year we became part-owners in a radio station. The year before, we decided to make an investment in a new venture being put together by my old friend Harvey Glatt, the former owner of Ottawa's Le Hibou. Glatt was now in concert promotion and owned the Treble Clef record store chain. When the licence for the 106.1 FM frequency became available, he applied to the CRTC and, on March 25, 1977, CHEZ-FM started broadcasting in Ottawa. We had to scramble to raise our share of the investment and, looking back, I wish we had found more loose cash, since being involved in that station turned out to be a great move. Although my involvement was quite hands-off, I had the pleasure of seeing the station grow into a regional powerhouse. By 1985, CHEZ would end up owning a majority stake in CKIK, a large station in Calgary. A year later it acquired two sister stations in Smiths Falls, located an hour southwest of Ottawa. I continued to own my shares in CHEZ until Harvey sold the company to Rogers Radio, a division of media giant Rogers Communications Inc., in 1999. I find it ironic that despite my ongoing battles with broadcasters over the years, in the end the most successful investment I ever made was in radio.

We helped Dan Hill get a deal with ATV Music, a large music publisher in L.A., where the idea was hatched of hooking Dan up with the great songwriter Barry Mann. Barry and his wife, Cynthia Weil, had written some of the biggest and best pop songs of all time. "You've Lost That Loving Feeling" (the Righteous Brothers), "On Broadway" (the Drifters), "Uptown" (the Crystals), and "We Got to Get Out of This Place" (The Animals) were among their monster hits. Seeing himself as a singer-songwriter, Dan understandably had some initial concerns about this kind of co-writing arrangement, but he went along with it and the results were magic.

I'll never forget the morning Fiedler and I were having breakfast with Dan at the Polo Lounge in the Beverly Hills Hotel. The Polo Lounge was right out of the movies. You had the feeling that Errol Flynn, Rita Hayworth, and Elizabeth Taylor might still have been in the cabanas located just behind the restaurant. Everyone there was in show business in one way or another. This was Hollywood and Beverly Hills at their most extravagant.

Suddenly we heard Dan being paged by a dwarf dressed to the nines in a very fancy, quasi-military style uniform and carrying a portable phone. Barry Mann was on the line. Dan and Barry had been working the day before on a set of Dan's older lyrics. Barry had put new music to the words and had more or less finished the core of a song called "Sometimes When We Touch." Barry played us the song over the phone. It struck me right from the beginning that this was something special. Dan returned to Barry's place and the two of them put the finishing touches on the song and then recorded a minimalist demo of it that we took back to Canada. Everyone who heard the demo had the same feeling we did. This was a song that seemed destined to be a hit of some kind.

The sessions for *Longer Fuse*, the album that would contain the single "Sometimes When We Touch," began almost immediately upon Dan's return from L.A. Matt and Fred were once again producing, and the sessions were moving along well, when I received a call from Dan. He wanted to have a meeting to discuss the recording. He had written a song called "McCarthy's Day," a poignant retelling of his parents' trials as an interracial couple living in the U.S. during the 1950s. Matt and Fred, perhaps prompted by the feelings of the U.S. record company, didn't think so overtly political a song belonged on the album and, despite their adroit handling of "Sometimes When We Touch," which was truly a magnificent production, they weren't that moved by the idea of recording "McCarthy's Day." They had given it a shot but it just didn't seem to be working out. Despite this, Dan was determined to record the song and have it released on the album.

Dan and I cooked up the following idea. Dan was recording the *Longer Fuse* sessions at Toronto's Manta Sound on Adelaide Street. We would go into another studio without informing Matt and Fred, in this case Eastern Sound located on Yorkville Avenue, where I had been working with Murray, and record "McCarthy's Day." We'd then present it to Matt and Fred as a *fait accompli*. Our thinking was that once they heard it recorded and had it in their hands, it would be easier to accept the idea of putting it on the album.

This song was important to Dan. He was very proud of his parents' accomplishments and wanted to tell the tale. Dan's father was black and his mother was white. They had moved to Canada hoping to find a better life. Dan Hill, Sr., was a human rights activist who became the Chair of the Ontario Human Rights Commission.

Dan and Matt had been friends since their early primary school days in Toronto and certainly Dan owed the McCauley family a lot for having taken an early chance on him by signing him to a production deal. Still, the trouble he had with the recording, or should I say the non-recording, of "McCarthy's Day," had left a bad taste with Dan. Later Bernie and I would get dragged into a lawsuit with the McCauleys in an attempt to have Dan's contract changed. This was not fun for anyone and one of the few times I was ever involved in an action that went to court. I always thought Dan's willingness to leave the McCauleys was somewhat provoked by the difficulties he had in getting "McCarthy's Day" recorded.

Anyway, our idea worked, and "McCarthy's Day" ended up on the album. During the same session we did the song "Friends," which eventually ended up on the follow-up record to *Longer Fuse*, called *Frozen in the Night*. Matt and Fred did an admirable job of finishing the tracks and I ended up with a co-production credit on both of those songs. "Sometimes When We Touch" turned out to be a monster hit and eventually went to number 3 on the *Billboard* chart and actually to number 1 on the *Record World* chart, a competing Top 100 chart in the U.S. There were days when the single would sell over 35,000 records, an astounding number, at least in my experience.

Dan had been doing some touring in the U.S. before the release of "Sometimes When We Touch," but we didn't have a formal arrangement with an agent involved in booking shows there. As the record started to climb the charts we fielded calls from every top agent in America. The most aggressive suitor was Jeff Franklin, from a New York–based company called ATI. Jeff was a scrappy kind of guy who somehow seemed to know where Bernie and I were at every moment, day or night. Fiedler thought that Jeff must have been having us followed, especially after he managed to reach Bernie on the phone at a restaurant in Toronto one evening. One night, he asked Bernie and me if he needed to come to Toronto to wine and dine us. We told him that would be fine but why didn't he just offer us something concrete, like a great opening spot on a U.S. tour. A few hours later he was back on the phone, asking us if getting Dan ten Art Garfunkel dates would do the trick. We jumped at it. This would be Art's first tour since the breakup of Simon & Garfunkel and he would be in the finest mid-size theatres in the U.S. It promised to be a national media event as well as the perfect audience for Dan. The next morning, Jeff called to confirm we had the Garfunkel tour. We were overjoyed and signed Dan to Franklin's ATI Agency.

Bernie and I agreed that I would accompany Dan on the tour. Meanwhile, the single started to take off worldwide, especially in the U.K. As a result, Dan was offered an opportunity to appear on *Top of the Pops*, a TV show that was by far the largest and most important music program in England. An appearance on *TOTP* pretty much guaranteed a top-ten record in the U.K. But there was one catch: they wouldn't book Dan until the single broke into the top forty and it was only just beginning to move up the charts. There was another problem: the available slot for Dan on *TOTP* was right in the middle of the Garfunkel tour. However, that actual date was during a day off in New York. It turned out that we could do *TOTP* if we took the Concorde to England, taped the show the next evening, flew the Concorde back to New York, and immediately transferred to a flight bound for Cleveland, the next date on the tour. If everything went smoothly we could make it back to the tour and even have enough time to do a sound check. Of course, given Murphy's Law, we would need some luck. We needed the single to have moved into the top forty by the time we arrived in England. Nothing was guaranteed, but we were ready to give it a shot, providing the record company would pick up the tab.

So in early 1978 we boarded the Concorde to England. The flight was an amazing experience. Kind of science fiction–like, the Concorde was essentially a long tube that could fly at supersonic speeds faster than any other commercial airliner, crossing the Atlantic in just under three and a half hours. The plane was so narrow that once they started serving dinner you just couldn't get past the serving carts but, oh, what a dinner. Russian caviar, lobster, truffles, fois gras, and many of the world's finest wines, as well as copious amounts of champagne.

Once in London, we stayed at the Montcalm Hotel, located right across the road from the headquarters of ATV, where our English record company, Pye, was housed. ATV was run by Sir Lew Grade, a truly larger-than-life character. Dan and I were invited to meet him in his office. His various companies had been involved in everything from publishing the songs of the Beatles to television hits like *The Muppet Show* and *The Saint*. We were sitting in his office when we found out that the single had gone into the British top forty so there was no question that Dan would be appearing on *TOTP* that evening. I don't think it was a coincidence that we learned about our chart position while in Sir Lew's office.

The show went extremely well and within a few weeks the single would go top ten in the U.K. At ten the next morning we caught the Concorde back to New York, arriving around 10:30 a.m. Eastern Standard Time. We transferred to a flight bound for Cleveland and made it to the concert hall in time for Dan to do the sound check and have what turned out to be a very fine show. Life at the speed of sound.

My trip to England with Dan wasn't my only foreign travel in 1977. I'd been in touch with a young Japanese promoter named Hiroshi Asada who had been showing a great deal of interest in bringing both Bruce and Murray to Japan for an extensive tour. We had released some of their records in Japan through two companies, CBS and Victor Musical Industries. Our sales in Japan were modest but there was a growing interest in Canadian music, especially in True North's two great singer-songwriters. These days, many Canadian artists sell records and tour in Japan, but in

1977 it was a distant and mysterious land. This was still during the time that if you picked something up in a store in Canada and saw "Made in Japan" you thought twice before buying it. Of course, this was also before the advent of Sony's Walkman and the Japanese car-manufacturing powerhouses. It was even before the rock cliché of "being big in Japan."

Hiroshi put together an offer for a seven-city tour that would take us from one end of the island nation to the other, with shows in Sapporo, Kanazawa, Kyoto, Fukuoka, Morioka, and Yokohama, as well as four concerts in Tokyo. This would be the most exciting and profound road trip of my career, and remains right near the top of all of my experiences. With the tour booked I immersed myself in learning as much about Japan as I could. At this time, James Clavell's novel *Shōgun* was all the rage, and I was among the millions who devoured the book. But I also read John Toland's *The Rising Sun* — a fascinating account of the Second World War as seen through the eyes of the Japanese — and a few books by the great Japanese novelist Kenzaburo Oe. I also began reading as many travel books as I could. But nothing prepared me for the culture shock.

We arrived during the peak of summer and the combined heat and humidity was something I had never experienced in Canada. Tokyo was by far the most densely crowded city I had ever visited, even more so than New York. We began the tour in Kyoto, the old Imperial capital of Japan.

Our touring party consisted of Bruce, Murray, Dennis Pendrith, and me. We were to be accompanied by two Japanese tour managers, one of them Hiroshi himself. They were both about our age and were determined to show us a good time. Also, representatives from the Canadian embassy seemed extremely happy to see us and were quite helpful. Up to this time, Canadian artists had been coming to Japan, but not with any regularity and certainly not in large numbers. So even though our tour was, technically, a commercial venture, as the tour rolled along it began to seem more like a cultural exchange. At the end of each show, it became a ritual to visit a local restaurant and have what can only be described as a feast, always accompanied by copious amounts of sake, beer, and local moonshine. Our promoters were always interested in having drinking contests with us – a Japanese tradition – and we were only too happy to oblige them. Canada's reputation was on the line, although I can assure you it was never at risk. There was many a night I could barely make it to my bed and many a morning when I could barely get up. The shows, without exception, were a great success, with the theatres almost always sold out. At the end of the tour, the Canadian embassy hosted a wonderful Chinese dinner for us and our tour organizers as well as other Japanese dignitaries. I'll never forget the thousand-year-old eggs.

Murray and Bruce backstage in Tokyo, 1977
(Masashi Kuwamoto)

I had some trouble getting used to sushi although that would change in time. By my return trip with Bruce two years later, I was a serious convert to Japanese cuisine. I ended up on the cover of Japan's equivalent of *Billboard* magazine. The feature was all about Canadian music and I considered it an honour to be interviewed for it.

I make it to the cover of *Music Labo*, Japan's largest music business magazine, in 1979

Soon, "Made in Japan" became a status symbol in the Western world, but that didn't surprise me after travelling throughout the country and meeting the people. It was both the most foreign of all the places I had visited up to then and also the most vibrant. Visiting Japan had a profound effect on all of us, and both Murray and Bruce used the country as a reference point in several of their subsequent songs. Cockburn would even have a hit single three years later with a song called "Tokyo."

I don't know how with all the international travelling, constant touring, and meetings in New York and L.A. that I still found the time in 1977 to go back into the studio with Murray and co-produce his album *Hard Rock Town*. I was burning the candle at both ends and beginning to feel more than just a little flamed out. One night, while I was in L.A., the Bernies asked me to join them for dinner with Cathy Smith and a few others, but I declined. I was in my hotel room and had just tuned into a Dodgers game on TV. The soothing voice of Vin Scully giving the play-by-play seemed more attractive to me than another night on the town, snorting coke and drinking wine. That ball game may have saved my life.

I had always liked baseball as a kid but somewhere down the line I had forgotten about the game until Bob Sniderman from Sam the Record Man, Peter Goddard, the *Toronto Star*'s music journalist, and I purchased season tickets for the Toronto Blue Jays. I said yes to being part of the group, although at the time I wasn't truly sure why. But when the season opened in April of 1977 my love for the game instantly reignited. In 1985, I would get one of my rare gold singles with the Blue Jays theme song, "OK Blue Jays (Let's Play Ball)." It was written and produced by Tony Kosinec, a wonderful singer-songwriter in his own right, and Jack Lenz, whose accomplishments in the field of music production for television are unparalleled. They made the record for the Jays organization, which used it in the team's promotional spots and played it during the seventh-inning stretch at the ballgames. When the Jays finally won their division title and made it to the playoffs, the single immediately took off and went gold. Timing is everything. I've got to tell you that there isn't any greater thrill than sitting in the ballpark watching a game and hearing a record of yours being played during the seventh-inning stretch. Thank you, Tony and Jack.

I returned from that L.A. trip knowing that I had to slow things down, at least when it came to working 24-7. And for a while I did just that. I knew my days as a hands-on, in-the-studio record producer were coming to an end. It had been a blast working so closely with Murray, and the work we had done together was actually pretty good, but things were changing in the studio world. That, along with the fact that my business was becoming bigger and demanding even more time than ever, meant something had to change. I couldn't continue working all day and recording all night. Our concert promotion business had also substantially grown and we were presenting shows for everyone from Tom Waits and Paul Simon to Joni Mitchell and Kate & Anna McGarrigle. Murray, Dan, and Bruce continued playing sold-out shows from coast to coast in Canada and were making inroads internationally.

But the one thing that remains constant is change. It seemed that just as one thing was on the rise, another would fall. Bernie Fiedler decided it was time to close the Riverboat. This institution that had been the home to so much great music had outlived its days. Fortunately for Bernie, with our management, record company, and concert businesses growing, he could afford to close the club, as sad as that might have been. Suitably, Fiedler's last performers at the Riverboat were Murray McLauchlan and Dan Hill. I was there, and although their show was terrific, there was a tangible sadness in the air that evening. An era was coming to an end and, along with it, the last vestiges of the grand counter-culture days of Yorkville.

In 1978, Murray decided that he would self-produce his next record, a decision I fully supported. What a great one this would turn out to be. *Whispering Rain* became his bestselling album ever and the title cut would go on to be his most played song, even eclipsing "Farmer's Song." Murray had the inspired idea to see if he could get the Jordanaires, Elvis Presley's famous and fabulous backup singing group, to do the harmony vocal parts on the album. I put together the deal and Murray made his way to Nashville to record with them. Even after all of my experiences in my preceding fifteen years in the business, I was still able to be amazed. There was just no way in 1956, as I was loving Elvis's "Don't Be Cruel," that I would have imagined that one day I'd hire his extraordinary backup singers, but that's exactly what happened. One of the things I regret is not having made that Nashville trip, but I was so busy with the business that I could seldom afford the luxury of spending days in a recording studio.

The Riverboat closes. From left to right: Eddie Collero (CBS Records), Bernie Fiedler, me, and Charlie Camilleri (CBS Records)

In the midst of all these exciting developments, I faced a challenge. In early 1979, I received a phone call from Chris Blackwell, the founder and owner of Island Records. True North was being distributed in the U.S. by Island and reciprocally we had been looking after Island's business in Canada, providing them with the services of our marketing team even though Island was distributed in Canada by RCA. That's how I met Stuart Raven-Hill, who was the label manager for Island Canada prior to our deal with them. When True North was asked to take over the supervision of Island's activities, I had to decide what to do about Stuart's job. Island was giving us a monthly retainer and how to spend it was left entirely to me. I didn't really need another staff member, but I had grown to like Stuart. His knowledge of the artists recording on Island was comprehensive, and his love for reggae, at that time the label's dominant music, was obvious, so I decided to keep him on. It turned out to be a good decision. During the few years that True North worked the Island label, we had the extreme good fortune to put out Bob Marley's seminal album *Exodus*, Steve Winwood's *Arc of a Diver*, and Robert Palmer's *Double Fun*.

At the same time, Island's U.S. operation had been releasing Bruce's and Murray's albums in America, but now Chris was on the phone telling me that things were changing. He was moving Island away from being an independently distributed label in America to being part of the Warner Brothers family. He was also going to remove Charlie Nuccio, who had been running the American operation. Seeing how it was Charlie who had negotiated the Island deal with me in America, this was not good news. With Island now going to Warner, they would only need a skeleton staff in North America, and because of that Chris no longer wanted to continue our distribution deal in the U.S. Chris saw True North as too specialized a label for his new Warner's arrangement and he would no longer need us to oversee Island in Canada because Warner Canada would now provide all of the marketing and promotional duties. I can't say I was entirely heartbroken by this turn of events, especially with Nuccio and all of his key people gone. Charlie had been our main day-to-day contact, so I could understand Chris's point of view. Even though we had made some progress in America, True North's artists weren't exactly boffo box-office, so a change might do us good.

But despite all that, there was one other thing that I did want to speak to Blackwell about. True North had just finished Bruce's album *Dancing in the Dragon's Jaws* and I was especially interested in what Chris would think about "Wondering Where the Lions Are." The session for that song had been particularly interesting. Some time before the album's recording sessions began, Bruce had been on the road, with Stuart Raven-Hill acting as tour manager. When Stuart heard Bruce playing "Wondering Where the Lions Are" with a light reggae lilt to it, he had some good ideas of which local reggae musicians might be effective on the recording. When Bruce entered the studio he remembered that conversation and, along with Gene Martynec, they put together a terrific and interesting backup band for that cut. The band consisted of two Jamaican-born, Toronto-based musicians, Larry "Sticky Fingers" Silvera on bass and backing vocals and Ben Bow on drums and vocals. The group also featured keyboardist Patrick Godfrey. I remember this well since they rehearsed that song, along with others, in the basement of the house that I then owned in midtown Toronto. "Wondering Where the Lions Are" was truly a product of Toronto's diverse, multicultural society, and when the single went on to be an international hit, it was one of the early examples of a reggae-influenced radio hit.

So it was with this in mind that I approached Chris to suggest he hear the album and especially the track "Wondering Where the Lions Are." Chris agreed and I immediately messengered the record down to him in New York. We made arrangements to talk again in a week or so. It was clear to me that the current deal we had was over but I thought this just might make an interesting record for the new Island Records to release in the U.S. I'm nothing if not pragmatic.

It turned out that Chris didn't agree with me. He liked the album but circumstances being what they were with his label's new direction, he just wasn't interested. I'm not even sure he listened to the record but I took his word for it. Unfortunately, he wasn't the only one turning us down. I was finding it very hard to get anyone in America interested in releasing *Dancing in the Dragon's Jaws*. I went to everyone I knew, sometimes twice, but to no avail. In the meantime we had released the single in Canada and to my astonishment it was beginning to get airplay on some of the top-forty stations across the country. I'll never forget the day J. Robert Wood, the program director of CHUM-AM in Toronto, called me and said he was going to add "Lions" to their playlist. CHUM was the most powerful station in Canada by a long shot. I was floored. It was a moment that I had been working toward for Bruce but had begun to think might never happen.

Bruce had now released an album a year with no appreciable airplay on any of Canada's leading top 40 commercial stations. It remained one of my daily goals to somehow find a way to cross him over to a bigger audience. Although Bruce may not have been overly concerned about commercial acceptance, it mattered to me, mainly because I thought he was so damn good. With CHUM playing the record there was now a very real possibility of Bruce finding that larger audience.

Bob Wood was as good as his word. CHUM started playing the record and presto, like magic, the phones at the station rang off the hook, and both the single and the album started to sell faster than anything Bruce had previously released. This made me even more determined to get this single out in America, even though I was running out of potential buyers. It was my lawyer Berni Solomon who recommended that I talk to Jimmy Ienner, who had just launched his own independent label called Millennium. Meeting Jimmy would be just about my last chance to get a deal in the U.S.

I met Jimmy in New York and immediately liked him. He was a big friendly guy with immaculate hair right out of a 1950s teen movie and the biggest smile you've ever seen, set off by a gleaming set of white teeth. In fact, his nickname was "Teeth." Jimmy had long been one of the top record producers in America, with a major list of credits on his resumé that included work with Three Dog Night, Grand Funk Railroad, and the Canadian band Lighthouse, co-led by my old client from the Paupers, Skip Prokop. It was hard not to like Jimmy.

I handed him the album and asked him to play "Wondering Where the Lions Are." He put it on his turntable and we listened to the distinctive opening guitar lick followed, twenty or so seconds later, by Ben Bow's opening drum lick. Jimmy stopped the record player and said to me in a loud voice, "What the hell was that?" I thought, *Oh no, here comes another rebuff, and this time we haven't even got to the vocal.* Before I had a chance to reply, Jimmy restarted the song from the top and, again, when it came to the drum entry, he stopped the record.

"God, that sounds like someone just fell down stairs," he said. "I've got to hear that again."

This time he played the record all the way through, and by the time the song ended we worked out the details of the deal on the spot. Jimmy was in love with that song, and his enthusiasm

Bruce signs with Millennium Records in the U.S. From left to right: Jimmy Ienner, Bruce, and me. A few months later, Bruce hits the Top 30 in the U.S.

for the entire album was contagious. He called in his younger brother, Donnie, who was his in-house promo man, and that was the beginning of my long relationship with the Ienners. Donnie, whose personality was as big as Jimmy's, was equally excited about the song. I would end up working with Donnie once more, some ten years later, when he became the president of Columbia Records in the U.S.

The Ienners worked that record like there was no tomorrow and they delivered it right into the top 30, peaking at number 21 on *Billboard*. Bruce had his first hit in America.

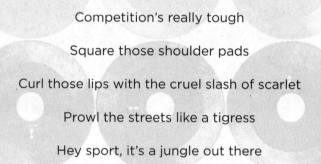

Competition's really tough

Square those shoulder pads

Curl those lips with the cruel slash of scarlet

Prowl the streets like a tigress

Hey sport, it's a jungle out there

"It's a Jungle"
(Carole Pope and Kevan Staples)
Rough Trade

CHAPTER THIRTEEN

I was thrilled of course. We had our second worldwide hit single in a three-year period. Like Dan's "Sometimes When We Touch," Bruce's single also did well in many countries around the world. What a remarkable period: between our management company and the record company we had a string of Canadian hits, including Murray's biggest-selling Canadian album *Whispering Rain*, as well as the two bona fide international hits. Not bad for an air force brat who only fifteen years earlier was trying to find his way from Downsview to Yorkville.

As good fortune would have it, True North's distribution agreement with CBS was coming to an end. That meant I could negotiate from a position of strength. The new agreement that CBS signed gave the label the ability to sign more acts, all with guaranteed marketing and promotion commitments. Arnold Gosewich was the president of CBS and he was anxious to keep us in the CBS family. Although Arnold is long gone from the record business we remain friends to this day. In essence, CBS would be advancing me the money needed to sign and record more artists. In return, CBS would have exclusive distribution rights for five to seven years – depending on the performance of the records – and then all of the distribution rights would return to my company. A sweet deal.

The time had come to sign another act to the label. As much as I loved working with singer-songwriters, and as good as that genre had been to me, deep down I missed the excitement that a great rock band can generate. A good song was still the most important thing on my mind, but I also wanted something that would be new and fresh and strikingly original. It didn't take me long to find that something, although the truth is, I didn't find it at all; it found me.

Carole Pope and Kevan Staples had been around Yorkville in the sixties and had been through various band incarnations, most notably O and then the Bullwhip Brothers. Yet somehow I just plain missed them during that period. It was as if we were living in parallel worlds even though we were right there on the same street. For me that whole period of the seventies was spent almost entirely in the world of "folk music," or more specifically, of modern singer-songwriters. I had become something of an expert in that field. I knew every song and every artist, from the most successful to the completely obscure. The music was in my blood and certainly I had skin on the table; every move, and every song, mattered to me. There was never a moment, even when I was dreaming, that songs didn't keep rolling around in my consciousness, 24-7.

So it was easy to understand how I might have missed the rising popularity of Carole and Kevan's latest creation: Rough Trade. One day, in early 1980, I noticed that the band would be doing a show at the Danforth Music Hall, the former Roxy movie theatre in the east end, and decided to check them out. I was blown away. The show was sold out, a feat unto itself, and it struck me that Rough Trade might have been the best white R&B band that I'd seen since the early Rolling Stones. I was so caught up in the music that night that I almost missed the whole social movement that had helped to fill that theatre.

In the mid-to-late seventies, another cultural revolution was bubbling up from the streets, one that, like almost all post-war cultural shifts, involved music, fashion, theatre, art, and a loosening of sexual codes of behaviour. Here was Carole, completely out of the closet, singing some of the most provocative, politically potent songs I'd ever heard to a very engaged and fashionably hip audience. It was a world that I knew little about, but as the saying goes, I knew what I liked. I went backstage to say hello and before I could say anything, Carole asked me, why hadn't I signed them yet? *Well, throw me in the briar patch*, I thought, or to put it another way, I invited Carole and Kevan to my office the next day, and we quickly worked out a contract that would include both records and music publishing. I really don't know why somebody else hadn't signed them before I did. Maybe the other labels were just plain scared of the sexual content of the songs, but the songwriting was just so good that I had no misgivings about giving them a deal.

Carole and Kevan agreed that Gene Martynec would be the ideal producer for their debut True North album. And why not? Gene had a strong reputation for bringing out the best in singer-songwriters, and both Carole and Kevan considered themselves to be just that. With that decision behind us, we embarked on what would be a short but illustrious recording partnership. Soon we began work on their debut for us, the groundbreaking and breathtaking *Avoid Freud*.

Avoid Freud featured artwork from the multi-media art collective General Idea, whose three members, AA Bronson, Jorge Zontal, and Felix Partz, were all close friends of the band. GI came up with one of the finest and most innovative album covers True North ever put out.

Album jackets were always important to me. It costs as much to print a bad or boring cover as it does a good one, so why not make it as great and as interesting as possible? I also liked the idea of using Canadian artists and photographers wherever possible. Of course, this went back to my early days and that chance meeting with Bart Schoales, a talented artist himself, who over the years contributed so much to the look and feel of True North. Arnaud Maggs, the internationally acclaimed Toronto photographer, did several covers for us, as did noted fashion photographer George Whiteside and General Idea's Jorge Zontal.

True North signs Rough Trade. From left to right:
Arnold Gosewich (Chairman, CBS Canada), Carole Pope,
me, Kevan Staples, and Bernie Fiedler

Many of Bruce's album covers truly were works of art. Painter and illustrator San Murata, who works in a folk art style, created a wonderful cover for *Salt, Sun and Time* and I particularly liked Blair Drawson's work on *Joy Will Find a Way* and *Stealing Fire*. We commissioned the great Aboriginal artist, Norval Morrisseau, who founded the Woodlands School of Canadian Art, to create the cover painting for *Dancing in the Dragon's Jaws*. We would later use Robert Davidson, another very fine Aboriginal artist, of the Haida nation, for the cover painting of *Waiting for a Miracle*. We had met Robert when Bruce was involved in the South Morseby benefit concerts in Vancouver supporting the campaign to stop the commercial logging that was devastating the Haida's homeland in the Queen Charlotte Islands. Those shows raised over $50,000 for the Haida's legal defence fund. And, of course, we had already used Alex Colville's painting *Horse and Train* for *Night Vision*.

The album jacket for Murray's *Whispering Rain* was a clever example of a great cover. It was done by the new-media artist Michael Hayden. He had at one time been a member of Intersystems, along with Moog synthesizer pioneer John Mills-Cockell. Michael had taken a look at the elements involved in doing a cover – photographs, typeface, layout, etc. – and condensed them all into one simple Polaroid picture. He die-cut both the album's title and Murray's name into a seven-by-four-foot piece of silver Mylar, then took the Mylar into a forest and stood Murray strategically in front of the cutout. Then he took Polaroid pictures until he had the one we all liked. No fuss, no muss, just a one-piece album front cover ready for printing.

I kept most of the original artwork for these covers and treasure them to this day. Later on, when compact disks replaced albums, I, along with many others, felt we had lost something

Covers Count

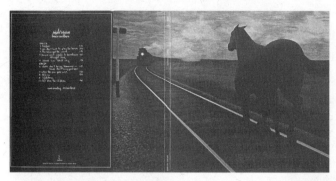

Alex Colville's *Horse and Train* on Bruce Cockburn's *Night Vision* album.

Murray McLauchlan's *Whispering Rain* cover, created by Michael Hayden

Robert Davidson's painting graces the cover of Bruce Cockburn's *Waiting for a Miracle*

Norval Morrisseau's painting for Bruce Cockburn's *Dancing in the Dragon's Jaws*

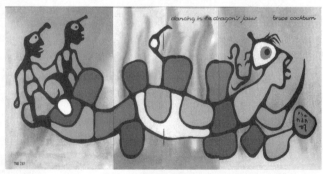

The front and back of Rough Trade's *Avoid Freud* by General Idea

special through the reduction of the package size. However, I continued to use Canadian painters where possible and had the good fortune to use a James Lahey painting for jazz guitarist's Michael Occhipinti's *Creation Dream*, an exquisite album of jazz interpretations of Bruce Cockburn's songs. In hindsight I wish I had used even more Canadian artists over the years. It surprises me that more people in our business never picked up on this idea.

As soon as General Idea finished the art we released *Avoid Freud* to the world. It turned out to be very successful in Canada, largely triggered by the raunchy "High School Confidential." The first single we released was called "Fashion Victim," and although it performed reasonably well, it didn't exactly light up the charts. I had thought "High School" had the potential to become a hit but didn't expect much airplay on top-forty radio. Not with lyrics that included the line, "She makes me cream my jeans when she comes my way." Still, we decided to put it out with the hope that maybe some adventurous radio station would pick it up and play it. And we knew if that happened, it was bound to be an attention-getter.

At first, little happened. The album was getting some notice and was beginning to sell, but top-forty radio wasn't on it at all. Yet it seemed obvious that once the commercial radio crowd heard this band, they were going to love them, and I hated the idea of a wasted opportunity.

About a month after we released the song I got a call from the music director of the mighty CHUM radio. They wondered if we would do an edit on the song, specifically to get rid of the word "cream." I took the idea to Carole and Kevan and although they were somewhat reluctant they were willing to give it a shot. We examined several ways to do it but settled on a simple beep to drown out the word as the best answer. We sent our handiwork over to CHUM. The powers-that-be approved it, and the song was added to its playlist. As soon as CHUM's listeners heard it, the phone lines lit up. For a while, it was the most requested song on the station. We rushed out copies of the edit to the other top-forty stations across the country and the record caught on from coast to coast. The bleep was like honey to a bear. Every time it was heard on radio, the curiosity of the listeners was heightened and out they went to buy the album that contained the unedited version. We sold well over 100,000 copies of that album in Canada alone. *Avoid Freud* was a great album but there can be no doubt that a simple little bleep helped push it over the top. As the record got bigger, radio actually started to play the unedited version and the world became a better place, at least for all of us at True North.

Carole Pope and Kevan Staples were true pioneers and visionaries. Carole, who was immensely creative, was also extraordinarily brave. She was open about her sexuality well before it became fashionable and safe to do so, and she did it gracefully and boldly. I'm extremely grateful to have had the opportunity to work with them.

But "High School Confidential" would not be Rough Trade's biggest single. Their next album, the aptly titled *For Those Who Think Young* (a play on the name Carl Jung) contained a song called "All Touch" that immediately hit radio with a bang, and not only in Canada. I had made a deal in Australia for the whole True North label and the first releases were Bruce's *The Trouble With Normal*, Murray's *Windows*, and *For Those Who Think Young*. "All Touch" was released as a single and took off down under, landing in the top ten. At the same time, I had made a deal for Rough Trade in the U.S. with a label called Boardwalk, a subsidiary of Casablanca, owned by music business legend Neil Bogart, who had almost singlehandedly launched the disco craze in America with Donna Summer's seventeen-minute single, "Love to Love You Baby."

Another renowned music man, Irv Biegel, ran Boardwalk.

He loved Rough Trade and was especially excited by the possibility of "All Touch" becoming a hit in America. We conceived a dynamic promotion campaign in the U.S. and the single started to take off. Irv was certain this was going to be at least a top-thirty *Billboard* single, and indeed it was beginning to move in that direction, but good fortune didn't come our way this time around.

When Neil Bogart became sick, his company began to flounder and things came unglued. Getting records on commercial radio in America is an expensive proposition and always a tricky exercise. Money wasn't the only necessary ingredient, although it seemed by far to be the most important. It also took a well-coordinated effort between all involved parties. With chaos reigning at the top of the company, things started to unravel. Just as the single hit number 58 on the *Billboard* Top 100 chart, officials at Boardwalk announced the company was going bankrupt. "All Touch" slowed down to a crawl. Sadly, a few months later Neil Bogart would die of cancer at the age of thirty-nine.

Jeff Franklin, Dan Hill's one-time agent, represented the buyers of Boardwalk's assets, so I flew down to New York to see if we could do something quickly to turn around the fortunes of the single and the album. Even though several weeks had passed since the single had peaked on the *Billboard* chart, I was still optimistic that we could turn it around. Why not, considering "All Touch" had been a top-ten hit in Australia and Canada and had been on the same trajectory in the U.S.? But Franklin was unmoved by my plea and the plight of the band; in fact, he was more than extremely unpleasant about the whole thing for reasons that I never understood. The meeting went nowhere, and although I did eventually get the rights back to the album, by the time that happened it was far too late to resuscitate the single. This was truly a tragedy. That song, at that moment, might well have broken Rough Trade in the States.

The next Rough Trade album was *Shaking the Foundations*, which we released in 1982. Arguably their best effort creatively, it didn't have a track with the same kind of commercial appeal needed to break them in America. "Crimes of Passion" was the top single, but its content was just too edgy for an increasingly conservative radio landscape. With lyrics like the following, even I understood that we didn't stand a chance at radio. But I couldn't resist the challenge of putting this record out.

> Her hand slipped down into the moistness of herself,
> She pulled her knees up spread eagle on the bed.
> Her chenille bathrobe, torn down the side,
> He was a willing victim, he couldn't resist her.

> Shower still dripping, coffee table overturned,
> The gun still smoking, scream caught in her throat.
> Her lungs still burning, her tempo throbbing,
> She reached for a crumpled pack and lit up a smoke.

> There's no limit to the depths you can sink to,
> There's no limit to the heights you can climb,
> Crimes of passion, crimes of passion, crimes.

While there may have been no limit to the depths that Carole and Kevan's characters might sink to, we did find the limit of what radio would play.

The video for "Crimes of Passion" was one of the most interesting made during those early days of the format. Whenever it was shown it would cause all kinds of talk. But we were never able to regain the momentum in America that had been lost with the untimely demise of Boardwalk. I can't help but wonder what might have happened to Rough Trade had "All Touch" been able to continue its natural growth in the U.S., but what the music business teaches you is that nothing is guaranteed and absolutely nothing can be taken for granted.

Years later, in the late nineties, long after the band had split up, I was attending a music conference in the U.K., where I spoke on a panel with Geoff Travis, the founder of England's seminal indie record label, Rough Trade Records. It was there that he told the assembled attendees and me that he had named his record store, and subsequently his label, after the band. Their legend lives on in many ways.

By 1981, finally, there truly was a Canadian music business. The Canadian-content regulations had done their job and I could see many positive spinoffs, not only for Canadian recording artists but also for many of the subsidiary interests tied to the business. Recording studios, equipment rentals, independent promotion companies, magazines, and many others directly benefited from the growing popularity of domestic artists. Our trade organization, CIRPA, was active in lobbying the federal government not just about regulations but also about funding. Although many of the leading artists of the time were signed to the independent labels who made up the vast majority of our membership, others were signed directly to the multinational labels whose executives, having seen that profits could be made, were beginning to take a very active role in signing and recording Canadian artists. Radio had been dragged unwillingly into the new world of Canadian-content regulations, but for the most part that fight was over. Yes, a few broadcasters still carried a grudge about being regulated, but by and large we were all working together to make things better. The one thing that CIRPA knew, though, was that its membership was chronically underfinanced, so we continually tried to induce the federal government to come up with a funding program to help our labels.

Independent labels, like True North, were entering an era of even greater competition now that our own distributors, the multinationals, were trying to sign the same acts as we were. Nothing was getting easier. The big companies at this time – CBS, RCA, EMI, Warner Brothers, PolyGram, and several others – not only had the advantage of large staffs and local offices across the country, but they also enjoyed a consistent revenue stream as hit after hit was delivered to them free from any real cost, since that had already been absorbed by their U.S. or U.K. owners. All they had to do was announce the release of a record that was already a hit in America (and perhaps in the U.K. as well) and Canadian radio programmers instantly put it on the air. The broadcasters even paid consultants whose main job was to read the foreign music trade magazines and tell them which songs were hits. When you consider that the album covers, posters, bios, and all the rest of the promotional material were supplied by their international parent companies, the Canadian-based multinationals really didn't have to do too much except wait for the money to flow in.

With radio already aware of the U.S. hits, it left our small Canadian companies fighting a pretty steep uphill battle. The idea that a station would ever play more than the required 30 per cent Canadian content never seemed to occur to any of the major radio stations, and there were many instances of the stations getting away with playing less. Of course the multinationals didn't mind this, since they owned the other 70 per cent. So it was left up to CIRPA and others to be on the front lines of monitoring this situation, and sometimes the front line is exactly what it felt like.

During this period, the federal and provincial governments had little interest in popular music. It always made me angry when I heard a politician or bureaucrat from Ottawa talking about funding the arts. I knew that when they mentioned music they weren't thinking about me or any of my colleagues. Although governments seemed quite at ease with film and books, when it came to funding music they seemed to think only of opera and classical music. Even though popular music was turning out to be the most successful of all of the Canadian "cultural industries," we remained chronically underfunded and mostly ignored.

So imagine my surprise when one day CHUM's Bob Wood – yes, the same Bob Wood who had added "Wondering Where the Lions Are" to his playlist – came to see me at the True North offices, by then located at 98 Queen Street East. He had been talking to Tom Williams, who, with Al Mair, was a co-owner of Attic Records, located on the floor right above us. Tom had given Bob the idea of redirecting some of CHUM's licence commitment money away from beneficiaries such as local student marching bands and putting it to better use directly inside the record industry. Radio broadcasters have always made various kinds of funding commitments to the CRTC as a method of insuring that they were able to receive and renew their licences. As a consequence, they were spending a fair buck on musical projects that had nothing to do with what they were broadcasting. The idea was to divert some of these dollars to a fund that would help the independents make more and better records.

I've got to say that I never liked the idea that we independents were making inferior records or that we weren't making enough records. I thought there were plenty of good records out there, and that this notion of "we need more and better" was just a euphemism for "we're never going to stop complaining about being regulated." However, I would be the first to admit that it wouldn't hurt if we could produce more and that we could all be better at what we do – radio included – so when Bob told me about the idea of redirecting some of his station's benefit money, I jumped at it, as did all of us at CIRPA.

It took about a year of behind-the-scenes negotiations but finally, in 1982, this innovative idea – hatched by Tom Williams and Bob Wood and midwifed by radio and CIRPA – gave birth to a private, non-profit funding organization, FACTOR (Foundation to Assist Canadian Talent On Record). Officially, FACTOR was founded by CIRPA, CMPA (the Canadian Music Publishers Association), and three of the big Canadian broadcasters: CHUM, Rogers Broadcasting, and Moffat Communications. The idea was to provide support to Canadian artists, songwriters, managers, labels, and distributors through programs directed toward recordings, marketing, promotion, touring, and other aspects of the business.

In 1986, the federal Department of Communications in Ottawa finally decided to help popular music through the Sound Recording Development Program (SRDP). As part of this initiative Ottawa also began to contribute to FACTOR. This was a first in Canadian arts funding, as FACTOR became the first organization of its kind to be funded by both the government and private industry but run quasi-independently of Ottawa.

There is much more that can be said about all of this, and indeed about every one of the institutions that have helped in so many ways to propel the Canadian music scene forward. I don't want to get bogged down in a lot of detail about the complexities and politics of funding, but one thing is certain, the many funding and regulatory initiatives have undoubtedly helped Canadian music to become more popular both at home and abroad. When I started in the sixties there were barely any well-known Canadian acts, and those few that there were, had, in almost every case, moved to the States. Today the number of successful acts has bountifully multiplied. Even though I sometimes regretted living in a world of reports and deadlines, brought on by a world full of funding regulations and bureaucracy, it remains certain that these institutions have worked. And there was still more to come.

Thinking back to this period, nothing is more important to me than the day, in 1980, that I met Elizabeth Blomme, who would become my wife and, by what can only be described as a miracle, remains my wife till this day. Remembering how we met brings a smile to my face. Late one afternoon I was on Yorkville Avenue, shopping at the Book Cellar just across the road from the Four Seasons Hotel. On my way to the parking lot I heard a voice calling my name. It was my old friend, and very first business partner, Peter Simpson. I hadn't seen Peter, who had become a film producer, for some time, and when he asked me if I wanted to have a drink with him at the hotel, I was happy to join him. It turned out he was there doing interviews for *Prom Night*, which he had produced and was setting up to release. He invited me to hang out with Elizabeth, his publicist, while he finished up the interviews. For me it was love at first sight. Although it took a couple of years of both dating and living together, in April 1982 we were married. This was almost exactly twenty years to the day since I had surreptitiously helped Peter elope with his high-school sweetheart Gordine. Symmetry can be a wonderful thing and I've had plenty of it in my life, but my chance meeting with Peter that led to Elizabeth is certainly the most special of all those events. We have two wonderful boys, Edan and Noah, whom I love dearly.

There were professional milestones in 1980 as well. That year we put out the follow-up album to *Dancing in the Dragon's Jaws*. At the time, many considered *Humans* to be Bruce's finest record. The first single, "Tokyo," became a hit in Canada and a few other countries but didn't do as well as "Wondering Where the Lions Are" in the States. Despite that, we were all excited about the album and its reception. There are many observations to make about that great record but what I remember most is that "Tokyo" was playing on my car radio the night of my first date with Elizabeth. I turned the radio up as loud as I could and proudly announced that this was on my label. At precisely that moment I was pulled over by the police. Apparently I had been repeatedly and precipitously changing lanes. The officer was quite nice about it, especially after concluding I wasn't drunk or in any way incapacitated. He told me to park my car and walk home. Not the best way to start a relationship, but I walked Elizabeth back to her place and thankfully she had a sense of humour, so there was a second date. I've always thought "Tokyo" was a special record, but it will always occupy a very important place in my heart because of that night.

During that same year our management company signed another new act: Graham Shaw & the Sincere Serenaders. Graham's first single, "Can I Come Near," immediately went top fifteen across Canada, and we got a pretty good shot at the American market from Capitol Records, though as hard as we all tried, it just didn't quite catch on there. Later that year, Graham won a Juno as most promising Male Artist of the Year. A year later we would do another album with Graham, but by the end of 1982 I would no longer be working with him or, for that matter, Bernie Fiedler. Change was once again coming my way, but at the time I was oblivious to it.

That same year, 1980, I sat down with my old friend Bob Ezrin, one the world's top record producers, with credits as long as your arm, including world-class hits like Pink Floyd's *The Wall*, Lou Reed's *Berlin*, Kiss's *Destroyer*, all of Alice Cooper's early albums, and Peter Gabriel's magnificent "Solsbury Hill." You get the idea. Bob was as hot as you could get in our business without spontaneously combusting. He was back in Toronto and looking for something interesting to do.

Bob had an arrangement with Asylum Records that pretty much gave him an "open door" to bring in new projects. Asylum was then being run by Joe Smith, whom you'll remember I had worked with during the time that he was with Warner Brothers and had signed Kensington Market. Bob told me that he had always liked Murray's music and if he could produce the next McLauchlan album he would be able to guarantee us a contract with Asylum, the home of artists like Joni Mitchell and Jackson Browne.

It was an intriguing idea. The marriage of Bob and Murray in the studio might lead to something interesting, given Murray's interest in rock and Bob's continuing interest in Canadian roots music. Certainly the idea of getting Murray another strong shot in America with both a first-class label like Asylum and a world-topping producer like Bob was more than compelling. I set up a meeting for Murray and Bob and the chemistry seemed to be right, so we rolled the dice and took a shot. In a matter of weeks the deal with Asylum was done and we flew out to Los Angeles to do the inevitable signing ceremony and then shortly after began the recording process.

Now, as a manager, I knew this was a potentially risky gambit, and so did Murray. There was never any question of Bob's ability or desire but he had never produced a Murray-style singer-songwriter and Murray had grown accustomed to producing his own records. Working with Bob was going to require Murray to give up a lot of control and take a leap into the unknown. But you never know what the results of anything are going to be and, let's face it, we were nothing if not optimists. You had to be just to survive in this crazy game, and besides, the lure of another kick at the can in America was seductive.

So off went Murray and Bob, unfortunately not always in the same direction, and there was little I could do about it. There were lots of drugs being consumed during the sessions, which only helped to exacerbate the situation. Bob would sometimes show up to the sessions several hours late, which drove Murray crazy. Still, they soldiered on, and some of the record was turning out amazingly well. There was this one song Murray had written called "If the Wind Could Blow My Troubles Away." It was like a little folk-hymn but by the time Bob was finished with it, it had become an immense full-on cathedral anthem.

Murray McLauchlan signs with Asylum Records. From left to right: me, Kenny Buttice (Asylum A & R), Murray, Bob Ezrin, and Joe Smith

I really liked that cut, and thought it might have a real chance to break Murray through in the States. When we delivered it to Joe Smith and the Asylum staff they seemed pretty excited about the song's chances. Asylum worked the record, but when little happened right out of the gate, they soon gave up promoting it, and unfortunately the record just didn't have the right spin to work on its own. The last time we tried a similar move it had led to "Farmer's Song." This time we just didn't get as lucky. *Storm Warning* was the title of the album, and it was aptly named.

By 1982 I felt my life had changed. The music business, which I had fallen into almost by accident, had become all-consuming. Elizabeth and I had married. Having watched the constant break-ups and heartache that plagued the personal lives of so many of my friends I was determined to give us a real chance. I was also questioning my ability to continue working with Bernie Fiedler. It had been an intense ten years that had brought many rewards and wonderful times but also the inevitable friction that can occur between partners under any circumstances, particularly when they're involved in the high stakes and constant pressure of the music business. As hard as it was, I came to the conclusion that the time had come to end our partnership. My thought was that this would reduce my workload, freeing up time for my family.

When I approached Bernie about the two of us going our separate ways, he really didn't fight it. I think he had probably gotten sick of me as well. The breakup went smoothly enough, although informing the acts was not easy. The plan was that I would keep True North Records, Murray, and Bruce, while Dan Hill and Graham Shaw would go with Fiedler. We made our deal, and although I'm not entirely sure how the artists truly felt about this new reality, I did have long private talks with each of them and no one expressed any deep reservations about it.

I was now on my own for the first time since 1972. It had been a great run; not without its disappointments, of course, but by and large it had been a remarkable and extremely productive time. I realized that I was now over an urge that seemed to have been deeply imbedded in me by my air force upbringing – to pick up and leave whatever I was doing every couple of years. Finkelstein-Fiedler had lasted a decade, and I had been working with Bruce for thirteen years and with Murray for twelve. That's a long time in the very fickle music business.

I kept my office on Queen Street East, which was right across the road from CityTV. City was a remarkable station run by my old acquaintance Moses Znaimer. I had first met Moses back in my early days when we were doing the early True North recordings at Thunder Sound. By 1982, he had not only become the pre-eminent television entrepreneur in Canada but also a kind of broadcasting guru. City was doing things no one else had even thought about – including lots of innovative music programming – and from time to time I would drop by the City studios to check in on what Moses and his gang were up to.

We had all been closely watching the new marvel of music videos. MTV had launched a year earlier. It was becoming very successful while revolutionizing the music business, with its concept of providing an outlet for the new promotional medium of music videos, interspersed with occasional live events and music business news. The combination of TV exposure with radio airtime was a new phenomenon in the culture and turned out to be a potent force for selling records.

The CRTC had scheduled a hearing, with the aim of licensing one or two music channels in Canada. Moses was going to be one of the applicants for a licence, which made sense as City was already playing music clips on many of its programs. I had been approached by several different groups to take a role in their applications and had actually accepted a position with a group headed by Allan Gregg, the well-known pollster and political commentator, and Bev Oda, who today is a Conservative federal cabinet minister. As the hearing date approached, Allan and Bev's group lost their funding and dropped out of the upcoming hearings in Ottawa. This was disappointing news, but I quickly went across the road to meet with Moses and asked him if there was anything I could do to help with his application for "MuchMusic." We quickly cooked up an idea that would eventually become VideoFACT (the FACT standing for Foundation to Assist Canadian Talent).

I've always been very proud of my role in VideoFACT. All of the applicants for the music channel were promising to play Canadian videos, but there were hardly any Canadian videos to play. Moses and I estimated that at the time of the hearings there were only twenty-two Canadian videos suitable for airplay. Our solution was simple and elegant: MuchMusic, if licensed, would commit to putting a percentage of its gross revenue into a fund that would be solely dedicated to financing Canadian videos in both official languages. We carefully developed the plan right down to the last detail. Our fund would be independent from Much but would include a couple of board members from the channel. I would be the first chair of VideoFACT, a role I figured I might take on for a few years to ensure that it got off the ground in the right manner. So I went to Ottawa with Moses and the rest of his team to appear in front of the commission and present the VideoFACT idea to the CRTC. It was a memorable event. I clearly remember the impressive and dedicated staff Moses had assembled for the proposed channel, especially John Martin, who would go on to become Much's first program director. For John and several of his colleagues, music television seemed to be a matter of life and death, which I found inspiring.

The first board of VideoFACT. Seated, from left to right: Sylvia Tyson, me, and Victor Wilson. Standing: Robert Brooks, John Martin, Moses Znaimer, and Pierre Boivin

At the time, City was largely owned by CHUM, so during the hearing I also worked with Allan Waters, the founder and owner of CHUM. Although we often had been at odds regarding Canadian content, I found Allan to be personable and easy to get along with. The CHUM group, consisting of Moses, Allan, and the rest of the team, was a formidable force. We arrived in Ottawa a few days early for rehearsals, which were organized to be as similar as possible to what the hearing itself would be like. CHUM brought in Jerry Grafstein (later Senator Grafstein) to play the role of a commissioner running us through the potential questions we might be asked. At one point, Jerry put a question to me that might have had any one of several answers, so I asked him what the right response might be. Allan jumped in and told me and the assembled group that the right answer was always the truth; that was what CHUM stood for. I was impressed with his candour, and my opinion of him, which was already high, jumped up a few more notches.

Finally the big day of the hearing came. I remember sitting in front of the commission and glancing back at the rows of seats behind me. I didn't see a single person from the music business, even though this hearing was arguably the most important industry event since the Canadian-content rules in 1971. When Much finally went to air in April 1984, and I would hear the not infrequent complaints levelled against it, I always wondered where these people were when they had the chance to make an impact on the outcome.

Our presentation went very well and the VideoFACT part of the proposal seemed to be a big hit with the commissioners. About six months after the hearing ended, we were informed that the CHUM group had been successful and that the commission expected MuchMusic to live up to its commitment to start a fund to finance Canadian videos, with me as its first chair. In our first year we had a budget of $100,000. Over the years that has grown to an annual budget in excess of $4 million. With no minimum distribution or sales requirements, VideoFACT has always taken a leading role in funding independent Canadian music. We ask only that the applicant be Canadian and that the song and video meet the Canadian-content rules. As a consequence we have often been at the cutting edge of support for up-and-coming young artists who at the time of our approval were essentially unknown: artists like k.d. lang, Arcade Fire, Barenaked Ladies, K-os, Celine Dion, Sam Roberts, and Sarah McLachlan. I remained Chair of VideoFACT (now known as MuchFACT) until February of 2011 when I finally stepped down to make room for new blood. MuchFACT has now spent over $65 million on videos and websites and funded some 5,400 different projects. Moses is no longer involved in the station and, sadly, John Martin has passed away, but I have fond memories of those early board meetings. We had fun and at the same time we thought we were making a difference.

Big Circumstance comes looming

Like a darkly roaring train –

Rushes like a sucking wound

Across a winter plain

Recognizing neither polished shine

Nor spot nor stain –

And wherever you are on the compass rose

You'll never be again

"Shipwrecked at the Stable Door"
Bruce Cockburn

CHAPTER FOURTEEN

In February of 1983, Bruce Cockburn took a trip to Central America on behalf of Oxfam Canada and it literally changed his life, personally and musically. He was to visit Nicaragua, Honduras, Guatemala, and Mexico on a fact-finding mission and, upon his return to Canada, report back to Canadians on what he saw. He did exactly that but what he saw affected him to such a degree that he ended up reporting to the whole world.

While visiting a refugee camp in southern Mexico he witnessed the after-effects of helicopter gunships strafing a camp where mothers were holding onto babies already so weak from malnutrition that even simple diarrhea would be enough to kill them, never mind machine-gun bullets from American-supplied gunships. What Bruce witnessed outraged him, and while still in Mexico he wrote "If I Had a Rocket Launcher." This song, along with several others, most notably "Lovers in a Dangerous Time," would become his next album, the classic *Stealing Fire*.

Stealing Fire's success caught me by surprise in more ways than one. First, the album was the most overtly political album

Bruce had ever done. Like all of his records, *Stealing Fire* dealt with many subjects, but the overriding theme was his time spent in Central America. His conclusions were not particularly friendly to America and he wasn't hiding any of those feelings. This was the America of Ronald Reagan, and the citizens of that country, along with many of us here in Canada, had been lulled into thinking that America was firmly on the side of all that was right and righteous. However, when most of us weren't looking, the U.S. had been fighting a dirty little war by proxy in Central America, trying to topple the Sandinista government in Nicaragua. It occurred to me that Americans might not be too interested in hearing Bruce tell them a very different story from the one they were hearing from their government and most of their media.

I first heard "If I Had a Rocket Launcher" while I was on tour with Bruce in Australia. He played it for me in his dressing room backstage in Melbourne. I was blown away. Hearing the line "Some son of a bitch would die" took my breath away. Bruce was quite torn about whether he should even record the song and was deeply concerned about the real possibility of it being misunderstood as some kind of rallying cry, urging people to incite violence. I'm happy to say that Bruce's good sense not to censor himself won out, and the song became a powerful track on an epic album.

I knew that getting a label to release that album in the U.S. would be quite an undertaking. Once again I found myself being turned down by all of the major companies, despite the fact that just four years earlier Bruce had had a major hit with "Wondering Where the Lions Are." I think I could sum up the problem by saying that the people I was meeting with were all aware of the old adage, "Nobody gets rich being ahead of the curve." In 1983, Bruce was clearly ahead of the curve, both musically and lyrically, with *Stealing Fire*.

As usual, I was persistent, buoyed in part by the positive early response to "Lovers in a Dangerous Time," our first single in Canada; I sensed that we had something good going on with this album. I met with everyone I knew in New York and Los Angeles, sometimes seeing the same person two or three times. While people were intrigued by the record, no one thought it would sell, although I firmly suspected that many of them were simply afraid of Bruce's outspoken take on American foreign policy, which in 1983 just wasn't part of the conversation, especially in the record business.

Finally I arranged a meeting in L.A. with Danny Goldberg, who owned a small label called Gold Castle. Danny would go on to become president of Atlantic Records, and later chairman and CEO of first Warner Brothers and then the Mercury Records Group, as well as Nirvana's manager. But at the time I met with him he was best known for having been the publicist who had worked with Led Zeppelin. He had recently launched Gold Castle on the lot of his distributor, A&M Records, and he was deeply involved in the American Civil Liberties Union (ACLU). We had found our man.

Danny immediately liked the album and thought "Lovers in a Dangerous Time" had a strong chance to make waves in America. We made a deal for the release of the record in the U.S. and then came the surprise; although the single became a top-ten hit in Canada, it got modest airplay in America and never really took off. (Over the years, however, it gained more and more popularity and eventually became one of Bruce's most covered songs.)

What both Danny and I noticed was that the most talked-about song on the record was "If I Had a Rocket Launcher." We decided to take a shot with it as a single in America. It caught on immediately with an FM radio format called AOR (Album

Orientated Rock), which had developed as a kind of middle ground between commercial top-forty and the free-form progressive rock radio of the sixties. Whenever the song was played, it garnered strong phone requests. Although AOR didn't have the same commercial sales potential as top forty, it was still a very powerful medium, one very well suited to Bruce's music. The record went top ten across the States on AOR and even crossed over to some top-forty stations. Suddenly Bruce had himself another hit, one that was even more left field than "Wondering Where the Lions Are." I don't think you'll be surprised to hear that back in Melbourne, when Bruce was first playing me the song, we didn't once discuss whether it might be a potential hit.

We made a very potent video for the song that was at once very political and very moving, and it was added and played in heavy rotation on MTV. It has to be one of the earliest politically charged rock videos and at the time it was very widely seen. I'm still proud of it.

Bruce's audience was expanding once again and we started playing all of the first-class concert theatres in America as well as multiple shows in most of Canada's leading concert halls. Bruce was not shy about speaking his mind during these shows, especially when it came to American foreign policy, and I've got to admit that there were nights in some U.S. cities when I worried for his safety. We were living in very polarized times and there was often a feeling of danger in the air. Still, they were also exhilarating times, and it was apparent that many Americans were receptive to hearing someone speaking out about what they themselves felt was their government's wrong-headed militarism in Latin America. But internationally, *Stealing Fire* became so successful – it was especially popular in Germany, where it sold more than 70,000 copies alone – that Bruce's touring schedule became increasingly global.

Although I had actually thought I would be working less after I parted ways with Bernie Fiedler, it turned out that the mid-eighties would be one of the busiest periods in my life. It wasn't what I had planned, but by now I was used to the fact that my own plans often went astray. So I did what I have always done when good things come my way – I worked harder. Perhaps I should have taken my winnings and left the table, but instead I got involved with two talented and interesting new artists in rapid succession: Doug Cameron and Tony Kosinec.

Doug Cameron's record contained a track called "Mona with the Children," which also became a political hot potato. The song told the story of Mona Mahmudnizhad, an Iranian Baha'i who had been executed in June of 1983 for teaching children expelled from school because of their beliefs. Doug and his producer, Jack Lenz, were Baha'i and they had made a very impressive video for "Mona with the Children" that quite graphically told the story of Mona's persecution by Iranian authorities. I did my research on the subject and decided that I should release this album and video and I'm glad I did. But for a while we were on extra alert around our office because we'd been warned we might face reprisals for releasing and promoting this record. Just another day around the True North offices.

It was about this time too that I released Tony Kosinec's album, *The Passerby*. As I mentioned earlier, I also got involved in the release of the theme song he had co-written with Jack Lenz for the Toronto Blue Jays, "OK Blue Jays." Although Tony's album didn't fare so well in the commercial market, the Blue Jays theme became a gold single.

But not all was well at True North. More and more I was feeling that I had somehow lost the way with Murray. We remained good friends, but it bothered me that despite all of my efforts I had never found a way to find him a bigger audience in the States, and in Canada things weren't going as well as they once had. I was confident that things would turn around for Murray, but I wasn't sure I was the one to do it. It was impossible for me to imagine a day when I wouldn't be working with Bruce and Murray, but I could see that that day might be coming whether I liked it or not. No one, as an artist – or indeed, as a person – mattered more to me than Murray, so it was heartbreaking to sense that things were kind of falling apart. We had made a few more records since *Storm Warning* – and one of them, *Timberline*, remains among my all-time favourites – but none of them was commercially successful.

During this same period, though, Murray also did a very neat CBC radio series called *Timberline* (we collected the songs from this series and collated them into the album *Heroes*, released in 1984). We had also pulled off a very fine TV special called *Floating Across Canada* with special guests like Gordon Lighfoot, Buffy Sainte-Marie, and Levon Helm. Murray had his commercial pilot's licence and for the special, which was broadcast on PBS in the U.S. as well as on the CBC in Canada, he flew a Cessna 186 floatplane across Canada. Murray was showing that he had a talent for radio and TV as well as for music, and I could see he had a growing interest in these types of new projects. Although I had helped him somewhat with both of these endeavours, I wasn't sure I was the best person to help with his transition into these new areas. I sat down with Murray one day and what I thought would never happen, happened: we decided to go our separate ways. It was a mutual decision.

It was the end of an era for me. My times with Murray were very special to me and he was as big a part of True North as I was, but life went on for both of us. Many years later we reunited to do one more album. I'm happy to be able to tell you that we remain great friends and even though we've both had our ups and downs, things turned out fine for both of us.

I had pretty much stopped doing all drugs of any kind and was splitting my time equally between my family and my business. I had cut back my staff to two people: Jehanne Languedoc, who was my assistant and did promotion, and Julie Thorburn, who was primarily administrating VideoFACT. Between the various industry boards I was on and Bruce's continuing success I was still plenty busy. In some ways I think back to these days being an idyllic and happy time. There was lots of international travel with Bruce that was often exciting, informative, and fun. His follow-up to *Stealing Fire* was the equally politically potent *World of Wonders*. One of the tracks on that album, "Call It Democracy," caused us no end of strange problems and also reunited me for a brief moment with Irving Azoff.

"Call It Democracy" contained the lines:

North South East West
Kill the best and buy the rest
It's just spend a buck to make a buck
You don't really give a flying fuck
About the people in misery

We released this record in 1986, one year after the Parents Music Resource Center – a group dedicated to giving parents more control over music that they felt was violent or sexually suggestive – was formed. The founders, known as the "Washington Wives," included Tipper Gore, Senator Al Gore's wife; Susan Baker, married to then-Treasury Secretary James Baker; and two other women whose husbands had senior government jobs in Washington.

By the time we were getting ready to release *World of Wonders*, Danny Goldberg had moved his label from A&M to MCA, for distribution. One day, Danny called me sounding pretty uncomfortable. The legal minds at MCA had decided that Bruce's album would have to be stickered with a Parental Advisory Explicit Content label, otherwise known as a "Tipper Sticker." The reason given was that the record contained the word "fuck." I had the unpleasant task of having to inform Bruce of this. Not surprisingly, Bruce wasn't too happy about it, but after we'd talked about it for a while, we concluded (or maybe the more accurate word would be *rationalized*), that the sticker would actually bring more attention to the song than it might otherwise receive. So I gave Danny and MCA the go-ahead to sticker the LP jacket in the States. A few days later, we got another call from Danny, telling us that the executives at MCA had changed their minds about stickering the album. I think they were embarrassed at having to sticker a Bruce Cockburn album. I had also been advancing the idea that maybe it was the political content of the song "Call It Democracy" that was really being singled out, rather than the word "fuck."

MCA was now asking if we would allow them to print the song lyrics on the back cover of the album jacket. Their thinking was that this way they would no longer have to sticker the record, because the public would be given fair warning that the word "fuck" appeared on the record. This proposed solution didn't really go over well with either Bruce or me, mostly because it would mean meddling with our artwork. We had a contractual right to say no to any changes, but on the other hand this would also draw attention to the track, so once again we agreed. Several days later, Danny called again. The MCA legal department now thought we would need to not only print the lyrics on the back of the cover but also make sure that "fuck" really stood out, just in case any record buyers failed to notice it. How to do this? Highlight the line "You don't really give a flying fuck" in yellow, they suggested, so that it'd grab the browser's attention on the back cover.

In fairness to Danny and the people at MCA, they, along with the rest of the American record business, were under big pressure from the government in Washington to conform to the PMRC. I happened to be in L.A. when this last request was made. I really wasn't looking forward to calling Bruce again to tell him about this latest turn of events, even though, in some ways, it was turning out to be a pretty fabulous situation. About the only thing left for them to do, if they wanted to draw even more attention to the word "fuck," was print it in 3D and hand out those stereoscopic glasses.

I paid a visit to Irving Azoff, MCA's chief, to get a better read on the situation. (As you might remember from earlier in the story, I had first met Irving when he was road-managing Neil Young's *Tonight's the Night* tour.) Irving and I had a brief but pleasant meeting that included some discussion about the idea of highlighting the lyrics in yellow. Irving said he would see what could be done but, as it turned out, several thousand copies of the album had already been printed – with "fuck" highlighted – and sent to various people in the business, including some stores, without our permission. After discussions over several days, MCA finally agreed that the official release would not use the highlighting. Once again, events had proved that sometimes life is indeed stranger than fiction, nowhere more so than in the record business. Today, copies of *World of Wonders* with "fuck" highlighted, which are hard to find, have become collectors' items.

This wasn't the only problem we would have with this song. Although we hadn't planned to release "Call It Democracy" as a single — that particular honour was reserved for "People See Through You" — we decided to go ahead and make a video right away. Even though it was still early in the history of music videos, we'd learned from "If I Had a Rocket Launcher" that you could deliver a strong message with the right song on video. The video makers, working closely with Bruce, came up with a wonderfully strong combination of found footage and original shots cleverly edited to make a strong visual statement that both enhanced and illuminated the song. One of the scenes showed a map of Latin America being fed into the top funnel of an old-fashioned meat grinder and coming out the bottom as a Coke bottle. Once we realized how powerful the video was, we decided to release "Call It Democracy" as a single, even though we knew it would take a miracle for it to get much play on commercial radio. Of course, we had anticipated that we would have to edit out the "fuck" to get any TV airplay, but sent the unedited video to MTV (in the U.S.) and MuchMusic (in Canada) anyway, just to see what would happen. We weren't surprised to hear that both channels wanted an edited version. Like most artists, Bruce never wants to have his songs edited for any purpose, but the idea of a song and video as compelling as "Call It Democracy" broadcast on TV made it worthwhile and, besides, the album version would be unedited.

However, there was one more surprise to come. MTV executives told us that before they would agree to play the video, we would have to take out a Coke bottle visible briefly on two occasions in the song — because, they said, it was product endorsement.

In my view, anyone who thinks putting Central America into a meat grinder and having it come out the other end as a Coke bottle is a product endorsement has some serious perception problems. But that was the world we were living in. I did my best to find out whether the concern was really about product endorsement or actually to do with the song's political message. I could never get a satisfactory answer, but I was assured that if we removed the Coke label they would play the video. Bruce and I decided we could live with that trade-off. We'd lose about two seconds of the Coke bottle but the point of that particular scene would be left intact and a very powerful message would be broadcast right across the U.S. I should mention that MuchMusic in Canada had no problem with the Coke bottle.

We did the requested edits and gave the video back to the officials at MTV and, true to their word, they started playing the video. It would turn out to be the last Bruce Cockburn video that MTV would play. I won't jump to any conclusions about that – after all, things were changing with the channel and, along with it, the music business, but sometimes you have to wonder. A couple of years later, however, we got some airplay on VH1, MTV's sister station, with another politically potent song and video: "If a Tree Falls," from Bruce's 1988 album *Big Circumstance*.

Meanwhile, "Call It Democracy" continued to make waves. Many U.S. radio stations also banned it, because the song was perceived as somehow being anti-American. You might say that Bruce's experiences were something of an advance warning of the society we would see come to prominence in the U.S. some fifteen years later. Despite all this, or perhaps because of all this, his popularity continued to grow in the States, where he found plenty of support – often tempered by hostility from some quarters, a situation that continues to this day.

The sun's going down on the midway tonight

The red stripes are turning to grey

But old Emmett's still out in the big top tonight

Sweeping the spotlight away

"Sweeping the Spotlight Away"
Murray McLauchlan

CHAPTER FIFTEEN

For the first time since I'd managed the Paupers at the beginning of my career, I was back to managing just one act: Bruce Cockburn. Not that I didn't have plenty to do. Bruce was having a commercially successful run and it seemed as though he was always on the road somewhere in the world, performing concerts in Germany, the U.K., Italy, Australia, and America. And often I was there with him. Italy was a particularly interesting place to play. There was a certain kind of casual approach to presenting a show there that was, well, quite foreign to just about everything I had trained myself to do.

A manager has many duties and one of them is to make things work on time and according to a schedule. I've often thought that if a bicycle tire was a metaphor for the music business then a manager would be right at the wheel's hub, along with the artist, and each spoke going outwards would be a different discipline within the business. One spoke might represent accounting, another might represent promotion, and yet another booking shows, and so on. And although a manager is not necessarily doing each of these different things by himself or herself, he or she would have to be conversant with them all and be able to hire and work with the right people in all of these specialized areas.

One of our tours in Italy tested the idea that things had to happen on time. One evening before Bruce's show in Milan, our Italian promoters were treating us to a particularly fabulous meal. (I might add that it's almost impossible *not* to have a fabulous meal in Italy.) The show began at 9 p.m. During the meal I took a quick look at my watch and was startled to see that it was 8:45. I anxiously pointed this out to our hosts, but they were not alarmed at

Me and Bruce fooling around at Tivoli Gardens, in Copenhagen (1980)

all, and they assured us that the three thousand people waiting in the venue would agree with them that enjoying our meal was more important than getting on stage on time. Both Bruce and I were quite taken aback by this, but the promoters turned out to be right, at least that night, because the show was a huge success. Things have changed now in Italy, so fortunately we didn't pick up the habit of being late – in fact, Bruce rarely eats before a show – but that was an exceptionally memorable evening in Milan.

I continued to run True North and had by now built up a tidy little catalogue of around eighty albums. I had taught myself to treat that catalogue like a garden. I knew if I looked after it properly, it would continue to grow and flourish, so I tended to it every single day, making sure the albums were available everywhere possible and that the songs would be available for other uses.

Also, I continued to serve on many industry-related boards: CIRPA, VideoFACT, Massey Hall, and others. One of the most interesting was the Ontario Film Development Corporation (OFDC), today known as the Ontario Media Development Corporation (OMDC). I had been asked to join the board by Wayne Clarkson and Bill House. Wayne had run Toronto's Festival of Festivals in its infancy (today the Toronto International Film Festival, or TIFF), and was about to become the first chairman and CEO of the OFDC when it launched in 1986. I had met Bill, a veteran film producer who was to be executive coordinator of the new agency, when he approached me to do a film about Bruce. Although we had grand ideas for creating a full-blown documentary, we had to settle for a concert film, *Rumours of Glory*. Nevertheless, it's a wonderful film made by the award-winning dramatic and documentary director Martin Lavut.

I was floored when Bill and Wayne asked me to join the board. It included such luminaries as Adrienne Clarkson, director

Norman Jewison, and long-time broadcasting executive Peter Herrndorf, among others. When I asked Wayne and Bill why they wanted me, they replied "Sex, drugs, and rock 'n' roll." *Aha*, I thought, *we're being noticed*. I loved serving on that board. I was immediately appointed to the executive committee and had the satisfying experience of seeing, from the inside, another arts organization grow from its inception. The OFDC was also a tremendous learning curve for me. To date most of my experience had been related to the music business. Now I was surrounded by a smart group of people from not only the film business but also many other areas of Canada's cultural and business worlds, and they had plenty to teach me. The OFDC was, at that point, directly funding some of Ontario's emerging young talents, and it impressed me the way that Wayne, Bill, and the staff at the OFDC were picking some real winners, among them Atom Egoyan, Patricia Rozema, and Bruce McDonald.

But not everyone at True North was as satisfied with the status quo as I was. Jehanne Languedoc, who was pretty much my whole support system, was forever fielding calls from musicians looking to hook up with me in one way or another; she was adept at moving them on to more likely situations, since I'd made it clear that I wasn't interested in working with new talent. Still, I think she knew me well enough to sense that I might be getting restless. She kept talking to me about an artist from Vancouver named Barney Bentall who, with his band the Legendary Hearts, was starting to make some noise on the West Coast. Jehanne was convinced that Barney was going to be big and kept giving me demos to listen to, which I kept ignoring. One day in 1987 I was having lunch directly across the road from my office at a fine little café called Emilio's. Was it a coincidence that Jehanne just happened to be eating there with Barney? She casually walked over to my table with him in tow and introduced us. I saw why Jehanne was so high on him. Barney is one of the nicest and most charming people I've ever met; it was hard not to instantly like him. I made a note to listen to his demos that evening. I liked what I heard and made arrangements to meet with Barney before he returned to Vancouver.

As it turned out, my good fortune was that CBS/Sony was considering signing Barney to a record deal at the same time that I initiated talks with him. True North was still being distributed by Sony (Sony had bought CBS but my distribution deal hadn't changed) so there was great synergy between our two companies and I quickly came to the conclusion that if I was going to expand again, having Barney directly signed to Sony would be a good thing for both the artist and me. I would represent Barney for management and publishing while Sony absorbed part of the burden of start-up costs. Barney had a terrific video for his song "Something to Live For," which was already being played on MuchMusic. There seemed little doubt, at least in my mind, that this song could be a hit if worked properly.

Once the deals were signed, we embarked on recording Barney's debut album and commercially releasing the first single. I wasn't surprised that "Something to Live For" became quite a hit. In fact the album, entitled *Barney Bentall & the Legendary Hearts*, eventually went platinum. We would go on to do four albums together, all of which went gold, while two reached platinum sales. Barney had a string of Canadian hits, including "Come Back to Me," "Life Could Be Worse," "Do Ya," and, of course, "Something to Live For." He was always a pleasure to work with and I owe Jehanne a great debt of gratitude for keeping after me to work with him.

In 1989 Barney and the Legendary Hearts won a Juno for Most Promising Group of the Year and we were set to have the self-titled debut album released in the U.S. At this point, CBS in the States was being run by Donnie Ienner, my old friend from back in the days of Bruce's "Wondering Where the Lions Are." Bruce's records were being released in the U.S. on Jimmy and Donnie's Millennium Records, but their company had begun to run into financial troubles in 1981, right around the release of *Inner City Front*. That's one of the ever-present dangers in the independent record business – you work with some very creative and fabulously talented record people but there is the constant threat of money problems. One day I got a call from Jimmy informing me that he was going to close down Millennium. I immediately got on a plane and headed to Manhattan. I'm sure that this was a very trying time for the Ienner brothers and I wanted to let them both know how much I had appreciated the great job they had done for us. I wasn't there to complicate their lives any further but to see

Barney Bentall gets the first of his four gold records

what I could do to get back the U.S. rights to our Cockburn masters. I think they were quite pleased that I wasn't there to pour oil on the fire, and we quickly worked out a deal to get our records back. As you'll see shortly, I would later resell those very same records to Donnie after he began running Columbia Records.

With Barney awaiting the release of his album in the States, I arranged for both of us to be guests of CBS at its annual international convention, being held that year in Boca Raton, Florida. This would be a great opportunity for Barney to meet a lot of the key people who would potentially play an important role supporting his international career. Only a selective number of CBS artists attended this exclusive convention, so the fact that Barney had been invited was an indication of the company's support and, because of Barney's winning personality, it had the potential to be an important event for him. The first evening was an introductory dinner with around four hundred CBS employees and their guests in attendance. While I was watching one of the acts performing onstage, someone came up behind me and put their hands over my eyes. It was Donnie Ienner, newly installed as President of the Columbia Records Group. We had a happy reunion. He liked Barney, as I suspected he would, and we quickly agreed during the convention to have Barney do a promo tour of some of America's key radio stations.

Then, unexpectedly, Donnie asked me what Bruce was up to. I explained that we were just ending our contract with Gold Castle, and Donnie asked me to contact him in New York after the convention. When I did, he made me an offer to start releasing Bruce's records in the U.S. on Columbia. It didn't take too long to work out the details and so, just like that, Bruce's records were being distributed on the most powerful label in America. While he was still signed directly to True North, we would now license our next several records to Columbia in America as well as other parts of the world. At the same time, we made another deal with Donnie for Bruce's available back catalogue – basically licensing back to Donnie the same albums that I had licensed to him at his previous company, Millennium, including *Dancing in the Dragon's Jaws*. I would eventually get those records back again, when we left Columbia several years later. Each time these records changed hands, both Bruce and I made money, and, even more importantly, the records received another lease on life and more shelf time in record stores around the world.

Working with Columbia was interesting, chaotic, and fun. It was a large company but there were lots of terrific music people who were in the business for all the right reasons. With their help, Bruce hooked up with producer T-Bone Burnett, already admired for his work with Los Lobos and Elvis Costello. Years later T-Bone would break through to wider public acclaim with his production of the Grammy-winning soundtrack to Joel and Ethan Coen's film *O Brother, Where Art Thou* as well as of *Raising Sand*, the Grammy-winning 2009 collaboration between Alison Krauss and Robert Plant. Bruce would do two albums with T-Bone – 1991's *Nothing But a Burning Light* and 1993's *Dart to the Heart*.

By the early 1990s, a whole new radio format, called Triple A, or Adult Album Alternative, had begun to catch on in the U.S. Simply put, it was music from the fringes of the mainstream aimed at a more mature audience whose taste in music hadn't drifted to the middle of the road. It wasn't quite the free-form radio of the sixties but was better, in my opinion, than the staid and overly formatted choices being offered elsewhere on the dial. Sadly, Triple A barely existed in Canada; there might have been one or two stations at any one time here, compared to more than one hundred in the States. Ironically, many of the artists getting exposed in the American Triple A universe were Canadian, among them Cowboy Junkies, k.d. lang, Barenaked Ladies, and Bruce. With the muscle of the American promotion team behind him, Bruce had several of his songs make the top five in this format.

One of the most interesting records we did during our Columbia years was Bruce's Christmas album released in 1993, titled simply *Christmas*. It was one of the few times Bruce produced himself and the album is a wonderfully eccentric mix of songs that includes "The Huron Carol" sung in the original Huron language and an obscure gospel number called "Mary Had a Baby."

Our experience with Columbia makes me think about how it's become quite fashionable to slam the large record companies. Those companies get hit with accusations ranging right across the spectrum, everything from blatant thievery to ruining good music to being populated by idiots who can't see where the future lies. If it's true, you wouldn't know it from my experience. Sure, the deals were not always fair, and they did make the companies and many of the entrepreneurs and executives rich, but they also made many of the artists rich, and brought their music into millions of homes. I've been an "indie" all my life and I'm proud of it, but I don't need to see the major companies attacked to feel good about what I've done. There is no doubt that today everything is in flux and the hold the multinationals once had on the marketplace is slipping. Maybe that's a good thing, but we'll have to wait and see what the new model brings, especially where it counts the most: with the music.

In the early 1990s I signed two brilliant songwriters to True North: Gregory Hoskins and Stephen Fearing. They were unique artists, and although I would only make two albums with Gregory, I would have a sixteen-year relationship with Stephen.

I always considered Stephen to be a very special talent and it was a constant disappointment for me that I couldn't break him bigger than I did, although I think I helped him have a consistently rewarding career in music. Stephen did bring to me one of the most fun projects I have ever been involved with – Blackie & the Rodeo Kings. And to think, I almost turned it down.

One day in 1996 Stephen called to tell me about an idea that he and Colin Linden had come up with and to see if I'd like to get involved. Just to back up for a moment, Colin was someone I had known or known about for most of my life. He would come to the Riverboat with his mother when he was just a kid and also show up at many of the shows we were promoting at Massey Hall. Colin was something of a child prodigy, an amazing guitar player with an encyclopedic knowledge of music, both its history and the players. This was especially true when it came to his first love, the blues.

When Bruce made *Nothing But a Burning Light* with T-Bone Burnett, he hired an all-star band that included Booker T. Jones of "Green Onions" fame, drummer Jim Keltner, and bassist Edgar Meyer, whose credits range from Alison Krauss to Yo-Yo Ma. When it came time for Bruce to tour, we were not going to be able to get these very, very busy studio musicians to go on the road with us at the drop of a hat, so Bruce suggested that we call Colin Linden, who knew the best roots players in Canada. In the end, we used Colin's band and spent a couple of great years on the road together. Bruce went on to use Colin's band as his studio group for *Dart to the Heart*. Eventually Colin succeeded T-Bone as Bruce's producer and made several albums with Bruce, including what I consider one of his best, *The Charity of Night*.

However, when Stephen called me to say that he and Colin had been kicking around the idea of forming a group to record a tribute album to songwriter Willie P. Bennett, using as the name of their band the title of one of Willie P.'s songs, I was less than impressed. Fortunately for me, I agreed to have lunch with Stephen, Colin, and Tom Wilson. Tom, who was going to be the third member of Blackie, is a big, talented, lovable guy you could easily mistake for a biker. He had already received one gold record for his work with the group Junkhouse. By the time the four of us had finished lunch I was completely sold on the idea of Blackie & the Rodeo Kings. (A little-known bit of trivia: I became known as Blackie, a title I kept until I stopped working with the band in 2007.)

Willie P. Bennett was truly one of the great songwriters of his generation and I had almost completely missed him – another reason to keep an open mind and listen to the musicians you work with. So even though I was unable to get Stephen the hit records I think he deserved, I was able to get him some airplay with the Blackie project. Indeed, both Stephen, as a solo artist, and Blackie & the Rodeo Kings would go on to win Juno Awards.

Working with Blackie was a joy. Sure, it was chaotic, and coordinating the schedules of the three principals could be maddening, but the music was always stimulating. I'm confident that had the three of them come along in the late sixties or early seventies, they would have been a huge success. As it was, they've done quite well, and it was always fun to work with them. Certainly they made some of the best records, and did some of the best live shows, that I had ever been involved in. But the business had now changed, and to be truthful I was having trouble finding the key that would unlock those doors and take a group like this onward to bigger and better things.

The world had moved on, as it must, and although I think I changed along with the times, I was finding it harder to keep the music I loved in the public eye. Nonetheless, True North continued to grow. I started releasing music from around the world, no longer restricting myself to Canadian records. By doing this I ended up putting out music by such greats as Richard Thompson, Echo & the Bunnymen, Shawn Colvin, Kelly Joe Phelps, Jethro Tull, and many others. The growth wasn't only confined to foreign acts. I also released records by Canadian acts such as the Rheostatics, Moxy Früvous, Zubot & Dawson, 54-40, Howie Beck, Lynn Miles, the Golden Dogs, Randy Bachman, and the late jazz guitarist Lenny Breau. By the new millennium, True North had grown from a scrappy one-man band in Canada's infant music business into one of the country's biggest and most successful independent record companies.

Blackie & the Rodeo Kings (Colin Linden, Stephen Fearing, and Tom Wilson) help me celebrate my induction into the Music Managers' Honour Roll (barryrodon.com)

By the time I sold True North we had put out over five hundred albums and countless singles. True North had collected more than forty gold and platinum albums, and around fifty Juno Awards. Our artists had received almost every type of award there was and many of them had become so well known that they were icons in the music business. But for me, it felt like my time had come and gone. Yes, I could still compete, and on any given day I could do my job as well as anyone anywhere in the world. In fact, on a good day I was even unbeatable. But I had promised myself many years ago when I was starting out that if I ever began feeling that I would rather be somewhere else more often than I felt like being at work, I would find a way to get out of the business. And sure enough, that day had arrived. But before that time came, I had to spend some time in the hospital with a heart condition that almost killed me.

For years I had abused myself with everything from drugs to overeating. I'd been mostly sedentary and had never bothered with doctors or annual checkups. I suppose I was lucky to be alive. By 2005, though, I had been noticing that I was frequently out of breath. It was particularly noticeable when I was arriving at airports. I would leave the plane and start the long trek towards the baggage claim area but would almost always have to stop, put down my carry-on bag, and catch my breath. Nonetheless, I ignored these signs, until early one morning when I woke up and immediately vomited. Given that I hadn't been out drinking the night before, the message finally sank in. Something was wrong. I called the office of the last doctor I'd visited and miraculously convinced his assistant to have the doctor see me that morning. Elizabeth drove me to the appointment. The doctor checked my heart rate, then took my blood pressure, and before he had even removed the inflatable cuff he told me that I should go immediately to the nearest hospital. My systolic blood pressure was up near 200 and he felt I could have a cardiac event at any moment.

We drove downtown to Mount Sinai, the hospital where I'd been born sixty-one years earlier. Of course, it had relocated to University Avenue from Yorkville decades before. When I presented myself at the emergency department that day, I hadn't been near a doctor for over five years and hadn't been in a hospital, other than for the odd broken finger or toe, for some forty years. When the admitting doctor asked me who my physician was, or if I had any idea of where my medical records might be, I wasn't able to give him anything. Furthermore, he wasn't able to find a single bit of information from the medical system citywide. The first thing he told me was that I was about to get my "money's worth" from Canada's medical care system. It took a few hours, but finally I was admitted.

How serious was it? I was in the hospital for close to two months. While there I had a quadruple bypass and a heart valve replaced. I was told the night before my operation that I was a bit of a high-risk patient and that I had the option to delay the operation for a month or so while I lost more weight and generally got into better shape. The surgeon told me that the normal odds of success for my kind of surgery were about 95 per cent but that in my case it was more like 85 per cent. I told him that in my world 85 per cent odds were better than anything I was used to and that we should go ahead as planned.

I'd like to tell you that I had an epiphany while in the hospital but I didn't. I did get control of my weight to some degree and I certainly cleaned up a lot of my bad habits. But as far as my working life, I didn't really come to any conclusions. In fact, I booked a ten-city tour for Cockburn from my hospital bed while attached to a morphine drip. (Turned out to be a good little tour, too.)

No, it wasn't until well after I left the hospital that I came to the conclusion I should make a change.

I had come face to face with the fact that for me the music business was no longer the fun it had been. In some respects I'd been hoisted by my own petard. I was now spending more time filling out grant applications and collecting backup material than I was in the studio. I was spending more time listening to my employees' problems than listening to music, and I was constantly trying to figure out how to keep the business going and growing, in a climate that was less and less conducive to growth, at least for someone with my skill set. Simply put, my due date had come and gone, and I had to do something about it.

Feet fall on the road

Bound to motion

Though chains be of gold

They are chains all the same

"Feet Fall on the Road"
Bruce Cockburn

EPILOGUE

One of my favourite stories involves a major-league baseball manager, I don't know which one, who had a sign on the wall behind his desk that simply had the number 1330 written on it. When a reporter asked him why he kept that sign there, and what it meant, the manager told him that it was the number of times that Babe Ruth had struck out in his career. And though I don't claim in any way to be Babe Ruth, I feel like I struck out at least that many times, but on the way I hit a few out of the park, and on balance I think I did okay.

The odds of success in the music business are stacked against you. I learned a long time ago that the reason to be in this crazy game was not because you wanted to be rich but simply because you wanted to put out the music that you loved. No matter how well it sold or was accepted, if, in the end, you liked what you were doing, then you could draw some real satisfaction from that alone. By that measure, I'm indeed satisfied.

There is no doubt that I am a product of the music business, for better or worse. The poetry I love comes from song lyrics.

I couldn't quote you Homer or Shakespeare but I know all the lyrics to the songs of Bob Dylan, Joni Mitchell, Gordon Lightfoot, and Leonard Cohen, and certainly all the songs of Bruce Cockburn and Murray McLauchlan. They contained the wisdom of the novels I missed through my early departure from high school. I'm the first to admit that my life revolved around the dynamics of being involved in the rough-and-tumble of the music world, and I feel all the better for it.

Where's it all going now that we're in the digital age? To be truthful, I don't really care. I trust that there will always be young people with ideas, and with ears for what is good, and they will find the way just as I did. It was a beautiful trip, one that I would gladly do all over again, and to quote the old saying, I would only change getting to my mistakes quicker the next time around.

I receive the Walt Grealis Award
(Juno Hall of Fame)

ACKNOWLEDGEMENTS

There would be no book without the help of the following kind people:

Sheila McCook for looking it over and giving me the feeling that it might be okay to let others read it.

Susan Abramovitch for finding the book a great home.

Doug Pepper for opening the door and being so enthusiastic.

I'm especially indebted to David Hayes who helped to bring this project to fruition.

And a special thanks to Philip Rappaport for making the book shine despite the odds.

And Elizabeth Blomme for, well, everything.

These are some of the people who have both helped and worked with me along the way over the past 45 years at True North and Finkelstein Management. Thanks for all your energy and help.

Alana Rouso, Bart Schoales, Bernie Fiedler, Bernie Solomon, Bessie Markouzis, Beverley McKee, Bob Farmer, Brenda Biseau, Buzz Chertkoff, Chris Vautour, Daniel Broome, Debra Sherman, Donna Wagg, Doug Flavelle, Edan Blomme, Elizabeth Blomme, Graham Henderson, Graham Stairs, Isobel Harry, James Grimes, Jason Mulcock, Jeanne Languedoc, Jenna Schiff, Jeremie Poirer, Joanne Smale, Julian Tuck, Julie Thorburn, Karin Doherty, Linda Hagen, Liz Braun, Marcus MacDonald, Mark Kozar, Melissa Hames, Michelle Murphy, Morris Snow, Mukesh Sachdeva, Murray Silver, Naz Etessam, Noah Finkelstein, Paul Gagnon, Richard Grasley, Rob Bennett, Robyn Taylor, Robyn Taylor, Sarah Scott, Sherri Sare, Stephen Ehrlick, Steve Jordan, Stewart Duncan, Stuart Raven-Hill, Sue McCallum, Susan Abramovitch, Tiffany Ferguson, Vee Popat, William Hinkson.

If I left anyone out it was a mistake. Sorry.

SONG CREDITS

INDEX

191-92, 193, 194-95, 229, 233, 234-37, 241, 275-76
Canadian-content regulations, 44, 88, 105-06, 111, 143-44, 148, 149-51, 233-34, 235-36, 244, 245
Canadian Federation of Musicians, 167
Canadian Independent Music Association (CIMA), 149
Canadian Independent Record Production Association (CIRPA), 148-49, 233, 234, 236, 261
Canadian Music Publishers Association (CMPA), 236
Canadian National Exhibition (CNE), 187, 189, 190-91, 192-94, 195
"Can I Come Near," 238
Capitol Records, 238
"Carmelita," 159
Carpetbaggers (Robbins), *The*, 28
Cashbox, 203
"Cathy's Clown," 25
CBC, 187, 189, 191, 252
CBS Canada, 138-39, 154, 158, 160, 168, 178, 179, 223-24, 234
CBS International, 160, 164, 165, 168, 210
CBS/Sony, 263, 264, 265
Central America, 247, 248, 250, 256
Century Sound, 86
CFGM, 31-32
CFOX, 84
Chapin, Harry, 174
Charity of Night, The, 268
Château Laurier, 153
Chateau Records, 147
Chater, Brian, 148, 149
CHED, 154
Chertkoff, Buzz, 113
CHEZ-FM, 205
Chez Piggy, 133
Chicago, 101
Chicago, IL, 102, 103, 199
Children, 133
"Child's Song," 10, 141
Chilliwack, 161

CHOM-FM, 84
Christmas, 267
Christopher's Movie Matinee, 133
CHUM, 43, 84, 148, 149, 219-20, 229-30, 235-36, 244
CIMA (formerly CIRPA), 149
Circles in the Stream, 205
CIRPA. *See* Canadian Independent Record Production Association
City Lights, 96
CityTV, 242, 244
CKIK-FM, 205
Clapton, Eric, 85
Clark, Dick, 23
Clarkson, Adrienne, 261
Clarkson, Wayne, 261, 262
Clavell, James, 211
Clayton-Thomas, David, 42, 43, 79, 110
Cleveland, OH, 209, 210
Climbing!, 109
Clinch, Paul, 147
Clouds, 91
Club 71, 134
CMPA (Canadian Music Publishers Association), 236
CNE. *See* Canadian National Exhibition
Coasters, 20, 21
Coast to Coast Fever, 181, 182
Cochrane, Tom, 147
Cockburn, Bruce, viii, x, 5, 132-33, 140, 144-45, 164, 180-81, 188, 193, 197, 229, 241, 242, 247
    performances, 6, 7, 8, 74, 133-34, 152-53, 157, 161-62, 173, 204, 210-12, 250, 259-61, 272
    recordings, 4, 19, 78, 92, 116, 134-37, 138, 141-42, 151-52, 156, 172, 181-83, 186, 203, 205, 213, 218-21, 228, 230, 238, 246, 247-48, 249, 250-51, 253, 254-57, 265-66, 267, 268, 274
Cockburn, Kitty, 140
Cohen, Leonard, 32, 174
Cohl, Michael, 6, 7